HELLENISM IN JEWISH PALESTINE

TEXTS and STUDIES

OF

THE JEWISH THEOLOGICAL SEMINARY
OF AMERICA

VOL. XVIII

HELLENISM IN JEWISH PALESTINE

THE STROOCK PUBLICATION FUND

Established in Memory of Sol M. and Hilda W. Stroock and Robert L. Stroock

ḤELLENISM IN JEWISH PALESTINE.

STUDIES IN THE LITERARY TRANSMISSION
BELIEFS AND MANNERS OF PALESTINE IN
THE I CENTURY B.C.E. — IV CENTURY C.E.

by

SAUL ⌊LIEBERMAN

NEW YORK
THE JEWISH THEOLOGICAL SEMINARY OF AMERICA
5722–1962

To the sainted memory of

LOUIS S. BRUSH

IN GRATITUDE

LOUIS S. BRUSH*

By Professor Alexander Marx

One of the many persons who were attracted by the magnetic personality of Professor Schechter and the hospitable home presided over by Mrs. Schechter was Mr. Louis S. Brush.

Like many others, he also became a frequent visitor of the model services in the Seminary Synagogue, which offered a rare combination of beauty and dignity and in which Dr. Schechter took particular pride. It was there that I first met Mr. Brush, some forty-five years ago.

He was a quiet, unostentatious person, a tall man of dignified bearing, meticulously dressed and well-mannered who had endeared himself to the Schechters by the apparent reverence and devotion he felt for them. He was a deeply religious man. I remember how one day he brought to the Seminary his Sefer Torah with breastplate, headpieces and pointer in a special case. He had inherited it from his father and had taken it away from another synagogue where, he felt, it was not sufficiently cared for. Once a year he would send his chauffeur to fetch the fine silver ornaments and have them looked over and polished at Tiffany's.

In the early years after the reorganization of the Seminary (1907), one of our promising students, Alexander Cohen, underwent a minor operation which proved fatal. The physician ascribed the unexpected tragedy to apparent malnutrition.

We all were very deeply moved by the sad event, and Mrs. Schechter tried to prevent similar conditions by seeing that more care should be taken of the physical welfare of the stu-

---

* Address delivered on April 5, 1949, on the occasion of the inauguration of the Brush Lectures.

dents. The establishment some years later of the Students' House was a consequence of this event.

At the time, Mrs. Schechter spoke to a number of friends urging the building of a dormitory. Mr. Brush promised her to do something some day and we expected that he would make some provision in his will for this purpose. He lived for many more years but never mentioned the subject again. After Dr. and Mrs. Schechter's death, he showed less and less interest in the Seminary; his visits to the Seminary Synagogue became rarer and rarer and finally ceased altogether. He kept up the care of his Torah ornaments and, as I heard later from Dr. Adler, made an anonymous gift of $1,000.00 every Hanukah. He was approached in vain for a contribution to the Students' House. When I happened to meet him two years before his death and asked him why he did not visit our Synagogue of late, he answered that he was not interested in the Seminary any longer.

To our greatest surprise, we learned on his death, that he had left the bulk of his fortune, one and a half million dollars, for the building of a dormitory. One half of the money should be devoted to the building, the other half to its upkeep expenses and to scholarships for the students. Nobody but his Christian lawyer had known anything of this will. What was the reason for so deep a secrecy we can only surmise.

His relatives were, naturally, very much disappointed and thought of fighting the will, but the lawyer declared that he was ready to swear that Mr. Brush was in full possession of his faculties when he made his will and they realized that they could do nothing about it.

The Seminary Board for a moment considered the building of some additional stories on top of the old Seminary on 123rd Street. However, there was a clause in the will that the dormitory had to be built in strict colonial style and the condition had to be adhered to. Fortunately, the large plot of ground on Broadway opposite the old building was available at that time. The picturesque high rocks on the vacant lot had been cleared away with the view of putting up here a high structure. That plan had been abandoned for various reasons. And thus, through

Mr. Brush's grandiose gift, it was made possible to erect the imposing building.

The Brush gift came at a psychological moment. In the 1920's, the Library had outgrown its quarters, partly through the acquisition of the Adler Library and the other rich gifts of Mortimer L. Schiff. It had occupied rooms on the first and second floors and the building which had looked so spacious when it opened, had become quite inadequate. It was contemplated to remodel two neighboring houses when the Brush gift offered entirely new possibilities. There was room enough on the new plot for adequate accommodations to house the Library and the Teachers Institute, which had its equally insufficient quarters downtown. Mr. Schiff's family decided to erect the Jacob H. Schiff building for the Library, and Mr. Unterberg donated the one for the Teachers Institute.

The Rabbinical Department carried on for a year or two in the building on 123rd Street which Mr. Jacob H. Schiff had presented in 1902, but during the depression it turned out to be too expensive to keep up the two buildings and so the instruction of the Rabbinical department was transferred to the Teachers Institute building.

The Synagogue also, after some time, was transferred to the new buildings and only recently, after the removal of the Museum to the Warburg House, found room in the Library building.

And thus it is due to the generosity of Mr. Brush that our Seminary has the most magnificent building that has ever housed a Jewish institution of learning. We have every reason to feel a lasting debt of gratitude to him and to keep the memory of the noble, generous donor alive.

The Brush lectures will, we trust, fulfill this purpose and will connect his name permanently with the scholarly pursuits of this institution which owes so much of its growth to Mr. Brush's vision.

CONTENTS

PREFACE TO THE SECOND EDITION

The first edition has been exhausted for a number of years, but I have had no opportunity to take time from my regular duties to revise it. The accumulation of new material in the field of archaeology and the publication of many important works relating to the subject dealt with in the present book justified a considerable revision of the book.

However, I have decided to content myself for the present with the most necessary additions and modifications, abstaining from a complete revision which would require many months of additional work.

The main purpose of the book remains what it was originally: the elucidation of difficult passages in rabbinic literature which were hitherto either unexplained or misinterpreted, and sometimes unknown altogether; the examination of certain customs and practices and the treatment of the literary methods used by the rabbis. This content is discussed against the background of Hellenism in Jewish Palestine. The well known facts are used only as a kind of cement to make the citations coherent. The rabbinic material which form the elementary knowledge of every serious student of rabbinics is given without any reference to scholars who have dealt with it.

S. L.

March 8, 1962

PREFACE

The following chapters are the outgrowth of lectures delivered on various occasions. They include the first Louis S. Brush Lecture delivered on April 5, 1949; an academic address given on May 7, 1950, at the Hebrew University in Jerusalem on the occasion of its twenty-fifth anniversary; a lecture in the *thiasos* at the Hebrew University and several other papers read at the Jewish Theological Seminary of America.

As far as possible I tried to avoid detailed and complicated *Halakhic* discussions which might divert the reader's attention from the main thesis. For this reason I have not, in my discussion of the literary transmission, concerned myself with investigations of the credibility of certain historic traditions in rabbinic literature. In these chapters our interest was fixed on literary activity, not on historic truth. In examining what the Rabbis report concerning by-gone times what was important to us was *not* the historic fact, but the view which the Rabbis held and their reaction to it.

Keeping in mind the two types of readers whom this book may attract — classical scholars who are not familiar with Jewish writings and rabbinic students who do not pursue Hellenic studies — I have generally avoided the usual abbreviations, and have fully spelled out the names of books and journals.

In order to explain clearly the rabbinic sources, I often had to disregard the Greek classics and give preference to later Hellenistic and Roman writings which were nearer in time (and sometimes in place) to those of the rabbinic tradition. I have always worked on the assumption that actual contact (in the times under discussion) between Jew and Gentile exerted greater influence on the former than literary works.

Prof. Abraham Halkin spent many evenings with me reading through the whole manuscript. I am glad to repeat my words in the Preface to *Greek in Jewish Palestine*: I am indebted to Dr. Halkin not only for the revision of the English style but also for many suggestions in connection with the presentation of the subject-matter. I frequently relied on his good taste and lucid judgment.

The proofs were read by my dear wife, Dr. Judith Lieberman, and Rabbi Gershon Cohen, both of whom I wish to thank.

I am grateful to Professor Louis Finkelstein, President of the Jewish Theological Seminary, to Professor Henri Grégoire of Brussels and to Professor M. Schwabe of Jerusalem for their constructive critical remarks, generous help and advice. Professor Elias Bickerman was of continuous aid with his erudition and acumen. My indebtedness to him is greater than I can express.

The authorities and staff of the Libraries of the Jewish Theological Seminary, and our good neighbors at the Union Theological Seminary, were exceedingly kind and helpful in supplying me with the necessary books. To all of them I extend my sincerest thanks.

My thanks are also due to Dr. Maurice Jacobs and his intelligent type-setters and proof reader for their conscientious and careful work.

S. L.

The First of Kislev 5711 — November 10, 1950.

The Jewish Theological Seminary of America

N. B. Unless otherwise specified all the dates mentioned in this book are C. E.

The English translations of Greek and Latin authors which are available in the Loeb Classical Library were mostly checked with and sometimes copied in the pertinent quotations cited in this book.

HELLENISM IN JEWISH PALESTINE

INTRODUCTION

More than half a century has passed since the publication of S. Krauss' *Griechische und Lateinische Lehnwörter im Talmud, Midrasch und Targum*. The abundance of Greek words recorded in this dictionary has been properly regarded as an indication of the close contact between the Jews of Palestine and their Greek-speaking neighbors. This deduction is, of course, correct. But no systematic effort has been made to examine fully and analyze the Greek words contained in rabbinic literature. It goes without saying that as a result of the close relations between Aramaic and Greek certain words of the latter have become an integral part of the former. But many Greek words occur in rabbinic literature only rarely; they give the impression of being a foreign body in the language. This category needs special investigation.

It is pertinent to inquire why the Rabbis employed the particular Greek word when an adequate Hebrew or Aramaic term was seemingly available. "Almost every foreign word and phrase have their 'raison d'être' in rabbinic literature. We shall try to demonstrate that all Greek phrases in rabbinic literature are quotations."[1] If a common Greek word is employed by the Rabbis only very rarely, whereas they generally use its Aramaic equivalent, some reason must lie behind the rabbinic choice of a Greek term in a particular case.[2] In a previous volume[3] we tried to outline the underlying principles of the method of linguistic investigation in the study of Greek words employed by the Rabbis.

Here we are concerned with a wider problem: an inquiry

---

[1] S. Lieberman, *Greek in Jewish Palestine*, N. Y. 1942 (Hereafter referred to as *GJP*), p. 6.

[2] See Lieberman, *J. N. Epstein Jubilee Volume* (*Tarbiz* XX), Jerusalem 1950, p. 113 ff.

[3] *GJP*.

into the spirit of many rabbinic observations and an investigation of the facts, incidents, opinions, notions and beliefs to which the Rabbis allude in their statements. The insinuations and the suggestions contained in the remarks by the ancient Jewish sages, which were understandable to their contemporaries, are now often quite obscure to us. But the study of the events, customs and manners in the environment of the particular Rabbi may often reveal to us the inner sense of a rabbinic statement; the latter, or its part, often sheds light on the given events, customs and manners.

Here we should like to lay down an important principle in the investigation of the *Aggadah*. The utterances of the Rabbis are not as a rule pointless. Their homilies and parables in which they utilized the current events of their time always contain something which must have appealed to the mind or heart of their contemporaries. The interpretations and explanations of certain rabbinic passages in the commentaries and the dictionaries sometimes make them colorless and even insipid. We shall quote a few examples.[4]

We read in the *Midrash*:[5] משל למלך שאמ' לבניו הוו יודעין שאני דן דיני נפשות ומחייב הקריבו לי קרבן (דורון)[6] שאם תעלו לפני לבימה שאעביר אולונין שלכם (לאחֹר)[7]. כך אמר הב"ה לישראל בדיני נפשות אני הורג. ראו איך אני חס עליכם ברחמים בדם פסח ובדם מילה "Like a king who said to *his children*: Remember that I am going to try

---

4 *Die Königsgleichnisse des Midrasch* by I. Ziegler, Breslau 1903, is a valuable book illuminating the king-parables of the Rabbis in the light of Greek and Roman literature. However, the book suffers from two considerable faults. The rabbinic texts are copied from erroneous editions and are not treated in a critical manner. Secondly, the author did not discriminate between information which was likely to be known to the ordinary people in the East and between literary knowledge which was predominantly the apanage of the learned in the Greco-Roman world. The explanations offered below were unknown to Ziegler, and for this reason no reference to his book will be found in this work.

5 *Shemoth Rabba* XV. 12. I copy from cod. Oxf., Ebr. 147, f. 191b.

6 The word קרבן is missing in the editions. But in addition to our manuscript it is also extant in cod. New York. It is therefore obvious that דורון is a gloss to קרבן and, as usual, the original was dropped and the gloss retained.

7 The dots on the word apparently indicate that it is to be deleted.

capital cases and convict [people to death]; therefore offer a
sacrifice to me, so that when you come before my tribunal I
may dismiss your *elogium*.[8] So the Holy One blessed is He said
to Israel: I am now sentencing people to death (i. e. the first-
born of the Egyptians); note that I shall have pity on you by
virtue of the blood of the Paschal Lamb and the blood of circumcision." The parable appears to be tasteless and artificial. Who
is that king who declares in advance that he will issue wholesale convictions (as in the case of the Egyptians)? And what
king would enjoin his children under the threat of a death
penalty to offer a sacrifice to him? The parable can make sense
only if it is not fiction but an actual fact known to the people,
which the Rabbis utilized to illuminate the Bible.

Indeed, Lactantius tells us:[9] "And first of all he forced
his daughter Valeria and his wife Prisca to be polluted by
sacrificing . . . Altars were placed in the council chambers and
near the tribunal that the litigants might offer a sacrifice before
their case would be heard. Thus judges were approached as
gods."

Now the parable becomes perfectly understandable. In the
wholesale condemnation of the Christians during Diocletian's
persecutions, the emperor's own daughter[10] and wife were forced
to sacrifice; otherwise they might be condemned along with all
other Christians. The point of the parable is that the Jews,
the children of the Lord, were similarly spared during the wholesale conviction of the Egyptians by virtue of the blood of the
Paschal Lamb and the blood of circumcision; their *elogium* was
then dismissed.

---

[8] The report to the proconsul or the legate of the preliminary interrogation
conducted by the magistrate; it was brought in with the defendant. This
report was the first document read in the court of the proconsul (or legate)
when the accused appeared there. See *JQR* XXXV, 1944, p. 30 and nn. 189,
190 ibid.

[9] *De mort. pers.* XV: et primam omnium filiam Valeriam coniugemque
Priscam sacrificio pollui coegit . . . arae in secretariis ac pro tribunali positae,
ut litigatores prius sacrificarent atque ita causas suas dicerent, sic ergo ad
iudices tamquam ad deos adiretur.

[10] Comp. also Eusebius, *hist. eccl.* VIII. 6. 1 ff.

Again we read in the *Midrash*:[11] ולרבקה אח ושמו לבן. ר' יצחק אמר פרדיכסוס "*And Rebekah had a brother, and his name was Laban* (Gen. 24:29). R. Isaac said: *paradoxos*." All the commentaries and dictionaries explain the last word to mean παράδοξος or παραδόξως, i. e. Laban was extraordinarily and incredibly white.[12] This explanation blunts the whole point of the Rabbi's remark.

The truth is that he wanted to obviate a difficulty in the verse. The Jewish sages noticed that when mentioning wicked people the Bible usually indicates it by saying: And X was (or is) his name.[13] But when referring to a righteous person the expression is: And his name was (or is) X.[14] Now the question was raised:[15] Why in the case of the wicked Laban does the Bible say: *And his name was Laban*, instead of the expected "and Laban was his name"? Thereupon R. Isaac remarked: παράδοξος, i. e. it is a παράδοξος [λόγος], a paradox: You would expect the famous cheat to be called *Shaḥor* (Black), but the paradox was that his name was Laban (White). The Torah wanted to hint that the notorious trickster misled people even by his name.

Likewise, it is recorded in *TP*:[16] אמר ר' אלכסנדרי עובדא [הוה][17] בחד ארכון דהוה שמיה אלכסנדרוס. והוה קיים דיין חד ליסטיס אמר ליה מה שמך. [אמ'] אלכסנדרוס. אמ' ליה אלכסנדרוס פנה אלכסנדרי.[18] ומה אם מי ששמו כשמו של בשר ודם הוא ניצול, מי ששמו כשמו של הקב"ה על אחת כמה כמה. הה"ד כל אשר יקרא בשם ה' ימלט וכמה. "R. Alexander said: A certain magistrate (ἄρχων) whose name chanced to be Alexander was once trying a robber (λῃστής). The former asked him: What

---

[11] *Bereshith Rabba* LX. 7, 647; see the parallels referred to ibid.

[12] "Laban" means white in Hebrew.

[13] See *Midrash Samuel* I. 6 and parallels, where a number of passages are listed, such as I Sam. 7:14: *Goliath was his name* (גלית שמו); ibid. 25:25: *Nabal is his name* (נבל שמו) etc. But see below, p. 209.

[14] I Sam. 1:1: *And his name was Elkanah* (ושמו אלקנה); ibid. 17:12: *And his name was Jesse* (ושמו ישי) etc.

[15] See *Midrash Samuel* ibid. where this question is explicitly asked.

[16] *Berakhoth* IX. 1, 13b, top.

[17] So cod. Vat., '*Ein Jacob* passim.

[18] This is the reading of cod. Vat. and קונטרס אחרון in *Yalkut*. '*Ein Jacob*: לאלכסנדרי. *Midrash Tehilim* VI. 3, ed. Buber 21b: לאלכסנדרוס.

is your name?[19] He answered: Alexander. He (i. e. the magistrate) said: Alexander dismisses Alexander. Now if a man is saved because he bears the same name as a man of flesh and blood, he whose name is like the name of the Holy One blessed is He[20] will certainly be saved. This is the meaning of the Scriptural verse (Joel 3:5): *Whosoever shall be called[21] by the name of the Lord shall be delivered.*" S. Krauss[22] treats this passage as a curious anecdote which tends to indicate that justice became a farce in Rome. But the context of the Talmud shows that the Rabbis took it seriously.

In this instance they utilized the famous "Alexandromania" of some of the Roman dignitaries to illuminate Scripture. Dio Cassius[23] reports the following anecdote about the emperor Caracalla who believed himself to be an incarnation of Alexander the Great. A man who happened to be called Alexander was once tried for many crimes which he had committed. The accusing orator kept on saying "the bloodthirsty Alexander, the god-detested Alexander. Caracalla became angry as if he himself were being called those bad names, and said: If you cannot be satisfied with plain 'Alexander', you are dismissed."[24]

Special attention should be paid to rabbinic parables which include details that are not essential to the illustration of the particular Biblical passage. This usually proves that the Rabbis quoted a story *in extenso*, because it was known as such to the audience.

We read in the *Midrash*:[25] למלך ששלח כתבים ממדינה למדינה

---

[19] See *JQR* XXXV, 1944, p. 24, n. 153.

[20] The allusion is to Israel which contains the name of God. See *TP Ta'anith* II. 6, 65d; *Debarim Rabba* ed. Lieberman, p. 28 and n. 14 ibid.

[21] The Rabbis interpreted יְקְרָא as יִקְרָא, see *Sifre* II 49, ed. Finkelstein, p. 114; *TB Baba Bathra* 75b, according to the reading of *Yalkut Hamakhiri* to Joel 3:5, p. 25.

[22] פרס ורומי בתלמוד ובמדרשים, Jerusalem 1948, p. 278.

[23] LXXVIII. 8.

[24] ὠργίσθη τε ὡς καὶ αὐτὸς κακῶς ἀκούων, καὶ ἔφη "εἰ μὴ ἀρκέσει σοι ὁ 'Αλέξανδρος, ἀπολέλυσαι".

[25] *Esther Rabba*, proem, 11. Comp. *Vayyikra Rabba* XI. 7; *Tanḥuma* שמיני 9.

ובכל מדינה ומדינה שהיו מגיעים כתביו של מלך היו מחבקים
ומנשקים אותם ועומדים על רגליהם ופורעים ראשיהם וקורין אותם
ביראה באימה ברתת ובזיע וכיון שהגיעו למדינתו של מלך קראום וקרעום
ושרפום "Like a king who sent rescripts[26] to every city. In every
city where the king's rescripts arrived the people *embraced them
and kissed them*,[27] rose to their feet, uncovered their heads[28] and
read them in fear, in awe, in trembling and in trepidation.[29]
But *when they arrived at the king's own city the people* read them,
tore them and burnt them." This parable illustrates the verse in
Jer. 36:23, where it is stated that the king tore the scroll of
Jeremiah to pieces and destroyed it by fire.

At first glance it appears to be an elaborate and complicated
parable. For the illustration of the verse, the tearing of the
king's letters is sufficient. As a matter of fact in the earlier
Midrash[30] the example is short and concise: "Like a king who
sent his ordinance ($\pi\rho\acute{o}\sigma\tau\alpha\gamma\mu\alpha$) to a city. What did the people
of the city do to it? They tore it and burnt it." The elaborate
parable of the later *Midrash* can be properly understood only if
we suppose that an actual event was applied to our verse.

Lactantius[31] relates: "Next day an edict was promulgated
depriving the men of this religion (i. e. the Christians) of all
honors and dignities . . . [a certain person] tore it down and cut
it in pieces." The story is short; there is no record of the
behavior of the people in other places. Lactantius related a
fact which happened in his own city, in Nicomedia, where the

---

[26] $\gamma\rho\alpha\varphi\alpha\acute{\iota}$ or $\gamma\rho\acute{\alpha}\mu\mu\alpha\tau\alpha$.

[27] These italicized words are missing in the parallel *Midrashim* noted
above n. 25.

[28] Comp. the *International Critical Commentary* to I Corinth. XI. 4,
p. 229.

[29] From Chrysostom's (Migne *PG* LIII, 112) description of the reading of
the imperial rescripts ($\beta\alpha\sigma\iota\lambda\iota\kappa\grave{\alpha}$ $\gamma\rho\acute{\alpha}\mu\mu\alpha\tau\alpha$) it is obvious that the people read
them "with fear and trepidation" ($\mu\epsilon\tau\grave{\alpha}$ $\varphi\acute{o}\beta\text{ou}$ $\kappa\alpha\grave{\iota}$ $\tau\rho\acute{o}\mu\text{ou}$), see Le Blant,
Les actes des martyrs, p. 34; idem, *Les persécuteurs et les martyrs*, p. 140; Lieber-
man, *JQR* XXXV, 1944, p. 7 ff.

[30] *Bereshith Rabba* XLII. 3, p. 402.

[31] *De mortib. pers.* XIII: Postridie propositum est edictum quo cavebatur,
ut religionis illius homines carerent omni honore ac dignitate . . . deripuit et
conscidit.

emperors then resided. For our purpose the words of Eusebius, a Palestinian, and probably a contemporary of the anonymous homilist in our *Midrash* are of greater importance.

He tells[32] us that when the edict was published in Nicomedia a Christian tore it, and he devotes a few words to emphasizing the fact that the outrage was committed in a city where the two emperors were present.[33] It is almost certain that the anonymous Rabbi refers to the same incident. He stresses the fact that whereas in all other cities the people *embraced and kissed the edicts*[34] of the emperor, in his own city their fate was altogether different.[35] This fact was certainly widely known

[32] *Hist. eccl.* VIII. 5.

[33] δυεῖν ἐπιπαρόντων κατὰ τὴν αὐτὴν πόλιν βασιλέων.

[34] The Hebrew here is unequivocal: the edicts were adored by embracing and kissing. A. Alföldi (*Mitteilungen d. deutch. archaeol. Inst.*, Roemische Abteil. vol. 49, 1934, pp. 8 ff. and 58 ff.) has convincingly demonstrated that, contrary to the accepted opinion, the various forms of the *adoratio* of the emperor were *not* first introduced by Diocletian. They were taken over by the Roman Emperors from their Oriental colleagues. Herodotus (III. 128) recounts that the Persian guards of Oroetes "rendered much reverence to the rolls [of Darius] and still more to what was written therein" (τά τε βυβλία σεβομένους μεγάλως καὶ τὰ λεγόμενα ἐκ τῶν βυβλίων ἔτι μεζόνως). The προσκύνησις in connection with the imperial letters is often the same as the σεβασμός mentioned by Herodotus: general reverence, and perhaps actual genuflexion (Comp. Alföldi ibid., p. 46 ff.). Nevertheless in the light of the explicit rabbinic statement (see also below n. 35) we may assume that προσ-κυνεῖν in regard to the edict sometimes means (like κυνεῖν) to kiss (See Liddell and Scott s. v. προσκυνέω II. 1; II. 3. Comp. also C. Sittl, *Die Gebärden d. Griechen und Römer*, p. 172, n. 4). Philostratus (*vit. sophist.* 590) relates about the sophist Adrian: προσκυνήσας δὲ τὰς βασιλείους δέλτους τὴν ψυχὴν πρὸς αὐταῖς ἀφῆκεν. "Kissing the emperor's (i. e. Commodus') letters he breathed out his soul over them".

[35] The burning of the edicts and the remainder of the conclusion of our *Midrash* are an adaptation of a historic fact to the verse of Jeremiah. True, there is a Christian legend (*acta sanctorum, Sept.* vol. VI, p. 686d) that when a martyr (in Egypt) wanted to see the edict of Diocletian, it was brought and adored (= kissed). Then the proconsul also rose to his feet and *embraced* the edict (similiter et praeses assurexit et edictum *amplexatus* est). The Christian, however, took it, read it and threw it into the fire (accepisset et legisset ... imperatoris edictum in ignem coniecit). An exact repetition of our *Midrash*! But this Christian legend has no historic value; the only reliable information contained therein is the general treatment of the edict.

among the Christians,[36] and it is no wonder that it reached the Synagogue.

The later Rabbis elaborated the simple parable used by the earlier *Midrash*,[37] and on the basis of an actual event added to it all the details which adhered to it. An instance taken from life[38] appealed to the people more than an abstract example employed by the earlier Rabbi.

As stated above, we assume that the Rabbis were guided by special reasons in their choice of Greek words which were not incorporated in the spoken Aramaic. Very often the good sense of the choice is revealed when we can surmise the source from which they borrowed these words.

For instance, Rab homiletically explains[39] the etymology of the word קלנדס (calendas,[40] calendae, καλάνδαι). According to the *Aggadah* it was Adam who first invented this word. "When he saw [for the first time] that the day is growing longer he exclaimed: *Calendas, calon dio*" (קלנדס. קלון דיאו). The explanations of the connection between *calendas* and *calon dio* offered by the dictionaries and commentaries are untenable. The most plausible among them is that given by Israel Lewy[41] who suggests that, according to Rab, Adam exclaimed: καλόν. *dies*,

---

[36] The latter ascribe the tearing of the edict to various saints, but all of them are connected with the same occurrence. We find in the *Synaxaria Selecta* (*Synaxarium of Constantinople*, ed. H. Delehaye, p. 538. Comp. also ibid., p. 248 and *acta Sanctorum, Martii*, vol. II, p. 391) that a certain Menignus (in the time of the Decian persecutions), a fuller by profession, trampled the king's letters under his feet after snatching them from the hands of the judge and cutting them in pieces (Μένιγνος . . . τὰ τοῦ βασιλέως ἁρπάσας γράμματα ἐκ τῶν χειρῶν τοῦ ἄρχοντος καὶ εἰς λεπτὰ κατακόψας κατεπάτησεν). But this story too has just as little historical basis.

[37] See above, n. 30.

[38] Philostratus (*vit. soph.* 565) tells about the famous Herodes Atticus that "when he wanted to move his hearers he drew not only on tragedy but also on the life of every day" (τῶν ἀνθρωπίνων συνελέξατο).

[39] *TP 'Abodah Zarah* I. 2, 39c.

[40] The Rabbis often used the Accusative instead of the Nominative.

[41] *Verhandlungen des Vereins deutsch. Philologen etc.*, vol. XXXIII, Leipzig 1878, p. 83. This was also the independent interpretation of H. Blaufuss, *Römische Feste und Feiertage nach den Traktaten über fremden Dienst* I, p. 7.

i. e. [How] good! [It is] day! If we accept this interpretation we may advance the conjecture that its origin lies in some incantation. Varro[42] reports that it is a Greek custom to say "good light" when light is brought in.[43] But following all the interpretations, including Lewy's, it is necessary to emend the text and read דיאס[44] instead of דיאו, with the result of a combination of Greek and Latin!

However, from the contents of *TP*[45] it is obvious that in the first year of his life Adam was frightened when he saw the day growing shorter and shorter. But after the midwinter solstice, observing that the days were becoming longer again, he was seized with joy. In other words, it was the early sunset which terrified him and after the midwinter solstice he realized that it was in the nature of things for the sun to set early in the fall. The light of the sun will shine again.

Therefore we may interpret his exclamation as an acclamation to the sun, a kind of farewell to it: $\kappa\alpha\lambda\grave{o}\nu$ $\delta\acute{v}\epsilon$, "Set well."[46] Indeed, in a magic papyrus[47] we find: $[\kappa]\alpha\lambda\acute{\eta}$ $\sigma o\upsilon$ $\kappa\alpha\tau\acute{\alpha}\delta\upsilon\sigma\iota\varsigma$, "Well be thy setting." Rab contended that the Calendae originated in the primitive sun festivals, and its name was derived from Adam's first joyful farewell to the sun when it was about to set.

The comparison of some of the Hebrew (or Aramaic) rabbinic terms with their Greek equivalents sometimes proves to be mutually helpful. For instance, the *Talmudim*[48] report that R. Dosa b. Archinus called his younger brother בכור שטן "The first-born of Satan." Rab Zemaḥ Gaon[49] read instead בכור שוטה

---

[42] *De lingua Latina* VII. 4 (end).

[43] Graeci cum lumen affertur, solent dicere $\varphi\tilde{\omega}\varsigma$ $\mathring{\alpha}\gamma\alpha\vartheta\acute{o}\nu$. Comp. the Aramaic נהורא מעליא.

[44] In accordance with the Accusative: *calendas*.

[45] Ibid. and *TB* ibid. 8a. Comp. also *Bereshith Rabba* XI. 2, 88 ff.

[46] See *Mishnah Sukkah* IV. 5 (יופי לך מזבח) and Baneth's note in his German translation of the *Mishnah*, *Seder Mo'ed*, p. 534, n. 12. Comp. also the modern Greek farewell: $\sigma\tau\grave{o}$ $\kappa\alpha\lambda\acute{o}$.

[47] Pap. Louvre 2391, col. V, l. 124. Preisendanz, *Papyri graecae magicae* I, p. 38.

[48] *TP Yebamoth* I. 6, 3a; *TB* ibid. 16a.

[49] Cited in *Liber Juchassin*, ed. Filipowski 11b.

"A foolish first-born son."[50] S. Rapoport[51] called attention to the latter reading and added that this agrees with the text of *Seder Eliyyahu Zuta*.[52]

However, the reading בכור שטן, "The first-born of Satan," should not be altered.[53] Polycarpus[54] also styles Marcion πρωτό-τοκος τοῦ σατανᾶ," "The first-born of Satan." From the Talmud it appears to be a popular derogatory phrase used to designate a man who can "prove" whatever he wants. The Greek corroborates the Hebrew text; the Hebrew source explains the meaning of the term.

For an instance where the Hebrew is an aid to the Greek text we turn to the Testament of Job.[55] Eliphaz says about Elihu: ὅτι οὗτός ἐστιν ὁ τοῦ σκότους καὶ οὐχὶ τοῦ φωτός. "For this man is of darkness and not of light." The first edition, however, reads:[56] ὅτι υἱός ἐστι τοῦ σκότους κτλ. "For he is the *son of darkness* and not of light." This is most likely the original reading.

In rabbinic literature we find the term בר קבלאי[57] "The son of darkness." It also occurs in Hebrew:[58] בן אפלה.[59] In the

---

[50] According to most commentaries only a first-born by his mother and not by his father was termed בכור שוטה, see דקדוקי סופרים to *TB Baba Bathra*, p. 351, n. 70. Comp. however *Bereshith Rabba* XCI. 9, p. 1132₆ and Albeck's note ibid.

[51] תולדות רבינו נתן איש רומי, Warsaw, 1913, p. 27.

[52] Ch. I, ed. princ. 52b.

[53] For it is attested by both *Talmudim* and by mediaeval authorities who employ this expression. Moreover, *Seder Eliyyahu Zuta*, ed. Friedmann (published from a manuscript dated 1073), p. 169, as a matter of fact reads: בכור שטן.

[54] Irenaeus, *adv. haer.* III. 3. 4; Eusebius, *hist. eccl.* IV. 14. 7. Comp. Polycarpus, *ad Phil.* 7.

[55] XLIII, ed. James, *apocrypha anecdota*, second series, Cambridge, 1897, p. 131₂₇.

[56] See variants ibid.

[57] See *Vayyikra Rabba* XXV. 5 and parallel. Ibid. IV. 1 (according to codd. Vat. and London): קבלאי, "the dark one".

[58] II *Aboth deR. Nathan* XXXII, ed. Schechter 35a, according to the reading of Rabbi Simeon Duran in his מגן אבות on *Aboth* III. 10, ed. princ., 41b.

[59] The edition reads: בן מאירה, "The son of a curse". This is the Hebrew equivalent of the Aramaic בר פחין which is very frequent in Palestinian rabbinic

recently discovered scrolls of Jericho[60] the righteous are called
בני אור "The sons of light," and the wicked are named בני חושך
"The sons of darkness." Accordingly the remark of Eliphaz was
that Elihu was a "son of darkness" and not "of light." Here the
Hebrew idiom confirms the Greek variant.

Similarly, it is related in *TB*:[61] דרב יוסף בריה דר' יהושע בן לוי
חלש ואיתנגיד[62] כי הדר א"ל אבוה מאי חזית וכו' "R. Joseph the son of
R. Joshua b. Levi fell sick and *gave up his ghost*.[63] When he
revived his father asked him: What [vision] did you see?"
However, the exact translation of the word ואיתנגיד is extant in
Pirkei Rabbenu Hakkadosh:[64] ונמשך לאותו העולם "And he was
drawn (taken up) to the other world." Ps.-Jonathan (Gen. 5:24)
renders the Ἀνάληψις of Enoch: איתנגיד וסליק לרקיעא. Its Greek
equivalent would be: ἀνελήφθη καὶ ἀνέβη εἰς τὸν οὐρανον.[65]
Indeed, we read in the *Midrash*:[66] ר' מייאשה בר בריה דר' יהושע
[בן לוי][67] נשתקע שלשה שלשה ימים בחליו. לאחר שלשה ימים נתיישבה דעתו אמר
ליה אבוי ... ומה חמית תמן וכו'. The text is defective. It was

literature. See Jastrow, Dictionary etc., s. v. פחא II. All the dictionaries and
commentaries have misunderstood this term. The proverb (*TB ʿArakhin* 19a):
סבא בביתא פחא בביתא is to be translated: "An old man in the house is a curse in
the house". Likewise, in *Bereshith Rabba* (XXXVI. 2, p. 33610) Ham is termed:
אבוי דפחתא, "The father of the curse", i. e. of Canaan (see Gen. 9:25). In the
same way Simeon and Levi are called (ibid. XCIX, 6, see the variants in ed.
Albeck, p. 1206) אחים דפחתא, "The brothers of a curse" (See Gen. 49:7). Perhaps
פחת in Lev. 13:55 is synonymous with ממארת in 52 ibid. Comp. also my
translation of *TP Nedarim* IX. 3, 41c in *JQR* XXXVI, 1946, p. 346.

[60] L. Sukenik, מגילות גנוזות II, pp. 28–29. See also ibid. I, p. 18. Comp.
also the *International Crit. Comment.* to Luke XVI. 8.

[61] *Pesaḥim* 50a.

[62] See דקדוקי סופרים a. l.; ibid. *Baba Bathra*, p. 45, n. 300. Comp. the
Geonic responsa, ed. Harkavy, p. 179 and the commentary on the *Sefer Yetzirah*
by R. Jadah of Barcelona, p. 24 and p. 25.

[63] This is the translation of איתנגיד according to Rashi: נוע ופרחה נשמתו.
Rabbenu Hananel (and other commentaries): כאילו פרחה נשמתו "As if he gave
up his ghost," i. e. fainted. Comp. *Aruch Completum* s. v. נגד I and V.

[64] Ed. Schönblum, f. 28a; Grünhut, p. 48; Higger in *Horeb* VI, New York
1941, p. 125.

[65] It should be noted that וסליק לרקיעא has no equivalent in the Hebrew
text.

[66] *Ruth Rabba* III. 1.

[67] See below.

preserved in its complete form by Rabbi Samuel Jama[68] who
writes: ר' מייאשה בר בריה דר' יהושע בן לוי נשתקע בחולי' א נ ל י פ ת י ן
ג' ימים לאחר ג' ימים נתיישבה דעתו וכו'. The word אנליפתין, ἀνελήφθην,
was omitted by the scribes[69] in accordance with their usual
practice.[70] What does ἀνελήφθην mean in our context? Perles[71]
explains it to mean "he recuperated."[72] But this explanation is
utterly untenable. It requires considerable alteration of the
following sentence in the text. Besides, (as I learn from
Professor Henri Grégoire) the passive of ἀναλαμβάνω never
occurs in Greek in the sense of recovering.

However, we can read a similar anecdote in a Greek fragment of the Ascension of Isaiah.[73] It is related that Isaiah fell
into a trance (ἐγένετο ἐν ἐκστάσει) and was thought to be
dead. But when the king took his hand he learned that he
did not actually die, but was *taken up* (οὐκ ἀπέθανεν, ἀλλ'
ἀνελήφθη).[74]

Our *Midrashic* passage should accordingly be translated:
"R. Meyasha the grandson of R. Joshua b. Levi was made
unconscious by his illness. He was *taken up* (i. e. fell into a
trance) for three days. After three days he regained conscious-
ness. His father asked him . . . What did you see there?"
(i. e. in the other world). איתנגיד is therefore the literal and the
exact equivalent of ἀνελήφθη.

Moreover in the *Targumim* of the Pentateuch[75] the word
איתנגיד is used as a euphemistic expression for the death of the

[68] In his אגור, *Jubelschrift . . . Grätz*, Hebrew part, p. 25.

[69] Of the manuscript, or manuscripts, from which our printed editions were
published.

[70] See *GJP*, p. 152 and n. 43 ibid.

[71] *Festschrift Adolf Schwarz*, p. 294.

[72] This explanation was previously accepted by me in הירושלמי כפשוטו,
p. 187.

[73] Ed. Charles, London 1900, p. 142.

[74] Comp. also Hieron., *Epist.* XXII. 30 (Migne *PL* XXII, 416; *CSEL*
LIV, p. 190, 8): cum subito *raptus in spiritu* ad tribunal iudicis pertrahor.
"Suddenly I was spiritually taken up and dragged before the tribunal of the
Judge".

[75] Gen. 25:8; 17; 35:29; 49:33. Comp. *TB Baba Bathra* 16b and Nach-
manides' commentary on Gen. 25:17.

righteous. It also reappears on the fifteenth century tombs of the Yemenite Jews[76] who frequently preserved ancient traditions.[77] Professor Henri Grégoire[78] has shown that ἀνελήμφϑη which occurs on some Christian tombstones was a Montanistic term,[79] signifying the death of the righteous.[80] Here again איתגניד and ἀνελήφϑη are identical.

We find in *TP*:[81] מי הוא זה שמראה עצמו באצבע "Who is it that points himself out with his finger?" The parallel passage[82] reads: מי הוא זה שמראה גדולה בפנינו "Who is it that shows his greatness in our presence?" Thus להראות באצבע is nothing but to acclaim (δακτυλοδειξία, see below) by pointing with the finger.[83] In the same way it is stated in *Mishnath R. Eliezer*:[84] המראה עצמו באצבע (כיניו)[85] אין גס רוח כמו זה "There is none so presumptuous as he who points himself out with his finger."

This sense of the phrase is better clarified by the portrayal of a religious banquet in the future world. Seeking to lure the masses from the heathen religious orgies the Rabbis promised

---

[76] S. D. Goitein, *Joseph Halevy's Journey in Yemen*, Hebrew, p. 114; Arabic, p. 61. It is also noteworthy that the Yemenite sources (*Midrash Haggadol*, Gen., p. 429, ed. Margulies, p. 477₁₂; *The Exempla of the Rabbis*, ed. Gaster, p. 18) read in *Bereshith Rabba* (LXV, end, p. 743₅): איתנח ונגוד instead of נתנמנם, "Fell into a trance".

[77] See Lieberman הירושלמי כפשוטו, p. 520; *Yemenite Midrashim*, p. 16 ff.; *GJP*, p. 189, n. 30.

[78] *Byzantion* II, 1925, p. 329 ff.; ibid. X, 1935, p. 248.

[79] See in detail Lieberman, *Annuaire de l'Institut de Philol. et d'Hist. Orientales et Slaves* VII, 1944, p. 439 ff.

[80] Prof. A. Berger (*The Journal of Juristic Papyrology* I, 1945, p. 29 ff.) has demonstrated that the same verb also means "to be born" "to be procreated".

[81] *Berakhoth* II end, 5d; *Baba Bathra* V. 15a.

[82] *TB Baba Kamma* 81b.

[83] See also *Ekha Rabba* I, ed. Buber 27a. Comp. Daremberg et Saglio, *Dictionnaire* etc. I, s. v. *acclamatio*. The acclamation by the finger is also extant in the paintings of the Dura Europos synagogue.

[84] Ed. Enelow, p. 196.

[85] Read כינוי. The word makes no sense. It is very likely that the scribe who did not understand the expression took the following word עצמו as a euphemism for the name of the Almighty (see Rashi on *TB Gittin* 56b, s. v. עצמו) and inserted in the margin the gloss כינוי, i. e. euphemism, which subsequently crept in into the text.

them participation in the true festivals of the future world. They maintained:[86] והצדיקים מראים אותו באצבע ואומרים כי זה אלקים וכו' "And the righteous will point to Him with their fingers and say: 'For this is the Lord' (Ps. 48:15) etc."[87] We further read in *Debarim Rabba*:[88] היו מראים לאמותם באצבע ואומרים זה אלי ואנוהו להם "To their mothers they pointed Him out with their fingers saying: *This is my God, and I will glorify Him.*"[89]

Persius states:[90] "It is pleasant to be pointed out by the finger and [to hear it] said: 'This is the one'." Similarly, Lucian pictures[91] how Education persuades him by saying that even abroad "everyone who sees you . . . will point you out with his fingers saying 'This is the one'."[92] Thus the phrase להראות באצבע ולאמר זה הוא is nothing but δεικνύναι τῷ δακτύλῳ καὶ λέγειν οὗτος ἐκεῖνος, a frequent form of acclamation in antiquity.

It is likewise stated in the *Midrash*[93] that a Rabbi of the second century attributed to Jacob the following acclamation of Pharaoh: יתוספון משנותיי על שנותיך "May years from my years be added to yours." This is the exact equivalent of the acclamations

---

[86] *TP Mo'ed Katan* III. 7, 83b and parallels.

[87] Comp. הירושלמי כפשוטו, Introduction, p. IX. עוֹלִימתא means there ἑταῖραι. In the Palmyrene bilingual inscription (G. A. Cooke, *North-Semitic Inscriptions*, p. 330, l. 26) די עלימתא is translated (ibid. p. 320, l. 5): [ἑ]ταίρω[ν].

[88] Ed. Lieberman, p. 15 top.

[89] The parallel passage (*Pirkei R. Eliezer* ch. 42, ed. Luria 99b) reads simply וקילסוהו, "And they acclaimed Him".

[90] *Sat.* I. 28: At pulchrum est digito monstrari et dicier "Hic est."

[91] *Somn.* 11.

[92] τῶν ὁρώντων ἕκαστος . . . δείξει σε τῷ δακτύλῳ Οὗτος ἐκεῖνος λέγων. See C. Sittl, *Die Gebärden d. Griechen und Römer*, p. 52, n. 2. In addition to Persius and Lucius he cites many other instances.
There is also a δακτυλοδειξία in the negative sense, see Sittl ibid., p. 51, n. 5. Comp. Midrash *Ekha Rabba* I, ed. Buber 27a where it is stated that the Rabbi interpreted the pointing with the fingers (shown in a dream) to be a bad omen. Comp. also Wertheimer בתי מדרשות I, p. 40 where it is reported that whoever points with his finger to the image of the king saying "this is the king" is liable to be executed. See also ibid. III, p. 38 ff.

[93] *Bereshith Rabba*, ed. Albeck, p. 1233. Comp. also *Midrash Haggadol* Gen., p. 692, ed. Margulies, p. 788.

of the Roman emperors. Tertullian[94] formulates it: de nostris annis augeat tibi Jupiter annos. "May Jupiter add from our years to yours."[95]

According to the *Midrash* (ibid.) Jacob lived less than his ancestors because he donated part of his years to Pharaoh.[96] Suetonius[97] recounts that a certain man vowed that he would commit suicide if Caligula recovered from his illness. The emperor subsequently compelled the man to fulfill his vow. In the light of the preceding it is to be understood that the emperor believed in the efficacy of the donation of the years and did not want to forego the present.

In conclusion we have to remark about the tendency to find Latin words in rabbinic literature. The Palestinian Rabbis certainly did not know Latin. Except for military and judiciary terms (as well as names of objects imported from Latin speaking countries) which are usually also extant in Syriac and later Greek, Latin words are less than scarce in rabbinic literature. It is a matter of regret that this simple rule is neglected, and wrong Latin identifications have crept in even into popular Hebrew dictionaries. We shall quote a typical instance:[98]

ר' יהושע בן לוי אמר חנניה בן עזור נביא אמת היה אלא שהיה לו קיבוסת[99]
והיה שומע מה שירמיה מתנבא בשוק העליון ויורד ומתנבא בשוק התחתון

"R. Joshua b. Levi[100] said: Hananiah the son of Azzur[101] was [formerly] a true prophet, but he was a לוקיבוסת, and he used to listen to what Jeremiah prophesied in the Upper Market and then he would go down and deliver the same prophecy in the Lower Market." The word לוקיבוסת never occurs anywhere else in rabbinic literature, and its meaning can be guessed only by

---

[94] *Apol.* XXXV.

[95] Comp. also *acta fratrum Arvalium*, Dessau *I. L. S.*, 451.

[96] Comp. also *Pirkei R. Eliezer* XIX, ed. Rabbi David Luria, 45a, and n. 31 ibid., and the interpolation in *Midrash Tehilim* ch. 92, ed. Buber 205a.

[97] *Calig.* XIV. 2; XXVII. 2.

[98] *TP Sanhedrin* XI. 7, 30b.

[99] Read לוקיבוסת in one word.

[100] Flourished in the first half of the third century.

[101] See Jeremiah 28:1 ff.

the context. Prof. Torczyner[102] identifies it with the Latin *loquax*, i. e. Hananiah was loquacious etc. The connection of the latter's chattering with Jeremiah's prophecies is very weak. But above all it should be asked why did R. Joshua b. Levi use here a Latin word?[103] Is not פטפט in Hebrew as good an expression as *loquax* in Latin?

It is therefore most plausible that לוקיבוסת is corrupted from לוגקליפטס, λογοκλέπτης, plagiarist, as correctly suggested by I. Löw.[104] This identification is now corroborated by *Mishnath R. Eliezer*[105] where it is stated about Hananiah: היה מגנב דברים מירמיה "He plagiarized words from Jeremiah." The Rabbis had in mind Jeremiah 23:30: הנביאים ... מגנבי דברי *"The prophets . . . that steal My words."*[106] מגנב דברים is the literal equivalent of λογοκλέπτης. This term is not recorded in the Greek dictionaries, but λογοκλοπία[107] and λογοκλοπεία[108] occurs in Greek literature; it is therefore evident that the designation of the perpetrator of λογοκλοπία, the λογοκλέπτης, was also extant in Greek speech and literature.[109] The Rabbis employed the Greek word because it was the current technical term for plagiarism.

Perhaps, the same technical term was available in the *Yelamdenu*. Rabbi Nathanel[110] quotes in the name of *Midrash Yelamdenu*: היה עשו הולך לאחורי המדרשות ושומע(ין) מה שהן קוראין מאחורי המדרש ובא אל אביו וא"ל מה הלכה חדשת היום והוא אמר לו כך וכך. וקיבל ממנו אביו. והוא לא ידע שהוא ג ו נ ב ע נ י נ ו ת "Esau would go

---

[102] *Apud* Ben Yehuda, *A Complete Dictionary of Ancient and Modern Hebrew* XI, p. 5707, s. v. קבסת.

[103] Comp. the other note of Torczyner ibid. (on קבסתן) which propriety forbids us to reproduce here. Besides, how reasonable is it to assume that Babylonian Rabbis would employ this kind of a Greek word? As to the first explanation of Torczyner ibid. of קבסתן see Pineles דרכה של תורה, p. 152.

[104] *Apud* S. Krauss *LW* II, p. 527b.

[105] Ed. Enelow, p. 117. This is the source of *Midrasch Tannaïm*, ed. Hoffmann, p. 63.

[106] The Septuagint translates it: τοὺς προφήτας . . . τοὺς κλέπτοντας τοὺς λόγους μου. Rashi remarks that the verse alludes to our Hananiah.

[107] See Liddell and Scott s. v.

[108] See Sophocles, *Greek Lexicon*, s. v.

[109] As it exists in neo-Greek, see S. Koumanoudis, Συναγωγὴ νέων λέξων, p. 611, s. v. λογοκλέπτης.

[110] *Light of Shade etc.*, ed. A. Kohut, New York 1894, p. 96.

behind the schools and listen from behind the school[111] to what was being studied. Then he would come to his father, and when the latter asked him: 'What new *halakha* have you evolved today?' He would answer 'such and such'. His father would accept it, not knowing that he was a plagiarist."[112] It is the predilection of the *Tanḥuma*-type of *Midrashim* to translate the Greek words into Hebrew,[113] and it is therefore possible that in his original remark the Rabbi used the word לוגוקליפטיס, λογο-κλέπτης, which was correctly translated גונב עינות.[114]

Rabbinic literature is replete with valuable information about the life, manners and customs of the ancients. Many passages in it can be properly understood only in the general frame of its environment. The Jews of Palestine were by no means isolated from the ancient Mediterranean civilized world. They shared many of its general beliefs, conceptions and patterns of behavior.

---

[111] Comp. Tosefta *Baba Kamma* VII. 13, 55917 and *Tosefeth Rishonim* II p. 94, n. 17. [Prof. E. E. Urbach correctly remarked (*Zion*, vol. XVI, 1951, fasc. 3–4, p. 16, n. 109) that the Rabbis alluded to the Jewish legends which the Christian church fathers included in their works without mentioning their sources.]

[112] Literally a thief of subjects, of ideas.

[113] Comp. also *JQR* XXXV, 1944, p. 37, n. 241.

[114] Rabbi Salem Shabazi in his חמדת הימים 47b cites here: גונב דברים. Since his quotation seems to be a combination of various sources, the reading is probably the Rabbi's own formulation.

THE TEXTS OF SCRIPTURE IN THE EARLY
RABBINIC PERIOD

In the book *Greek in Jewish Palestine* we sought to prove that the general Hellenization of the Mediterranean world did not bypass the Jews, that they were affected by it in not a small degree. Our investigations were mainly based on Greek phrases, technical terms and single words available in rabbinic literature. We shall now try to trace Hellenistic influence in the behavior, rites, practices, conceptions and literary methods of the Jews.

We shall consider first the treatment of the manuscripts of Scripture by the early Rabbis[1] and compare it with the methods applied by the Alexandrian grammarians to the Greek Bible, the poems of Homer, the "Prophet of All."[2]

According to the rabbinic sources the Bible contained words which were read although not written in the text, words written in the text which were not read,[3] emendations by the Soferim[4] (literally: Scribes, see below), dots on certain letters[5] and special signs.[6] Most of these sources date from the second century C. E., but the tradition itself is, no doubt, of much earlier origin. The information provided by it deserves closer examination.

Following the rabbinic analysis, we may divide the textual

[1] I. e. the Soferim who, according to tradition, were active in Palestine during the Persian period and the beginning of the Hellenistic domination.

[2] Ὁ τοῦ Πάντος προφήτης (Aristid. Quint. III.26).

[3] *TB Nedarim* 37b; *Soferim* VI, 8–9, ed. Higger, p. 174 ff. The whole text is translated and discussed by Geiger (*Urschrift* etc. p. 251) and by Ginsburg (*Introduction to the Massoretico-Critical Edition of the Hebrew Bible*, London 1897, p. 308).

[4] *Tanḥuma, Beshalaḥ* 16. Comp. *Mekhilta Shirah* VI, ed. Horovitz, p. 134, ed. Lauterbach II, p. 43; *Sifre* I, 84, ed. Horovitz, p. 81 and parallels.

[5] *Sifre* ibid. 69, p. 64 ff. and parallels referred to in the editor's notes. Comp. also Ginsburg ibid., p. 319 ff.

[6] *Sifre* ibid. 84, p. 80 and parallels, see below; Ginsburg ibid., p. 342 ff.

activity of the Soferim into three categories: 1. They strove to establish the genuine text, as given by God to Moses. 2. They introduced dots and possibly other signs (see below) into the text. 3. In the view of some Rabbis of Southern Palestine, they deliberately emended the text on occasion for certain reasons (see below).

The system of the so called *Keri and Kethib*[7] undoubtedly belongs to the history of text criticism. In the preface to his commentary on Joshua, Rabbi David Kimḥi[8] remarks: "It seems that these words (i. e. of the category of *Keri and Kethib*) came into existence because the books were lost or dispersed during the first exile, and the sages who were skilled in Scripture were dead. Thereupon the men of the Great Synagogue, who restored the Torah to its former state, finding divergent readings in the books, adopted those which were supported by the majority of copies and seemed genuine to them. In those cases where they were not able to reach a decision, they wrote down one alternative but did not vocalize it (!), or noted it in the margin but omitted it from the text. Likewise they sometimes inserted one reading in the margin and another in the text."[9]

Part of this account is, of course, mainly based on the famous passage:[10] ובשנים . . . באחד מצאו כתוב‏[11] . . . שלשה ספרים נמצאו בעזרה ‏ מצאו כתוב . . . בטלו חכמים את האחד וקיימו את השנים. "Three Scrolls

---

[7] Words read but not written and vice versa, see above n. 3.

[8] Flourished in the twelfth and thirteenth centuries.

[9] ונראה כי המלות האלו נמצאו כן לפי שבגלות הראשונה אבדו הספרים ונטלטלו, והחכמים יודעי המקרא מתו ואנשי כנסת הגדולה שהחזירו התורה לישנה מצאו מחלוקות בספרים והלכו בהם אחר הרוב לפי דעתם ובמקום שלא השינה דעתם על הבירור כתבו האחד ולא נקדו או כתבו מבחוץ ולא כתבו מבפנים, וכן כתבו בדרש (צ'ל: בדרך) אחד מבפנים ובדרש (צ'ל: בדרך) אחר מבחוץ.

[10] *Sifre* II 356, ed. Finkelstein, p. 423; II *Aboth deR. Nathan* ch. 46, ed. Schechter, 65a; *TP Ta'anith* IV, 2, 68a; *Soferim* VI, 4, ed. Higger, p. 169.

[11] This is the reading of *Midrash Haggadol* in the *Sifre* a. l., *TP* and *Soferim* ibid. It is the *terminus technicus* of both the scholiasts on Homer (εὕρομεν γεγραμένον — מצאנו כתוב —, see Ludwich, *Aristarchs homerische Textkritik* I, p. 45) and the Rabbis. See *BR* IX.5, ed. Theodor, p. 70 and the parallels referred to in the notes ibid.; Rabbinovicz, *Variae lectiones* to *TB Yoma*, p. 140 n. ש, passim. The same can probably be applied to the term נמצאו בעזרה where *TP* reads: מצאו בעזרה.

of the Law were found in the Temple Court[12]. . . In one of
them they found written[13]. . . and in the other two they found
written . . . The sages discarded [the reading of] the one and
adopted [the reading of] the two."[14] Nothing in the text indicates when this event took place.[15] The sages established the
correct reading of the Temple Scroll on the basis of the majority of manuscripts[16] at some time during the Second Commonwealth. For our purpose we shall note only that there is
no reference in the sources to doing away with (גניזה) or cor-
recting (הגהה) any of the books which they collated. It is not
even stated that they were removed from the Temple library.[17]

Although it appears from the earlier rabbinic sources that
only one authoritative book was deposited in the [archives of]
the Temple[18] it does not follow that other copies were not to be
found there. It means only that this book was the standard
copy par excellence, the book, as the Rabbis tell us, from which
the Scroll of the king was corrected[19] under the supervision of
the High Court.[20] A special college of book readers (מגיהי ספרים),
who drew their fees from the Temple funds, checked the text
of the book of the Temple.[21] This was probably the only genuine
text which was *legally* authorized for the public service.

But it is highly doubtful that the public at large accepted
at once the alterations and corrections of the learned men. In
all likelihood they adhered to their old texts for a long time.
The *vulgata*, authoritative popular texts circulated among the
masses, in many synagogues and in the schools. The copies of

---

[12] Comp. Jos. *Antiq.* V. 1. 17 (61); see *JQR* N. S. XI, 1920, p. 133.

[13] See above n. 11.

[14] See Blau, *Studien zum althebräischen Buchwesen*, p. 101 ff.

[15] See Blau ibid., p. 104.

[16] See E. Bickerman, *A. Marx Jubilee Volume*, pp. 167–168.

[17] On the library of the Temple, see Blau ibid., p. 99 ff.

[18] See *Mishnah Mo'ed Katan* III.4; *Kelim* XV.6; *Tosefta* ibid., 584₉. The
reading עזרא does not affect our thesis, for the book of Ezra was deposited in
the Temple as the context of the *Tosefta* clearly indicates.

[19] *Mekhilta* on Deut. in *Sifre* ed. Finkelstein, p. 211; *TP Sanhedrin* II,
20c.

[20] Comp. *Tosefta* ibid. IV. 7, 421₁₉.

[21] *TP Shekalim* IV, 3, 48a. Comp. *TB Kethuboth* 106a.

the temple were the ἠκριβωμένα, the most exact books, but the *vulgata* continued to exist as the standard texts of the public.

We read in *Midrash Bereshith Rabbathi* (ed. Albeck, p. 209) by Rabbi Moshe Hadarshan:[22] דין הוא מן מליא דכתיבן באורייתא דנפקת מן ירושלם בשביתא וסלקת לרומי והות גניזא בכנישתא דאסוירוס וכו' "This is one of the words which were written in the Scroll which was captured in Jerusalem[23] and was brought to Rome and was stored in the synagogue of Severus[24] etc."[25] That our Scroll is of the Jerusalem type is confirmed by the fact that the medial מ occurs in it frequently instead of the final ם.[26] This agrees with the statement of a Rabbi of the third century who remarked:[27] אנשי ירושלים היו כותבים ירושלים ירושלימה ולא היו מקפידין "The people of Jerusalem used to write [in their scrolls] ירושלים and (ירושלימ(ה indiscriminately", i. e. they used the final ם and the medial מ promiscuously.[28] Furthermore, a *Baraitha* in tractate *Sefarim*[29] quoted by Rab Hai[30] states that the scroll found in Jerusalem was in a *different script* and that its number

[22] Flourished in the first half of the eleventh century. He used much earlier sources for his *Midrash*.

[23] Codd. Paris. and Damasc. (see below n. 25) do not mention that the book came from Jerusalem. But see Jos., *bel. Iud.* VII.5.7 (162). Comp. *Vita* 75 (418) and Blau, *Studien zum althebräischen Buchwesen*, p. 39, n. 3.

[24] See Momigliano, "Severo Alessandro Archisynagogus," *Athenaeum* XXII, 1934, p. 151 ff.

[25] The text was first published by A. Epstein in *MGWJ* 34, 1885, p. 342 and in the *Chwolson-Festschrift*, p. 49; by Neubauer in *MGWJ* 36, 1887, p. 508 from a Paris manuscript and by A. Harkavy in his חדשים גם ישנים No. 6, p. 4–5 (from a Damascus manuscript).

[26] See Albeck's notes p. 210, nn. 3, 5 and 6; p. 211 nn. 2 and 6.

[27] *TP Megillah* I. 9, 71d.

[28] Comp. A. Sperber in *HUCA* XVII, 1943, p. 332 ff. Prof. H. L. Ginsberg has kindly called my attention to H. Torczyner הלשון והספר, Jerusalem 1948, p. 19 who also associated (Comp. Sperber ibid., p. 333) the above text with the statement in *TP*. The observation of *TP* ibid. ודכוותה צפון צפונה etc. has to be understood as a question prompted by the fact that the anonymous Rabbi probably had never come across the promiscuous use of ן and נ in old books.

[29] Or *Soferim* II, see M. Higger שבע מסכתות קטנות, p. 10 ff.

[30] *Geonic Responsa*, ed. Harkavy 3, p. 3; *Otzar Hageonim* on *Kiddushin* I, p. 84 ff. See also below, p. 42, n. 37.

of verses[31] did not correspond to the number given in the *Baraitha* quoted in *TB Kiddushin* 30a. Comp. *Yalkut* I, 855.

These books of Jerusalem are thus quoted as possessing some authority; they probably represented the general *vulgata* of the Jews of the first centuries C. E.

R. Moshe Hadarshan (ibid.) and Rabbi David Kimḥi[32] already noted that some variants recorded in *Bereshith Rabba* as *"found[33]* in the book of Rabbi Meir"[34] also occur in the Jerusalem scroll which was stored in the synagogue of Severus. The expression "the book of R. Meir" is generally taken to mean R. Meir's personal copy. This is certainly true with regard to those variants which were apparently glossae introduced by the eminent Rabbi. But in addition this book had textual readings different from those in our accepted texts, as can now be ascertained by the excerpts from the scroll of the synagogue of Severus. Furthermore, R. Hiyya[35] once remarked[36] that if he could obtain the book of Psalms of R. Meir[37] he would be able to act in a certain manner. The context suggests[38] that R. Hiyya could have had in mind any of the copies written by R. Meir and not his personal volume. It is therefore obvious that there is no proof that to the Rabbis "the book of Rabbi Meir" always meant one and the same scroll, i. e. his personal copy.[39]

---

[31] On stichometry among the ancients, see F. Ritschl, *Opuscula philologica* I, p. 74 ff. and p. 86 ff. Among the Greeks, Callimachus (c. 305–240 B. C. E.) seems to have been the first to introduce stichometry in his πίνακες (See ibid., p. 84). Comp. also Th. Birt, *Das antike Buchwesen*, p. 162 ff.; idem, *Kritik und Hermeneutik etc.*, p. 39 ff.; Swete, *Introduction to the O. T. in Greek*, 1914, p. 346 ff. W. Schubart, *Das Buch bei d. Griechen²* etc., pp. 73 and 180; E. Bickerman, *JBL* LXIII, 1944, p. 340, n. 6.

[32] See Albeck ibid. nn. 12, 13.

[33] בספרו של ר'מ מצאו כתוב, see above, n. 11.

[34] Flourished in the second century.

[35] Flourished in the beginning of the third century.

[36] *TP Sukkah* III. 11, 53d and parallel.

[37] ספר תילים של ר' מאיר.

[38] As correctly understood by Blau, *Studien zum althebräischen Buchwesen*, p. 111, n. 3. Comp. n. 2 ibid.

[39] Comp. also כנסת הגדולה, ed. Suwalsky, III, part 3, p. 172 ff.

The Jews had no such big publishing houses as, for instance, that of T. Pomponius Atticus in Rome. Book trade marks like Ἀττικιανά[40] are not available in early Jewish manuscripts, but certain books were identified as coming from the hand of a careful scribe. TP[41] incidentally refers to an exact copy (ספר מוגה) "like those which are designated as the books of Assi" (כגון דאמרין אילין ספרוי דאסי).[42] From the context it is obvious that these exact books were written by Assi himself whose handwriting was well known. His books were renowned as "the books of Assi."

This is the sense to be attached to the phrase the "book of R. Meir." The Rabbi was a scribe by profession,[43] "a good copyist of the very best,"[44] and it is safe to assume that his copies were designated by his name. It was noted above[45] that several readings of his book were identical with those of the scrolls of Jerusalem. This is quite instructive. Rabbi Meir earned his livelihood as *librarius*; he transcribed books which were in demand by schools and individuals. He therefore copied the *vulgata*, the text to which the public was accustomed.

This practice parallels the one that was characteristic of the circulation of the Homeric texts. The publishing houses took little notice of the literary activity of the Alexandrian grammarians, and continued to copy the common text.[46] The copies designated as χαριέστατα and ἀστειότερα (*urbana*) were the appanage of the few; the κοινότερα were the possession of the public at large.

Thus the κοινά, the common texts, of the Bible were not simply erroneous texts. They represented a variant text which

---

[40] See Dziatzko in PW *RE* I, 1886, s. v. Ἀττικιανά; Schubart, *Das Buch bei d. Griechen*² etc., p. 188.

[41] *Kethuboth* II. 3, 26b.

[42] Comp. also *TB Baba Bathra*, 164b.

[43] *TB 'Erubin* 13a passim.

[44] *Koheleth Rabba* II, 17: ר' מאיר הוה כתבן טב מובחר.

[45] Regardless of how we understand the expression the "book of R. Meir," i. e. even if we assume that it refers to his personal copy, he might have used it as the standard book from which he transcribed the volumes for sale.

[46] See Th. W. Allen, *Homer* etc., p. 309 ff.

perhaps did not contain some of the emendations of the Soferim and corrections of the sages, for it is unlikely that all those alterations were immediately introduced into the popular texts. Some time later some of them were probably accepted and some rejected, much as in the case of the common classical texts.[47] The Jerusalem books, many of whose readings are identical with those in R. Meir's copies,[48] probably belonged to a certain type of common text.

We may safely assume that the Scriptures of the small Jewish localities in Palestine were inferior to the *vulgata* of Jerusalem, and that the school copies for the children's use in such localities were of the worst type, $\varphi\alpha\nu\lambda\acute{o}\tau\epsilon\rho\alpha$. The fact that R. 'Akiba urged his pupil, R. Simeon, to teach his son from a revised copy[49] indicates that such erroneous books were current in the schools.

On the other hand, rolls written by R. Meir were exact copies of the average *vulgata* of the Jerusalem type. A text of this kind was certainly treated as a good authority, at least for *Midrashic* purposes. The Rabbis used to base their exegesis both on the *Keri* and the *Kethib*.[50] It seems likely that they utilized for the same purpose the current vulgar text,[51] although they officially recognized the Temple copy of the Bible as the only genuine one for the use in the synagogue service.

We outlined here in general features the history of the Scriptural texts in the early rabbinic period. According to the Rabbis, the Soferim pursued their literary activity (comp. the following chapters) during the domination of the Persians over Palestine and the early years of the Hellenistic ascendency. If this is the case, the text criticism of the Alexandrian school,

---

[47] See Allen ibid., p. 311.

[48] See above, n. 32.

[49] *TB Pesaḥim* 112a. Comp. *TB Kethuboth* 19b.

[50] See Bacher, *Terminologie* etc. II, pp. 92–93; 194–195.

[51] Comp. יד מלאכי, sect. רפ׳ג and Rabbi 'Akiba Eiger's note in his גליון הש״ס to *Tosafoth* on *Shabbath* 55b, s. v. מעבירם. The current *vulgata* was not rated worse than לשון הדיוט, secular documents, which the Rabbis were in the habit of interpreting. See *Tosefta Kethuboth* IV. 9–12, 264 30 ff. and parallels.

which began with Zenodotus (c. 284 B. C. E.), could hardly have influenced the Soferim.[52]

However, the treatment of the text of the Bible and that of Homer shows striking parallels (see the following chapters), with one vital difference. The sacred text of the Bible was handled by Jews, whose general reverence and awe in religious matters need not be stressed. The copies of Homer, although a religious text, were handled by Greeks whose comparative levity even in the religious domain is well known. The rejection ($\dot{\alpha}\vartheta\acute{\epsilon}\tau\eta\sigma\iota\varsigma$) of many verses of Homer by Zenodotus, Aristophanes of Byzantium, Aristarchus etc.[53] and many of the reasons offered by them for such eliminations[54] speak for themselves.

[52] The division of the Bible into twenty four (See IV Ezra, end, and Charles, *The Apocrypha* etc. II, p. 624, n. 45) or twenty two (See Swete, *Introduction to the O. T. in Greek*, 1914, p. 220 ff.) books and the respective division of the Iliad and Odyssey in twenty four books (See Seneca, *Epist.* LXXXVIII. 40 and Th. Birt, *Kritik und Hermeneutik* etc., p. 296) may serve as a good illustration as to how careful we have to be in drawing conclusions from parallels.

[53] Although they affected our texts of Homer but slightly their very suggestions betray their attitude. Comp. also H. Wolfson, *Philo* I, p. 139.

[54] See, for instance, below, pp. 36–37.

CORRECTIONS OF THE SOFERIM

The term תיקון סופרים, correction of the Soferim, is first found in an utterance of R. Joshua b. Levi, a Rabbi who flourished in the first half of the third century. We read in *Shemoth Rabba* (XIII.1): כל הנוגע בהם כנוגע בבבת עינו. ר' יהושע ‏<‏בן לוי‏>‏[1] אמר תיקון סופרים הוא ביו"ד ה י ה כ ת ו ב[2] "[It is written]: '*He that toucheth you*[2a] *toucheth the apple of his eye*' (Zech. 2:12). R. Joshua b. Levi said: It is a correction of the Soferim, it was [originally] written with a יו"ד" (i. e. עיני, "*My eye*").

A similar statement is recorded in *Bereshith Rabba*:[3] ואברהם עידנו עומד לפני ה' אמר ר' סימון תיקון סופרים זה שכינה ממתנת לאברהם "[It is written]: '*But Abraham stood yet before the Lord*' (Gen. 18:22). R. Simeon[4] said: It is a correction of the Soferim, for the *Shekhinah* was waiting for Abraham."[5]

---

[1] This is the reading of *Yalkut Hamakhiri* (Zech., p. 32 and Prov. 27:3, f. 66a) and Rabbi Abraham Bucrat in his ספר הזכרון 9c. Cod. Oxford (147, f. 188a) also reads: רי"בל. Similar statements by his pupil which are recorded in many places in rabbinic literature (see below n. 5) indicate clearly that its ascription to R. Joshua b. Levi is not apocryphal.

[2] This is the reading of the *Yalkut* and Bucrat ibid. Cod. Oxford reads: ביו"ד כתי'. Ed. princeps: עיני כתוב, read כתוב [היה] עיני.

[2a] I have translated according to the M. T. The Hebrew is a rabbinic paraphrase.

[3] XXXIX. 7, ed. Theodor-Albeck, p. 505.

[4] The famous disciple of R. Joshua b. Levi, see above n. 1.

[5] Theodor a. l. quotes the numerous places where R. Simeon's statement is recorded. (The only genuine reading is in *BR*. In the later sources the text is elaborated). He further calls attention (Comp. מנחת שי a. l. and Geiger, *Urschrift* etc., p. 331 ff.) to *TP Bikkurim* III. 3, 65c (add: *TP Rosh Hashanah* I. 3, 57b): R. Simeon said (in ref. to Lev. 19:32): "The Holy One blessed is He said etc.: I was the first to observe [the law of] standing up before an 'old man' " (זקן =sage). The Talmud does not specify the case where the Lord stood in the presence of a sage. But it is most likely that our R. Simeon alludes to his own remark on the above mentioned verse in Genesis. Although

Tanḥuma (*Beshalaḥ* 16) cites a number of other verses which were slightly altered, with the explicit remark:[6] "And Scripture used a euphemistic expression, i. e. it is a correction of the Soferim, the men of the Great Synagogue . . . and the verse (Ezek. 8:17) '*to My nose*' was corrected by them: '*to their nose*' . . . But these verses were corrected by the men of the Great Synagogue."[7]

This tradition deserves closer examination. Mediaeval and modern scholars have assumed divergent attitudes towards it. Some of the former[8] denied that the Soferim ever altered the text of Scripture. They explained the *Midrashic* passages to mean that the Bible itself employed euphemistic expressions. The Soferim only taught the original *meaning* of these euphemisms. Some modern scholars[9] adopted the same attitude and maintained that the "corrections" are a later invention. Their main argument is that the *Tannaitic* sources[10] which cite some of the verses in question make no mention at all of the term

Theodor overlooked the passage in *Midrash Shir Hashirim*, ed. Grünhut, f. 38b where the same observation is made with an explicit reference to Deut. 5:28, he is right in his association of *TP* and *BR*, for in *Midrash Shir Hashirim* the statement is recorded anonymously, and it is probably based on a different tradition; see *TB Megillah* 21a.

The objections raised by Reifmann in *Beth Talmud*, ed. Weiss II, p. 377, are totally untenable, for he overlooked all the parallels cited by Theodor, where it is stated that our R. Simeon himself connected the verse in Genesis with Ps. 18:36.

[6] וכנהו הכתוב שהוא תיקון סופרים אנשי כנסת הגדולה . . . אל אפי והם תקנו אל אפם . . .
אלא שכינו פסוקים אלו אנשי כנסת הגדולה.

[7] For the mediaeval authorities dealing with the alteration of the Soferim, see Theodor to *BR* ibid.; Pinsker in כרם חמד IX, pp. 53 ff.; Ginsburg, *Introduction* etc., pp. 351 ff.; W. E. Barnes, *The Journal of Theological Studies* 1900, I, pp. 388 ff. and the articles referred to below. Add: Raimundus Martini, *Pugio Fidei*, ed. Carpzov, pp. 694–695. Comp. ibid. p. 227.

[8] See the list cited by Rabbi Abraham Bucrat in his ספר הזכרון 9b, Rabbi Azariah de Rossi in מאור עינים ch. XIX and Katzenellenbogen in נתיבות עולם to the ל״ב מדות, 33b ff.

[9] S. Sachs in his editorial remark to Pinsker's article in כרם חמד, IX, p. 60 (see above n. 7); H. J. Pollack in *Beth Ha-Midrash*, ed. Weiss, 1865, pp. 56 ff.; Barnes ibid. (see above, n. 7) and many others.

[10] *Mekhilta*, *Shirah* IV, ed. Horovitz, p. 135, ed. Lauterbach II, p. 43; *Sifre* I, 84, ed. Horovitz, p. 81.

"correction of the Soferim," but state explicitly: שכינה הכתוב, "Scripture" (and not the Soferim!) "used a euphemistic expression." As for the clear statement of the *Midrash Tanḥuma*, it is dismissed as a later interpolation. Indeed, Rabbi Azariah de Rossi[11] testifies that in two old manuscripts of the *Tanḥuma* the passage is missing.

However, the express statements of R. Simeon[12] and his teacher[13] can by no means be disregarded. It stands to reason that in the *Tanḥuma* manuscripts of Rabbi Azariah de Rossi the passage was deliberately eliminated on the very same grounds which prompted the Soferim to make their alterations (see below). Indeed, in *Yalkut Hamakhiri*[14] we find a quotation from *Tanḥuma* (on Num. 22:9) including a long list of the corrections of the Soferim with the same explicit description:[15] "And Scripture used a euphemistic expression, i. e. this is a correction of the Soferim, the men of the Great Synagogue,"[16] as in the *Tanḥuma*-passage quoted above. In all our editions of the *Tanḥuma* to *Bemidbar* the entire portion is missing.[17] The author of the *Yalkut* certainly did not invent the passage. He found it in his Spanish manuscripts.[18] The copies in possession of the editors of our *Tanḥuma* to *Bemidbar* were purged of this annoying portion.

Furthermore, the *Tanḥuma* section in question was extant

---

[11] See above, n. 8.

[12] In *Bereshith Rabba*. And this *Midrash* is not of the sixth century, as Barnes, p. 404 (see above n. 7) would have it, but was compiled by the end of the fourth century or the beginning of the fifth. The name R. Simeon which occurs also in the parallel places is evidently based on a sound tradition. The Palestinian Talmud confirms it, see above n. 5.

[13] According to the correct reading of both the name of the Rabbi and his statement, see above nn. 1–2.

[14] Zech. 2:12, pp. 29–30.

[15] Ibid., p. 30.

[16] Whether the apposition "the men of the Great Synagogue" is a later interpolation or not is of no import to our thesis, for the interpolation is probably based on an old tradition.

[17] Only the beginning of the passage is extant in *Bemidbar Rabba* XX. 6; the whole discussion of the corrected verses is missing.

[18] See A. Marx, *OLZ*, 1902, p. 295 ff.; Lieberman, Introduction to his edition of דברים רבה, p. XI.

in the manuscripts of Rabbi Nathan of Rome[19] who accepted it literally and at its face value.[20]

Some modern scholars[21] having credited the *Tanḥuma* tradition regarding the corrections of the Soferim used it as a point of departure to discredit our Massoretic text. They "discovered" additional corrections, maintaining that even the later Rabbis (until the second century C. E.) continued to emend the texts of Scriptures.

Thus, both Biblical and rabbinic scholars are divided into two camps. One contends that the original tradition about the euphemisms under discussion is preserved only in the earlier, *Tannaitic*, sources,[22] where the term תיקון סופרים, "correction of the Scribes," is not found, and they assert that the report contained in the *Tanḥuma* and in the mediaeval Jewish sources is a later invention which has no roots in earlier tradition. The other maintains that the genuine text is represented by the *Midrash Tanḥuma*, whereas the earlier sources were modified according to the prevailing rabbinic opinion that no human being has the right to alter even a dot in Scripture.

However, the attitude of both camps is wrong. We should neither read in our ideas into the texts nor do violence to the wording of the sources. The *Mekhilta* and *Sifre*[23] state in plain words that Scripture used euphemistic expressions, — Scripture itself and not the Soferim.[24] On the other hand in *Midrash Tanḥuma*[25] it is expressly recorded that the Soferim changed the text. The two opinions cannot possibly be reconciled. We are confronted with two divergent views of two different schools. We have no right to adapt one rabbinic source to the theory expounded in another rabbinic book. We must consider the sources as they are, independently of each other.

[19] Flourished in the eleventh century.

[20] See ערוך s. v. כבד I. Comp. also ibid. s. v. עטר I.

[21] Geiger, *Urschrift* etc., p. 309 ff.; J. H. Schorr, החלוץ I, p. 99 (second edition, p. 84) and others.

[22] See above, n. 10.   [23] See above, n. 10.

[24] The reading in both sources is absolutely sure: it is confirmed by all manuscripts.

[25] And the other *Midrashim*, see above, nn. 2, 3, 5.

Let us therefore examine the texts carefully. The *Mekhilta*[26] lists eleven instances of euphemistic expressions in Scripture.[27] The *Sifre* omitted four examples out of the eleven, counting only seven.[28]

Nine out of the eleven euphemisms recorded in the *Mekhilta* involve the change of only one letter in the pronominal suffixes. In one case the substitution of two letters (in the pronominal suffix) instead of one is implied,[29] and the last example concerns the transposition of two letters in the same word.[30]

In ten out of the eleven instances mentioned in the *Mekhilta* and in seventeen out of the eighteen listed in the late sources[31] the euphemism concerns the honor of the Lord only.

The single exception in all the sources is formed by Num. 12:12: בצאתו מרחם אמו מרחם אמנו אלא שכינה הכתוב. ויאכל חצי בשרו חצי בשרנו אלא שכינה הכתוב[32] " 'When he cometh out of his mother's womb' (Num. 12:12) means 'when he cometh out of OUR mother's womb', but Scripture has euphemized. 'Of whom the flesh is half consumed' means 'OUR flesh is half consumed', but Scripture has euphemized." One wonders what the Rabbis felt to be offensive in the expression אמנו (our mother's) and בשרנו (our flesh), and how it was obviated by the change to אמו (his mother's) and בשרו (his flesh). The difficulty was already noted by Abraham Ibn Ezra a. l.

However, an old parallel source[33] states clearly to this effect: מכאן היה ר' אלעזר בר' שמעון אומר צריך אדם להיות מושל בשל עצמו משל אחרים. "From here (i. e. Num. 12:12) R. Eleazar b. Simeon concluded that if a person has to mention [anything unpleasant with reference to] himself he should word it as if it referred to somebody else."

It is therefore evident that the early Rabbis never intended

---

[26] See above n. 10.

[27] An English translation is available in ed. Lauterbach. Comp. also Ginsburg, *Introduction* etc., p. 348.

[28] See Ginsburg ibid., p. 349.

[29] In I Sam. (3:13) להם is used instead of לי.

[30] In II Sam. (20:1) לאהליו is used instead of לאלהיו.

[31] See Ginsburg, *Introduction* etc., p. 351.

[32] This is the reading of some mss. in *Sifre* I, ed. Horovitz, p. 103.

[33] *Sifre Zuta*, ed. Horovitz, p. 277.

to say that Scripture had changed the words of Aaron. It is Aaron himself who employed a euphemism.[34] The compilers of the *Mekhilta* and the *Sifre* gathered the various euphemisms from several places and reckoned Aaron's turn of speech among the euphemisms of Scripture. The editor of the *Tanḥuma* simply introduced the whole section of the *Mekhilta* into his compilation,[35] although, of course, the last instance can under no circumstances be counted as a revision of the Soferim. The editor merely quoted his source in its entirety, although one of the instances did not fall under the general category according to his own views. It is a regular, well known, phenomenon in rabbinic literature.

Thus *all* the euphemistic alterations ascribed to the *Soferim* concerned His honor, and His honor only.

Indeed, some of the expressions in their original form (or meaning) practically border on blasphemy. The verse: *"And, lo they sent the Zemorah*[36] *to their nose"* (Ezek. 8:17), if the euphemism is removed reads: *"to My nose."* In this form it would be shocking even to the primitive ear. It is suitable only to the filthy slave of the Aristophanean comedy.[37] On the other hand, it is hard to understand why most of the other verses cited in the rabbinic sources were revised. Jacob Reifmann[38] collected a great number of Biblical passages which contain rougher expressions than many of those included among the corrections of the Soferim. Why then, he asks, did the Soferim (or the verse) modify some utterances while they left others unchanged? Why the inconsistency?

However, we cannot apply our modern standards to the

---

[34] The expression שכינה הכתוב, "Scripture has euphemized," is simply a cliché. Comp. also *Sifre Zuta* ibid., p. 277 15.

[35] The number "eighteen corrections" mentioned in the Massoretic sources has no sound basis. See Schechter's note *apud* Barnes (see above n. 7), p. 414, n. 1.

[36] See below, n. 37.

[37] *Plut.* 698: προσιόντος γὰρ αὐτοῦ (i. e. Asclepius) μέγα πάνυ ἀπέπαρδον. On the meaning of *Zemorah* in the sense of *crepitus ventris* see ספר השרשים by Rabbi Jonah Ibn G'anaḥ s. v. זמר and Rashi to Ezek. a. l. The other rabbinic interpretations of the word do not render the action less obscene. See *Aruch Completum* III, p. 300, s. v. זמר.

[38] *Beth Talmud*, ed. Weiss, II, p. 275 ff.

ancients. We are not in a position to measure their sensitivity to certain expressions and their definition of rudeness of style. We really find no consistency in the use of euphemisms even in later rabbinic literature.[39] We are in no position to judge the ancients for their seeming inconsistency; they were guided by their own standards and reasons. We must also take the individuals, times and places into consideration.

The Rabbis whose opinions are represented in the *Mekhilta* and the *Sifre* held the view that Scripture itself used euphemisms; there was no need for interference by the Soferim. R. Joshua b. Levi,[40] on the other hand, was of the opinion that the Soferim were responsible for the changes. His disciple, R. Simeon,[41] followed in his footsteps.[42]

---

[39] The Rabbis (*TB Mo'ed Katan* 18b, see Rabbinovicz, *variae lectiones* a. l., p. 60 n. 7 and ibid. *Sanhedrin*, p. 354, n. 9) relate that Moses was suspected by the masses of the worst sins, and they tell it explicitly without any circumlocution. But when they had to compare R. Johanan to a Sadducee they expressed it (*TP 'Erubin* I. 1, 18c): "The enemies of R. Johanan like a Sadducee." The *Tosefta* (*Baba Mezi'a* VI. 17, 385 6. Comp. *TP* ibid. V, end, 10d) remarks that the usurers declare that the Torah is a fraud and Moses a fool. No substitute is employed either for fraud or for fool. But *TB* (ibid. 75b) formulates it: "They declare Moses to be wise and his Law to be true." Bar Kappara (of Southern Palestine, Judea) maintains (*TP Yoma* VI. 2, 43c) that the High Priest omitted the words עמך בית ישראל (Thy nation Israel) from the official confession of sin on the Day of Atonement in order not to implicate Israel (שלא להזכיר גנויין של ישראל).

Sometimes the Rabbis are extremely particular about choosing decent language, לשון נקיה (See *TP Mo'ed Katan* I, 80d; *Sotah* I. 2, 16c; *Kethuboth* I. 8, 25c; ibid. V. 8, 30b; *TB Pesaḥim* 3a and parallels. Comp. also *BR* LXX. 4, 801 5; ibid. LXXXVI. 6, 1059 2 and parallels referred to in the notes ibid.; *Tanḥuma* מצורע 1; ed. Buber ibid. 3, 22b), and stress its importance. But they did not consistently employ דבר instead of בעל (At least three of the *Mishnayoth* which used this euphemism — *Sotah* I. 2, *Kethuboth* I. 8 and V. 9 — seem to be of Judean origin, as it appears from the names of the Rabbis mentioned there or in the preceding clauses). They sometimes uttered a phrase which is simply shocking to us, see *TB Zebaḥim* 31a and comp. Ps. 78:65, as already observed by Rabbi Hayyim Joseph David Azulai in his ברכי יוסף to יורה דעה sect. 334. 53.

[40] See above n. 1. He taught in Lydda, Judea.

[41] Who likewise lived in Lydda, see Bacher, *Die Agada d. Palaest. Amoräer* II, pp. 437–438.

[42] See above, nn. 4–5.

As said above, the euphemisms counted in the *Mekhilta* and *Sifre* consisted of the alterations of single letters of the pronominal suffixes (with one exception where transposition of letters was involved). The correction of the Soferim according to R. Joshua b. Levi was limited to one letter only. But his pupil, R. Simeon, contended that in one place the Soferim inverted the order of the subjects in the verse.[43] We do not know whether R. Simeon's statement was based on a tradition or whether he derived it from the context.

The fact is that this Rabbi is the only one who made the Soferim responsible for a transposition of subjects in a verse. All other sources talk about the change of single letters in the pronominal suffixes, alterations which remove irreverent connotations from expressions referring to the Lord.

It seems that the justification for such emendations was casually preserved in the Babylonian Talmud. We read there:[44]

אמר ר' חייא בר אבא א'ר יוחנן מוטב שתעקר אות אחת מן התורה ואל יתחלל שם שמים בפרהסיא . . . אמר ר' יוחנן משום ר' שמעון בן יהוצדק מוטב שתעקר אות אחת מן התורה ויתקדש שם שמים בפרהסיא "R. Ḥiyya b. Abba reported in the name of R. Johanan: It is better that *one letter be removed*[45] *from the Torah* than that the Divine name be publicly profaned . . . R. Johanan said in the name of R. Simeon b. Jehozodak:[46] It is preferable to have *one letter removed from the Torah* so that thereby the Divine name be publicly hallowed.''

The phrase "to remove a letter from the Torah" is used here as a figure of speech. The passage deals with the transgression of a law and not with the actual deletion of a letter from the Torah. The phrase does not quite fit the context, as already observed by a great mediaeval scholar.[47] It can be understood only as a stereotyped proverbial expres-

---

[43] See above, nn. 1, 4.

[44] *Yebamoth* 79a.

[45] Literally: be uprooted. The verb עקר was a technical term for deleting something from a text. See Bacher, *Terminologie* etc. I and II, s. v. עקר.

[46] Flourished in the beginning of the third century.

[47] *RITBA* a. l.: והא דאמרין אות אחת לאו דווקא דהא מקרא שלא עקרינן.

sion[48] which is also applied in another passage of the Babylonian Talmud.[49]

We may therefore safely assume that the origin of the phrase is a law in which it was interpreted literally. It offers a good explanation and justification for the corrections of the Soferim: "It is better that one letter be removed from the Torah than that the Divine name be publicly profaned." As conventions were crystallized, it was deemed insufficient to change only the Keri;[50] it was a question not of indelicate expressions, but of the honor of the Lord. A slight emendation of single letters in the text solved the problem. Everybody knew the meaning of a euphemism, both in the oral and the written Law;[51] the alteration did not entirely obliterate the original text.

We find exact parallels to this procedure of the Soferim in the treatment of the books of Homer by the early Alexandrians. In the passage:[52] "Ere now have I consorted with warriors that were better men than *ye*", Zenodotus found the language employed by Nestor regarding Agamemnon and Achilles indecent (ἀπρεπές) and coarse. He accordingly altered the word ὑμῖν into ἡμῖν,[53] i. e. "Better men than *we*;" he changed one letter in the pronoun.

Again we read:[54] "And the goddess, laughter-loving Aphrodite, took for her a chair, and set it before the face of Alexander. Thereon Helen sate her down etc." Zenodotus rejected these four lines (423–426) from the poem and substituted for them: "And herself (i. e. Helen) sat down over against Alexander the

---

[48] Comp. *TP Sanhedrin* II, 20c; See Strack und Billerbeck, *Kommentar* etc. I, p. 244.

[49] *Temurah* 14b, according to cod. Mun. and שטה מקובצת a. l. Comp. also the commentary ascribed to רבינו גרשם ibid.

[50] I. e. to modify the reading without altering the text. See *Tosefta Megillah* IV. 39–41, 228 20 ff.; *TB* ibid. 25b; *Soferim* IX. 8, ed. Higger, p. 204. Comp. Geiger, *Urschrift* etc., p. 385 ff.; Ginsburg, *Introduction* etc., p. 346.

[51] See *TB Shebu'oth* 36a.

[52] *Il.* I. 260: ἤδη γάρ ποτ' ἐγὼ καὶ ἀρείοσιν ἠέ περ ὑμῖν ἀνδράσιν ὡμίλησα.

[53] Ζηνόδοτος γράφει: ἠέ περ ἡμῖν. (Sch. A.).

[54] *Il.* III. 424: τῇ δ' ἄρα δίφρον ἑλοῦσα φιλομμειδὴς Ἀφροδίτη, ἀντί' Ἀλεξάνδροιο θεὰ κατέθηκε φέρουσα. ἔνθα κάθιζ' Ἑλένη κτλ.

prince."[55] "It seemed to him improper for Aphrodite to carry a chair for Helen,"[56] and for this reason he rewrote the text.

We have deliberately selected these two instances from the earliest Alexandrian grammarian because the first instance parallels the corrections of the Soferim consisting mainly of the alteration of one letter in pronominal suffixes and the second instance is similar to the correction ascribed to the Soferim by R. Simeon, for it was ἀπρεπές (indecent) that the Lord should wait for Abraham.[57]

However, we can hardly assert Alexandrian influence on the Soferim in regard of the above mentioned textual corrections, even if we extend their activity beyond the time set by the Rabbis. It may simply be a natural similarity in human attitudes. Furthermore, there is an immense difference between the Greek and the Jewish textual alterations. The Soferim altered the text only when the honor of the Lord was involved. The Alexandrians changed it whenever it was not in conformity with the manners of the court of the Ptolemies,[58] or the customs of certain Greeks.[59]

---

[55] αὐτὴ δ' ἀντίον ἷζεν 'Αλεξάνδροιο ἄνακτος. (Sch. A).

[56] ἀπρεπὲς γὰρ αὐτῷ ἐφαίνετο τὸ τῇ 'Ελενῇ τὴν 'Αφροδίτην δίφρον βαστάζειν. (ibid.).

[57] The Soferim, according to R. Simeon, objected only to a written statement which represented the Lord as standing before Abraham (See above n. 5), but not to the fact itself. The Greek grammarians who did not accept Zenodotus' rejection of the verses motivated their refusal by explaining that "he (i. e. Zenodotus) forgot that she (i. e. Aphrodite) was disguised as an old woman, and in that form she behaved in a fitting manner." (ἐπιλέλησται δέ, ὅτι γραῒ εἴκασται καὶ ταύτῃ τῇ μορφῇ τὰ προσήκοντα ἐπιτηδεύει. A. ibid.). Comp. also the remark of another scholiast who refers to Od. XIX. 34. See C. G. Cobet, Miscellanea critica, p. 228; K. Lehrs, de Aristarchi studiis homericis³, p. 333; A. Ludwich, Aristarchs Homerische Textkritik I, p. 241.

[58] See C. G. Cobet ibid., p. 225 ff.

[59] See Athen. Deipnosoph, V, 177c ff.

CRITICAL MARKS (σημεῖα κριτικά) IN THE HEBREW BIBLE

a. *The inverted Nuns*

We read in *Sifre*:[1] ויהי בנסוע הארון נקוד עליו מלמעלה ומלמטה מפני שלא היה זה מקומו רבי אומר מפני שהוא ספר בעצמו ... ר' שמעון אומר נקוד עליו מלמעלה ומלמטה מפני שלא היה זה מקומו ומה היה ראוי לכתוב תחתיו ויהי העם כמתאוננים.

"[It is written] '*When the ark set forward*' [etc. These two verses][2] are marked at the beginning and at the end to show that this is not their proper place. Rabbi said: [They are marked] to indicate that they form a separate book[3]. . . R. Simeon said they are marked to betoken that it is not their proper place; what should have been written in its place? '*And the people were as murmurers*'."[4]

A parallel *Baraitha*[5] states: ויהי בנסוע הארון ויאמר משה. פרשה זו "[It is written] 'עשה לה (והקב"ה)[6] סימניות מלמעלה ולמטה שאין זה מקומה וכו' written] '*And it came to pass when the ark set forward that Moses said etc.*' (Num. 10:35–36). Provide marks[7] above and below this section to show that this is not its place etc."

Again we find:[8] שני סמניות אמורות בתורה בפרשה קטנה. ואיזו היא פרשה קטנה ויהי בנסוע הארון וכו' "Two marks (σημεῖα) occur in the Torah in a small section.[9] Which is [the] small section? '*When the ark set forward etc.*'"

[1] I, 84, ed. Horovitz, p. 80.
[2] I. e. Num. 10:35–36.
[3] See *Mishnah Yadaim* III. 5; *Tosefta* ibid. II. 10, 6834; *BR* LXIV. 8, 7085; *Vayyikrah Rabba* XI. 3; *Midrash Mishle* XXVI. 24, ed. Buber, 50b and the sources quoted below.
[4] Num. 11:1. See below.
[5] *TB Shabbath* 115b, bot.
[6] Missing in *Rashi* and '*Ein Jacob* a. l. and *Mizraḥi* on Num. 11:35. Comp. also Rabbinovicz, *variae lectiones* to *Rosh Hashanah*, p. 37, n. 100.
[7] The Hebrew text uses here the Greek word σημεῖα.
[8] I *Aboth deR. Nathan* ch. 34, ed. Schechter, 50a.
[9] I. e. μικρον τμῆμα. See Birt, *Das antike Buchwesen*, p. 494–495.

Modern scholars[10] correctly associated these signs with the critical marks employed by the Alexandrians, but they did not fully evaluate their exact nature in our text. We must first establish the form of these signs. It was pointed out above that the *Sifre* states regularly that the section was "marked" (נקוד, περιεστιγμένον). *Aboth deR. Nathan* and *TB* (see above) specify that it was provided with signs σημεῖα. The minor tract *Soferim*[11] states: הכותב צריך לעשות ש י פ ו ר בפתיחה של ויהי בנסוע הארון מלמעלה ומלמטן "The scribe must provide [a sign in the form of] a *Shofar* (horn)[12] in the blank spaces of the section '*When the ark set forward etc.*,' at the beginning and at the end."

In our Biblical scrolls[13] these marks appear in the form of נ conforming to the Massoretic tradition. It is called נון הפוכה or נון מנוזרת, "an inverted Nun."[14] Rab Hai Gaon[15] also speaks of

[10] See Perles in *Magyar Szido Szemle* 1891, p. 359 (referred to by S. Klein in (מארץ הגר) הצופה לחכמת ישראל XI, p. 235); M. Rahmer, *Jüdisches Litteratur-Blatt* XXIV, 1900, p. 46; Kaminka in *Encyclopaedia Judaica* IV, p. 623 and, especially, S. Krauss, *Zeitschrift f. d. alttestam. Wissenschaft* XXII, 1902, p. 51.

[11] VI. 1, ed. Higger, p. 165.

[12] This explanation of שיפור was hesitatingly suggested by Rahmer ibid. Some mss. read שיפוד (See the variants by Higger ibid., p. 165, n. 2) or שפוד (See ibid., p. 166, n. 5). These readings support the conjecture of Krauss ibid. that it means spit, the ὄβελος. The majority of the codices read שיעור which at first sight makes no sense. However, *Midrash Haggadol* (to Num. 11:35, Horovitz, *Sifre Zuta*, p. 266) quotes: יש אומרין לא נאמרו כל ה ש י ע ו ר י ן הללו אלא שאינה מקומה של פרשה... שלא נאמרו כל ה ש י ע ו ר י ן הללו אלא שאינה מקומה של פרשה. The text is certainly taken from *Sifre Zuta*, as is obvious from the quotation by Rabbenu Hillel (23b, Jerusalem 1948), and the words יש אומרין, "some say" are undoubtedly the author's own introduction of the citation. The phrase לא נאמרו כל השיעורין הללו etc. is consequently to be ascribed to R. Simeon (as it is evident from the parallel in *Sifre*) in accordance with his usual style (See *Mishnah Schabbath* VIII. 1 and *Baba Bathra* II. 2). It seems to be a technical term in connection with verses which are not in their proper place. See *Mekhilta Amalek*, end, ed. Horovitz, p. 2028, Lauterbach II, p. 191 179.

[13] Num. 10:35–36.

[14] See Ginsburg, *Introduction* etc., p. 342; L. Blau, *Masoretische Untersuchungen*, p. 40 ff.

[15] Quoted by רשב׳א to *Shabbath* 103a, s. v. משני, by מגיד משנה to Maimonides הלכות שבת XI. 10 and in שלטי הגבורים to Alfasi *Shabbath ibid.*

נונין הפוכות, "inverted Nuns." An unknown author[16] of the eleventh century represents them in the form of $\mathcal{L} \, \mathcal{L}$, something like a $\delta\iota\pi\lambda\tilde{\eta}$. Finally the author of מחזור ויטרי (p. 668) writes them כ כ,[17] a mark which is identical with the $\dot{\alpha}\nu\tau\dot{\iota}\sigma\iota\gamma\mu\alpha$. Thus the term נון הפוכה, "inverted Nun," the form of a horn possibly suggested by the minor tract *Soferim*, and the position of the inverted Nun in a Hebrew text (which is written from right to left) all argue for the identification of those signs with the $\dot{\alpha}\nu\tau\dot{\iota}\sigma\iota\gamma\mu\alpha$.

We shall now analyze the opinions of the Rabbis who attempted an explanation of the nature of that sign. Let us examine the first rabbinic source, the *Sifre*.[18] Two opinions are expressed there. The one, by an anonymous Rabbi,[19] maintains that the purpose of the marks is to show that the section in question is not in its proper place. According to the explanation of Rab Ashi[20] its proper place is in [the section of] the Standards.[21] Mediaeval Jewish scholars suggested two divergent places for our section. According to חזקוני[22] it should follow verse 21 in Num. X. However רבינו בחיי[23] and בעל הטורים[24] point to Num. II verse 17, after which our section properly belongs.[25]

Rabbi Simeon[26] likewise contends that the marks designate a dislocation of the verses.[27]

---

[16] גנזי מצרים, ed. Adler, p. 37. See J. N. Epstein in *Tarbiz* VI. 3, p. 187.

[17] Comp. also the Responsa of Rabbi Solomon Luria (רש"ל) No. 73.

[18] See above, n. 1.

[19] According to *TB Shabbath* 116a this Rabbi is no other than R. Simeon b. Gamaliel (flourished in the middle of the second century).

[20] *TB Shabbath* 116a.

[21] In *Soferim* ibid., p. 116: בנסיעת דגלים, "In [the section of] the march of the Standards."

[22] In his commentary to Num. 10:21, ed. Cremona 1559, 116b.

[23] A. l., ed. Venice 1544, 170a, bot.

[24] In his רמזים, ed. Venice 1544, 45a.

[25] This is also the view of Geiger in his *Jüdische Zeitschrift* etc. III, p. 81. He, as well as Blau (*Masoretische Untersuchungen*, p. 45), overlooked the suggestions of the mediaeval Jewish sources.

[26] Flourished in the middle of the second century.

[27] Comp. *Sifre Zuta*, ed. Horovitz, p. 266 23 ff. and Rabbenu Hillel a. l. 23b. Comp. also *Soferim* ibid., p. 166. Geiger (ibid., see above, n. 25) called atten-

The second interpretation is that of Rabbi [Judah the Prince]. He maintains that the marks indicate that our small section is a separate book.[28]

The significance of the critical signs used by the Greek grammarians was by no means clearly defined.[29] The Greek books περὶ σημείων, treating the different meanings of the critical marks are lost.[30] The later grammarians were sometimes at a loss to explain them. As an instance, out of many, let us quote the divergence of opinions regarding the διπλῆ to Il. VIII.221, and the question of Aristonicus: τί ποτε σημαίνει; "What in the world does it designate?"[31] The same question was raised by our three Rabbis regarding the critical mark in Num. 10:35, similar in its external form to the ἀντίσιγμα and the διπλῆ.

The ἀντίσιγμα usually designates the transposition of verses.

---

tion to the Septuagint in which Num. X, verse 34 (of the Hebrew text) follows verse 36, i. e. our small section precedes verse 34.

[28] See the references above, n. 3.

גנזי מצרים (see above n. 16) quotes in the name of *"some Midrashim"*: מה ראו חכמ' ליתן נונין הפוכין על ויהי העם כמתאוננים אלא אמרו חכמים כל התורה כולה מיוחדת לנבואת משה חוץ מאילו שני פסוקים שהן מנבואת אלדד ומידד לפיכך סיינן בנון כפוף ונטפל בתורה "Why did the sages add inverted Nuns to the verse '*And the people were as murmurers?*' (Num. 11:1). The sages thereby declared: The whole Torah is exclusively the prophecy of Moses save those two verses (i. e. Num. 10:35–36) which are part of the prophecy of Eldad and Medad. Therefore it was marked with a curved Nun [to indicate that it is] attached to the Torah." Comp. the style in *Vayyikra Rabba* VI. 6, and my note in ed. Margulies, p. 872, bottom.

This passage, which is not extant in our *Midrashim*, may possibly shed some light on an obscure passage in *Midrash Mishle* (XXVI. 24, ed. Buber, 50b). We read there: ונ ג נ ו ספר היה בפני עצמו "[These two verses] stem from an independent book which existed *but was suppressed*" (i. e. declared apocryphal). It appears that the Rabbi alludes to the apocryphal book of Eldad and Medad (See Schürer, *Geschichte* etc. III[4], pp. 360–361), an excerpt of which was allegedly attached to the Bible. Comp. *TB Sanhedrin* 17a, *Sifre* I, 95 (end, ed. Horovitz, p. 96 and the sources referred to in note 11 ibid.). None of them mentions that our verses were taken from the prophecy of Eldad and Medad.

[29] See Gudeman in PW *RE* XI, s. v. Kritische Zeichen, p. 1916 ff.; Swete, *Introduction to the O. T. in Greek*, 1914, p. 71 ff.

[30] See Gudeman ibid.

[31] See A. Ludwich, *Aristarchs Homerische Textkritik* I, p. 40.

The scholion A[32] to *Il.* II.192 asserts[33] that Aristarchus designated by the inverted σίγμα that the verses 203–205 are to replace verses 193–197.[34] Both the anonymous Rabbi and R. Simeon followed this opinion, considering the marks to be a sign of transposition of verses.

On the other hand, according to Rabbi [Judah the Prince] the marks indicate that our small section is a separate book.[35] The legal sign for the beginning of a new book was a blank space of four lines.[36] Owing to the brevity of our book this procedure was abandoned and signs were provided in its stead.[37] The marks for division in antiquity had many and various forms as can now be ascertained from the papyri;[38] some of them closely resemble the signs attached to the section under dis-

[32] See A. Ludwich ibid. p. 209; W. Deecke, *Auswahl aus den Iliasscholien*, Bonn 1912, p. 19; Gudeman ibid., p. 1923.

[33] τὸ ἀντίσιγμα. ὅτι ὑπὸ τοῦτον ἐδεῖ τετάχϑαι τοὺς ἐξῆς παρεστιγμένους τρεῖς στίχους (203–205).

[34] Comp. also Sch. A to 188 ibid. and Diogenes Laertius III. 68.

[35] This would make the smallest sacred book, consisting of only eighty five letters. (See the sources referred to above n. 3). Comp. however *TB Baba Bathra* 14a. On small publications in antiquity see W. Schubart, *Das Buch bei d. Griechen*² etc., pp. 55–56 and 178.

[36] See *TP Megillah* I. 11, 71d; *TB Baba Bathra* 13b; *Soferim* II. 6, ed. Higger, p. 114.

[37] No special space was left between פסוקים, κόμματα, the so called verses. Comp. Swete, *Introduction to the O. T. in Greek*, 1914, p. 344 ff. Palestinian and Babylonian Rabbis disagreed about the division of verses. See *TB Kiddushin* 30a and above p. 23 ff., nn. 30–31. Comp. Graetz *MGWJ* XXXIV, 1885, p. 97 ff.; Friedmann, הקדם I, pp. 116 ff. and 149 ff.; ibid. II, 30 ff.

We read in *Soferim* (III. 7, ed. Higger, p. 125): ספר שפסקו או שניקד ראשי פסוקים שבו אל יקרא בו "A scroll the end of whose sentences was indicated by marks, or whose verses were interpunctuated, shall not be used for [public] reading." Such things were probably introduced for the convenience of school children. Comp. the signs of division in a fragment of Homer written on a wooden tablet reproduced by Schubart, *Das Buch bei d. Griechen*² etc., p. 23. On interpunctuation in ancient books see ibid., pp. 85 and 181; idem, *Einführung in die Papyruskunde*, p. 60, and *Palaeographie* I (München 1925), p. 173.

[38] See Schubart, *Das Buch bei d. Griechen*² etc., pp. 181 (n. to p. 85) and 182 (n. to p. 93); Hephaestio Grammaticus, ed. Consbruch, p. 73. 4; Schol. to Aristophanes *Eq.* 722 and Gudeman *PW RE* XI, p. 1919.

cussion. Our Rabbi had good reasons to explain the inverted Nuns as an indication that the section constitutes a separate unit.[39]

Furthermore, it seems that the critical marks in the Bible are not limited to inverted Nuns only; we shall demonstrate it in the following, supplementary, chapter.

b. *The ten dotted places in the Torah*

Aboth deR. Nathan[40] records: עשר נקודות בתורה וכו' "There are ten dots[41] in the Torah"[42] (i. e. in the Pentateuch only) etc. A number of modern scholars[43] have treated in detail both the tradition as a whole and every passage separately. For our purpose we have only to stress the general character of those dots, without entering into a detailed discussion of all the separate items.

However, it is necessary to establish the origin of this tradition, which has not thus far been undertaken. A *Baraitha* from the lost minor tract *Sefarim*[44] sheds interesting light on the provenance of our passage.[45] The name of the famous sage R. Jose figures there in the explanation of every dotted verse. In similar fashion, several clauses of our *Baraitha* scattered in

---

[39] According to the Babylonian Talmud (*Rosh Hashanah* 17b) similar critical signs were applied in Psalms 107:23–31, which aimed to suggest transposition of verses (See Blau, *Masoretische Untersuchungen*, p. 41 ff.; Ginsburg, *Introduction* etc., pp. 342–244; Klein, (מארץ הגר) הצופה לחכמת ישראל XI, 333 ff.), but we omit the discussion of the passage, because it adds nothing of importance to our foregoing study.

[40] I, ch. 34, ed. Schechter 50b and II ch. 37, 49a.

[41] From the context it is obvious that the Rabbis meant to say: ten dotted places.

[42] Comp. also *Sifre* I 69, ed. Horovitz, p. 64 ff.; *Bemidbar Rabba* III. 13; *Midrash Mishle* XXVI. 24, ed. Buber 50a; *Soferim* VI. 3, ed. Higger, p. 166 and the references ibid.; מדרש חסירות ויתירות, ed. Marmorstein, p. 30 ff.

[43] See Blau, *Masoretische Untersuchungen*, p. 7 ff., Ginsburg, *Introduction* etc., p. 318 ff. and the many references given by Marmorstein ibid., p. 31, n. 126.

[44] Quoted in גנזי מצרים, p. 38. See above, n. 16.

[45] Both the language and the contents of this *Baraitha* argue for its early date and its utter independence of the later sources.

the *Mishnah*[46] and the Babylonian Talmud[47] are attributed to
R. Jose. Consequently we can safely assume that the passage
in *Aboth deR. Nathan* and *Sifre* originates from the school of
that Rabbi.[48]

Regarding the character of these dots we are told in *Aboth
deR. Nathan*:[49] כך אמר עזרא אם יבא אליהו ויאמר לי מפני מה כתבת כך
אומר אני לו כבר נקדתי עליהן ואם אומר לי יפה כתבת אעבור נקודה מעליהן
"Thus said Ezra: If Elijah [the prophet] should come and say
to me, why did you write[50] in this manner? I will answer him:
I have already dotted them.[51] But if he should say: You have
written them correctly, I shall remove the dots from them."
It is therefore evident that the Rabbis considered the dots to
be a mark on doubtful words. This agrees entirely with the
purport of the dots in the Alexandrian school[52] (with the difference that in Scripture the dots were placed above the letters).
Doubtful passages were marked with points by the early Alexandrian grammarians. The dot was, naturally, the more primi-

---

[46] See *Pesaḥim* IX. 2 and parallels.

[47] *Baba Meẓi'a* 87a; *Menaḥoth* 87b. Comp. also *Berakhoth* 4a and Rabbinovicz דקדוקי סופרים to *Horayoth* 10b, p. 32, n. 50.
In the light of our source we may the better understand the reading of,
and the comments by, early authorities on the quotation in *TB Sanhedrin* 43b.
Rabbenu Hananel, *Yad Ramah* and *Aggadoth Hatalmud* read there ר' יוסה
(instead of ר' נחמיה in our editions and manuscripts). The very strange comment by Rabbenu Hananel can only be understood in the light of our *Baraitha*
(ibid., p. 39. In the respective statement of R. Jose שאני = שאיני).

[48] Flourished around the middle of the second century.

[49] Ibid. (see above, n. 40) 51a and 49b.

[50] I. e., these doubtful words.

[51] Dots (*superposita*) as a sign of deletion are extant in the Greek papyri.
See Pap. Oxyrh. V. 844 and p. 308, n. 21 ibid. Comp. Schubart, *Einführung
in die Papyruskunde*, p. 52; idem, *Das Buch bei d. Griechen*[2] etc., pp. 92 and
182 (n. to p. 90); K. Dziatzko, *Untersuchungen über ausgewählte Kapitel d.
antiken Buchwesens*, p. 155.

[52] See Sch. A to *Il.* VIII. 535. The Sch. to *Il.* X, 397 ff., reports: πρῶτον
μὲν στιγμαῖς φησι τὸν Ἀρίσταρχον παρασημειώσασθαι αὐτούς, εἶτα δὲ καὶ
τελέως ἐξελεῖν κτλ. "They say that Aristarchus marked them (i. e. the
verses) with dots, but afterwards removed them entirely" (And he marked
them with an obelus, see K. Lehrs, *De Aristarchi studiis homericis*[3], p. 340–341).
The references given by Blau, *Masoretische Untersuchungen*, p. 8, n. 1 are
both late and not entirely relevant to our passage.

tive sign; it meant: σημείωσαι, *nota bene*, which was subsequently taken over by the διπλῆ (see below).

A closer examination of the rabbinic source will show that the Rabbis did not always treat these dots as a mark of a doubtful reading. For instance, let us consider their interpretation of the points on the word וישקהו (Gen. 33:4). We read in the *Sifre*:[53] וישקהו נקוד עליו שלא נשקו בכל לבו ר"ש בן יוחי אומר הלכה בידוע שעשו שונא את יעקב אלא נהפכו רחמיו באותה שעה ונשקו בכל לבו " '*And he kissed him*' (Gen. 33:4), the word וישקהו is dotted to indicate that he did not kiss him sincerely. R. Simeon b. Yoḥai says: As a rule it is known that Esau hates Jacob but this time his love for his brother was stirred, and he kissed him sincerely."[54]

L. Blau[55] called attention to the anonymous note in two manuscripts,[56] which most probably[57] refers to Origenes. It reads: οὐεσσάκη, ἐν παντὶ Ἑβραϊκῷ βιβλίῳ περιέστικται, οὐχ ἵνα μὴ ἀναγινώσκηται ἀλλ' ὑπαινιττομένης ὥσπερ διὰ τούτου τῆς βίβλου τὴν πονηρίαν τοῦ Ἡσαῦ· κατὰ δόλον γὰρ κατεφίλησε τὸν Ἰακώβ. "[The word] *Vayyishakehu* is dotted in every Hebrew Bible, not [to indicate] that it should not be read, but the wickedness of Esau is hereby hinted by the Bible; he treacherously kissed Jacob."

The Rabbis also interpreted the dots not as a sign of spuriousness, but as a mark of an unusual allusion in the passage (σημειῶδες). This is particularly obvious from the opinion of R. Simeon b. Yoḥai who maintains that Esau kissed Jacob sincerely. According to him the dots point to the extraordinary situation. It is indeed remarkable: Esau kisses Jacob sincerely! It is in exactly the same spirit that the Rabbis interpreted the

---

[53] Ibid., p. 65. See the parallels referred to above, n. 42 and *BR*, LXXVIII.9, p. 927.

[54] גנזי מצרים (see above n. 44) preserves a divergent tradition to which I find no parallel (except *Midrash Mishle* XXVI, 50b); its meaning is not altogether clear to me. Perhaps the reading should be corrected according to all other parallels, as it is apparent from the verse (Prov. 21:1) cited there.

[55] *Masoretische Untersuchungen*, p. 22.

[56] Quoted by Field in the *Hexapla* a. l. n. 6.

[57] As surmised by Field ibid.

dots in many other instances quoted in the above sources. They took them to be signs calling for special interpretation.[58] In the classical Greek texts the διπλῆ served a similar purpose. It called attention to a remarkable passage,[59] to a πολύσημος λέξις,[60] to a text which has many significations. Any Greek grammarian upon finding such a critical mark in a classic text without a commentary would ask: τί ποτε σημαίνει;"[61] "What in the world does it signify?" The Rabbis did the same thing.

When R. 'Akiba interpreted and derived "mounds of rules" from every apex (κεράια) on the letters of the Torah[62] he was well appreciated by his fellows. He followed a classical tradition; he could rightly remark: ולא תהא תורה שלמה שלנו כשיחה בטלה שלהם[63] "Should our perfect Torah be less seriously treated than the idle talk of theirs"?!

To repeat, we do not enter into the discussion of the original intentions of him (or them) who inserted the critical marks in the Scriptures. Our purpose is to elucidate how the Rabbis treated them. It is quite apparent that the Rabbis of the second century interpreted the critical marks in the same way that the Alexandrian grammarians treated the critical signs in the classic texts.

---

[58] It goes without saying, that in everything unusual in the script of the sacred text the Rabbis saw a sign calling for special interpretation. They interpreted all the letters suspended between the lines (See Blau, *Masoretische Untersuchungen*, pp. 46 ff. and 54 ff.), although they certainly knew that this was the practice of the ancient correctors. See *TP Megillah* I. 11, 71c; *TB Menaḥoth* 30b; *Tosefta Gittin* IX. 8, 334₆ passim. It is also very frequent in the ancient Greek papyri. See Schubart, *Das Buch bei d. Griechen*², p. 92 passim.

The Rabbis also interpreted the special forms of single letters, see *Soferim* IX. 1–7, ed. Higger, p. 200 ff. This is quite natural and in no way invalidates our general argument.

[59] See Diog. Laert. III. 66; *Anecdotum Venetum* quoted by Gudeman in PW *RE* XI, p. 1918.

[60] See *Anecd. Ven.* ibid.

[61] See above n. 31.

[62] *TB Menaḥoth* 29b.

[63] See *TB Baba Bathra* 116a top, passim.

RABBINIC INTERPRETATION OF SCRIPTURE

The Rabbis never suggest a correction of the text of the Bible. In the entire rabbinic literature we never come across divergences of opinion regarding Biblical readings.[1] It is therefore obvious that the textual corrections of Greek classics practiced by the Alexandrian grammarians have no parallel in the rabbinic exegesis of Scripture.

It has been indicated in the previous chapters that in rabbinic tradition exceedingly few traces are left of the literary activity of the Soferim. The literal meaning of the word Soferim is scribes. The Rabbis interpreted it to mean "tellers"; the Soferim counted the letters of the Torah.[2] They probably knew the number of letters in every section.[3] In this they resembled the γραμματικός, grammarian,[4] but they came much closer to his character in the rest of their literary activity. The word *Sofer* in Is. 33:18 was understood by the Septuagint in the same sense. They translated this verse: ποῦ εἰσιν οἱ γραμματικοί; Where are the Grammarians?[5] Indeed the Soferim were grammarians,[6] and they engaged in the same activity which was pursued by the Alexandrian scholars. They elaborated the so called *Midrash* (interpretation) of the Bible. Although the word is already found in II Chron. (13:22 and 24:27) it is highly

---

[1] The only questions sometimes raised by the Rabbis in this connection have to do with the *matres lectionis* or vocalization. See *Mishnah Sotah* V. 5; *'Abodah Zarah* II. 5, passim. Comp. also *TP Kil'aim* III. 1, 28c; *Sanhedrin* VII. 11, 25b; *TB Kiddushin* 30a.

[2] *TB Ḥagigah* 15b; *Kiddushin* 30a.

[3] See above p. 42, n. 35. For the later *Massorah*, see Ginsburg, *Introduction* etc., p. 113.

[4] Concerning the number of letters in the Pentateuch, see A. Marx in *JBL* XXXVIII, 1919, p. 24 ff. On the counting of letters, see Th. Birt, *Das antike Buchwesen*, p. 161. On the stichometry of the ancients, see above p. 24, n. 31.

[5] Ezra the Scribe happened to be a grammarian as well.

[6] Of course, not in the strict sense of our modern usage of the word.

doubtful that it carries there the technical meaning of rabbinic times. The Septuagint translates it respectively: βιβλίον, γραφή.[7] However some copies of the *Hexapla*[8] translate מדרש (in II Chron. 13:22) ἐκζήτησις, enquiry, which is the exact equivalent of our word. "*Ezra has set his heart to inquire into the Law of the Lord*" (Ezra 7:10). The Hebrew לדרוש is correctly translated by the Septuagint: ζητῆσαι, to inquire.

One of the first fundamentals of research is to ask "why", to inquire into the reasons of a given matter. מפני מה, "why",[9] is the common term used by the Rabbis in their interpretation of Scripture. Similarly, Didymus the grammarian[10] likes to introduce his disquisitions with ζητεῖται, διὰ τί etc.,[11] and the ζητήματα[12] constituted a notable part of the philologic,[13] the philosophic and the juridic literature.[14] Ἐκζήτησις, as found in some copies of the *Hexapla* (see above), is the correct rendering of *Midrash*.

But the first rudiment of the interpretation of a text is the ἑρμηνεία, the literal and exact equivalent of the Hebrew תרגום, which means both translation and interpretation.[15] The Rabbis derived[16] from the verse in Nehemiah (8:8) that Ezra performed the functions of a ἑρμηνευτής (translator and interpreter) and γραμματικός.[17]

The elementary task of the interpreter of the Bible was to explain the *realia* and to render the rare and difficult terms in a simpler Hebrew, or, sometimes, in Aramaic. The *Tannaitic*

---

[7] See Bacher, *Terminologie* etc. I, p. 104. Comp. also M. H. Segal in *Tarbiz* XVII, 1946, p. 194 ff.

[8] See Field a. l.

[9] See Bacher, *Terminologie* etc. I, p. 113, s. v. מפני.

[10] Flourished in the first century B. C. E.

[11] See G. Zuntz, *Byzantion* XIII, 1938, p. 647, n. 3.

[12] In the Talmud בעיות, see below p. 183, n. 25.

[13] See K. Lehrs, *de Aristarchi studiis Homericis*[3], p. 217 ff. Comp. p. 213 ibid.

[14] See F. Schulz, *History of Roman Legal Science*, p. 342, Note DD.

[15] Comp. also Brockelmann, *Lexicon Syriacum*, 834a.

[16] *TP Megillah* IV. 1, 74d; *Bereshith Rabba* XXXVI. 8, p. 342; *TB Megillah* 3a and parallel.

[17] Comp. A. Kaminka, *Encyclopaedia Judaica* IV, p. 622.

Midrashim swarm with such translations.[18] The Rabbis like to introduce such simple renderings with the term: אלא . . . אין, "nothing else than."[19]

These translations are sometimes quite instructive. The Rabbis often explained the "Bible by the Bible,"[20] and their Hebrew translations are often quite illuminating. For instance, we read in *Sifra*:[21] מעל אין מעילה אלא שינוי. וכן הוא אומר וימעלו בה' אלהי אבותם ויזנו אחרי הבעלים, וכן הוא אומר בסוטה ואיש כי תשטה אשתו ומעלה בו מעל '' "*Ma'al*' (Lev. 5:15). '*Me'ilah*' is nothing but faithlessness, for it is written (I Chron. 5:25): '*And they broke faith (vayyim'alu) with the God of their fathers and they went a-whoring after the ba'alim*'.[22] Similarly it is written (Num. 5:12): '*If any man's wife go astray and act unfaithfully (ma'al) against him*'." Aquila translated מעל (in Lev. 5:15) παράβασις, transgression.[23] The Rabbis were more exact. They followed sound philological method and established its meaning from other places in the Bible where the word is explicitly associated with unfaithfulness. The Biblical מעל was rendered שינוי by the Rabbis, a word probably common in the current Hebrew of

---

[18] See *Mekhilta*, ed. Lauterbach I, p. 82 13; 204 231 passim. *Mekhilta deRashbi*, ed. Hoffmann, p. 12; *Sifra*, ed. Weiss 108d (comp. Lieberman, *JQR* XXXVI, 1946, p. 352, n. 179); ibid. 111a–d; *Sifre Zuta*, ed. Horovitz, p. 292 6; *Tarbiz* VI. 3, p. 105 and n. 3 ibid.; *Jubilee Volume in honor of Samuel Krauss*, Jerusalem 1937, p. 33, n. 16. Comp. also L. Dobschütz, *Die einfache Bibelexegese d. Tannaim*, pp. 20–25 and the instances quoted below.

[19] See, for instance, *Mekhilta*, ed. Lauterbach I, pp. 27 68; 44 3, 5; 48 65; 49 83; 56 75; 67 95; 110 42; 159 20; 160 41; 170 13; 174 70–73; 190 45; 191 47; 202 200; 225 29; 245 25; ibid. II, pp. 22 5; 38 18; 88 52; 151 41; 269 42; 289 66; ibid. III, p. 247 8; 259 0; 45 56–58 and 66 54–57. It is also very frequent in all the other *Halakhic Midrashim*, see Bacher, *Terminologie* etc. I and II, s. v. אין and לשון. Comp. Gen. 28:19. It corresponds to the Greek: οὐδὲν ἄλλο . . . ἤ.

[20] תורה מתוך תורה, see *TP Megillah* I. 13, 72b. For linguistic purposes the Rabbis considered the entire Bible as a unit. See *TB Baba Kamma* 2b.

[21] *Vayyikra*, Ḥoba XI. 1, ed. Weiss 25c. Comp. *TB Me'ila* 18a.

[22] This is also the reading of *TB ibid.* But our text of the Bible reads אלהי עמי הארץ, "*The gods of the peoples of the land.*" The rabbinic scribes most probably completed the quotation from memory, according to the more familiar verse (Jud. 8:33).

[23] On the rendering of the Septuagint, see Schleusner, *Lexicon in LXX* etc., s. v. λανθάνω.

the time. Indeed, *Sifre Zuta*[24] also renders ומעלה בו ("*And acts unfaithfully against him*." Num. 5:12) שינת בו.[25] It is likewise used in *Sifre*[26] with the same meaning.[27]

The Septuagint, the oldest of our preserved *Midrashim* often agrees with these simple interpretations of the Rabbis,[28] but the latter are sometimes more consistent. For instance, on Ex. 12:13 and 23 they remark:[29] אין פסיחה אלא חייס[30] שנאמר כצפרים עפות כן יגן ה' צבאות על ירושלם גנון והציל פסוח והמליט "The word פסיחה means nothing but protection, as it is said (Isa. 31:5): '*As birds hovering, so will the Lord of Hosts protect Jerusalem; He will guard and deliver it, He will protect and rescue it*'." The Rabbis prove the meaning of פסח from Isa. 31:5 where the context indicates that פסיחה signifies protection.[31] The Septuagint translates (Ex. 12:3) ופסחתי עליכם καὶ σκεπάσω ὑμᾶς (and I shall protect you)[32] and פסח (ibid. 27) ἐσκέπασεν (protected). But ופסח (ibid. 23) is translated: καὶ παρελεύσεται (And He will pass by). The latter agrees with R. Josia's interpretation[33] of the verb פסח, which is accepted by the Jewish commentaries.[34]

---

[24] Ed. Horovitz, p. 233 12.

[25] See *Sifre* ibid., p. 117 ff. and comp. *Mekhilta Nezikin* III, ed. Lauterbach, vol. III, p. 25 90.

[26] II, 306, ed. Finkelstein, p. 330. The Rabbis explain Mal. 3:6: כי אני ה' לא שניתי to mean "For I, the Lord, was not unfaithful." This is probably the true meaning of the verse, see below, n. 27.

[27] H. Yalon in the Hebrew periodical מלילה II, p. 172, adduces post-*Tannaitic* sources which employ the verb שנה with a similar meaning. He correctly associated it with Prov. 24:21: עם שונים אל תתערב. According to the sources quoted above in the text, the verse should be rendered: "*Meddle not with traitors*." Comp. also Liddell and Scott, *Greek Lexicon*, s. v. μεθίστημι. B. I. 4.

[28] It can be ascertained by comparing the sources referred to above, n. 19, with the Septuagint.

[29] *Mekhilta, Pisḥa* VII, ed. Lauterbach I, p. 56 75 (Comp. 57 87); ibid. XI, 87 90

[30] Variant reading: חסות.

[31] Comp. also *Tosefta Sotah* IV. 5, 299 12; *Mekhilta*, ed. Lauterbach I, 185 207. The correct English translation of the verse ibid. is: "The Lord will *protect* the door."

[32] אחסה in Ps. 61:5 is translated by the Septuagint: σκεπασθήσομαι.

[33] *Mekhilta* ibid., p. 57 84.

[34] Comp. also Field, *Hexapla* Ex. 12:11, n. 11, who refers to Philo and Josephus. See Riedel, *ZATW* XX, 320 ff. and below p. 209.

Aquila also translates (Ex. 12:11 and 27) the name פסח ὑπέρβασις (skipping over), but Symmachus renders it:[35] φασὲχ ὑπερμά-χησίν ἐστιν. "[The word] faseh means defence."[36]

Indeed the verb פסח certainly means to step over, to skip,[37] but from the Prophets the Rabbis proved that it also signified to protect, and their translation makes much better sense of Ex. 12:23. Since the word has two meanings they preferred the one which suited the context best.

It appears that comments formulated אלא...אין which are incorporated in the Halakhic Midrashim have their origin in a very ancient commentary of the Law. Most of these comments undoubtedly provide the plain meaning of the text. In course of time this vigorous assertion (i. e., it is nothing but . . .) was extended even to Midrashic exposition,[38] but as such it was almost exclusively limited to the narrative parts of the Bible. The use of this emphatic formula for a Midrashic comment therefore becomes one of the characteristic exaggerations of the Aggada; it degenerates into a mere literary phrase, and the Rabbis themselves will not take a comment introduced by these words more seriously than any other Midrashic interpretation in the Aggada.[39]

The Rabbinic sages sought to understand the meaning of the difficult and rare words in Scripture not only through parallels in the Bible itself where the sense of the expression is clear. They also sometimes explained them with the aid of other languages, remarking that the given word is לשון כנעני, Phoenician,[40] or לשון מצרי, Coptic,[41] or לשון סורסי, Syriac,[42] or derived from some other tongues.[43]

---

[35] Comp. Field ibid.   [36] Comp. also the Aramaic Targumim a. l.
[37] I Kings 18:21 and 26. See however Ibn Gānâh, ספר השרשים, p. 405.
[38] See Mekhilta, ed. Lauterbach I, 151₁₃₃; 169₁; 191₅₀; 196₆₀; 206₃₁; 207₃₅; 210₈₃; 221₇₄ (in the variants); 226₃₄; 229₈₈; 233₂₁; 241₁₂₅; ibid. vol. II, 22₁–₃; 264₇; 68₁₄; 139₅₆; 169₁₀₂; 186₁₁₀ and so in the other Halakhic Midrashim.
[39] See Lieberman שקיעין, p. 82 ff.
[40] See Sifre II, 306, ed. Finkelstein, p. 336₁₂ and notes ibid.
[41] See Pesikta deR. Kahana XII, 109b. Comp. A. Brüll, Fremdsprachliche Redensarten, p. 47.
[42] Mekhilta Pisḥa III, ed. Lauterbach I, 28.
[43] See Brüll ibid., p. 30 ff. Comp. also Samuel Rosenblatt, The Interpreta-

Some of them travelled to the provinces for the sole purpose of discovering the meaning of some rare Biblical words in
the dialects spoken there.[44]

In addition, they sometimes explained expressions of the
Bible by the customary usage (i. e. the χρῆσις, συνήθεια) of
the language,[45] although they were well aware that the meaning,
or usage, of a given word in the Bible often differed from their
own.[46]

There is no evidence that the Rabbis prepared special lexica
of the Bible; they had no need of them. The entire rabbinic
literature bears testimony to the fact that the Rabbis knew
the Bible by heart.[47] Jerome[48] testifies that the Palestinian Jews
of the fourth century were able to recite the Pentateuch and
the Prophets[49] by heart.[50] The Jewish sages could well manipu-
late their explanations without the help of special vocabularies
of the Bible.[51]

---

tion of the Bible in the Mishnah, p. 33. This method was subsequently extended
and pushed to the extreme by the *Aggadists*; they even tried to interpret
certain expressions of the Pentateuch according to the Greek language, see
Brüll ibid., p. 20 ff.

[44] *Bereshith Rabba* LXXIX. 9, p. 946 ff. The Rabbis mentioned there
flourished at the end of the second and the beginning of the third centuries.

[45] *Mishnah Nega'im* X. 6, *BR* LXXV.6, p. 8927.

[46] See *TB 'Abodah Zarah* 58b; *Hullin* 137b; *Esther Rabba* I.1 end, ed.
Rom, 3d; *Pesikta Rabbathi* III, 7b. Comp. *TB Shabbath* 36a.

[47] The exception in *TB Baba Kamma* 55a does not invalidate the general
rule. Comp. J. Brüll in בית תלמוד, ed. Weiss I, p. 207.

[48] *In Is.* 58:2.

[49] Comp. also Eusebius, *Praep. Ev.* XI. 5, 513b–c.

[50] *Libros Prophetarum ac Moysi memoriter revolventes*, quoted by Samuel
Krauss in *JQR* 1894, p. 232. Krauss, however, committed a serious error in
asserting (ibid., p. 233) that the Hebrew teacher of Jerome quoted Virgil in
the original. He certainly misunderstood the church father. The latter reports
(Praef. in Dan., Migne *PL* XXVIII. IX, 1292b) that the Jew convinced him
to study Aramaic by quoting a passage in his tongue (*in sua lingua ingerente*,
i. e. in the Jew's own language) that persistent labor will conquer everything.
It is Jerome who associated it with Virgil (*Georg.* I. 145): *Labor omnia vicit
improbus.* The Jew probably cited something like: אם יאמר לך אדם יגעתי ולא
מצאתי אל האמן "If a man says to you I have laboured but not found, do not
believe him" (*TB Megillah* 6b).

[51] On the rabbinic grammar of the Bible see L. Dobschütz, *Die einfache*

The early Jewish interpreters of Scripture did not have to embark for Alexandria in order to learn there the rudimentary methods of linguistic research. To make them travel to Egypt for this purpose would mean to do a cruel injustice to the intelligence and acumen of the Palestinian sages. Although they were not philologists in the modern sense of the word they nevertheless often adopted sound philological methods.

However, the Rabbis were confronted with a much more difficult problem than this simple linguistic research. They treated all of Scripture as one unit. They had to reconcile apparent contradictions in it. Moreover, the Bible, in addition to its narratives, contains the body of Jewish Law. No law book in the world explicitly encompasses all the possible cases. As life developed new legal questions rose which are not clearly stated in the Bible. It is only by way of comparison, inquiry into the spirit of the laws, and special interpretation that proper deductions could be made. Hence, the Rabbis had to introduce a complicated system of interpretation; the grammarians had sometimes to assume the functions of advocates and rhetors (see below).

We learn from the *Tosefta*[52] that Hillel the Elder applied seven norms of interpretation in his discussion with the Bene Bathyra.[53] The seven rules are: קל וחומר וגזירה שוה ובניין אב וכתוב אחד ובנין אב[54] ושני כתובין וכלל ופרט וכלל וכיוצא בו ממקום אחר ודבר הלמד מעניינו 1. Inference *a minori ad majus.* 2. Inference by analogy (*Gezerah Shawah*, explained in detail, below). 3. Constructing a family on the basis of one passage.[55] 4. The same rule as the preceding, but based on two Biblical passages. 5. The General and the Particular, the Particular and the

---

Bibelexegese d. Tannaim, p. 25 ff.; S. Rosenblatt, *The Interpretation of the Bible in the Mishnah*, p. 10 ff.

[52] *Sanhedrin* VII end, 427ᵃ. Comp. *Aboth deR. Nathan* ch. 37 and *Sifra*, Introduction, ed. Weiss, 3a.

[53] In the second half of the first century B. C. E.

[54] The last two words are missing in Cod. Erfurt but they are extant in ed. princ. and Cod. Vienna.

[55] I. e. a specific regulation which is found in only one Biblical passage is extended and applied to a number of passages.

General. 6. Exposition by means of another similar passage. 7. Deduction from the Context.[56]

The context suggests that Hillel was not the author of these rules and norms;[57] he simply used recognized arguments to prove that the Paschal Lamb is offered on the Sabbath, if the fourteenth of Nissan happens to fall on that day.[58] He employed seven norms of interpretation to prove one particular law from the Torah.

A *Baraitha* ascribed to R. Ishmael[59] enumerated thirteen norms of interpretation[60] of the Torah. Schürer[61] calls these norms "a kind of rabbinic logic." Many modern scholars have investigated these rules in detail.[62] A. Schwarz devoted six books[63] to the analytics of these norms of interpretations. Neither he nor any of the other scholars has been able to discover definite Greek influence in them.[64]

---

[56] See on these norms Strack, *Introduction to the Talmud and Midrash*, Philadelphia 1931, p. 94 and notes ibid., pp. 284–285; Schürer, *Geschichte* etc. II⁴, p. 397 and n. 20 ibid.

[57] See H. Housdorff, *Jahrbuch d. jüd.-lit. Gesellschaft* (Frankf. a. M. 1907), p. 382 ff. and especially Sh. H. Kook in (מארץ הגר) הצופה לחכמת ישראל XIII, p. 91.

[58] Hillel asserted (*Tosefta Pesaḥim* IV, 162₂₈; *TP* ibid., VI, 33a; *TB* ibid. 66a) that his opinion was based on the authority of his teachers Shemaiah and Abtalion. It appears that his tradition went only as far as the law itself was concerned. The proofs were his own (Comp. the style in the *Tosefta* ibid.); he utilized the *Gezerah Shawah* on his own initiative, because it supported his tradition. R. Abba b. Memel (flourished in the third century) remarked (*TP* ibid.): אדם דן גזירה שוה לקיים תלמודו "A man may utilize a *Gezerah Shawah* for the purpose of supporting his tradition."

[59] Flourished in the beginning of the second century.

[60] Introduction to the Sifra (Comp. M. Zucker, *Proceedings of the American Academy for Jewish Research* XVIII, 1949, p. י"ב, n. 15). See Strack, *Introduction* ibid. pp. 95 and 288, n. 8, where a list of selected literature and translations is given.

[61] *Geschichte* II⁴, p. 397.   [62] See Strack ibid.

[63] *Die hermeneutische Analogie*, Wien 1897; *Der hermen. Syllogismus in d. talmud. Litteratur*, ibid. 1901; *Die hermeneut. Induktion* etc. ibid. 1909; *Die hermeneut. Antinomie* ibid. 1913; *Die hermeneut. Quantitätsrelation*, ibid. 1916; *Der hermeneut. Kontext in d. Talm. Literatur* ibid. 1921.

[64] An article by D. Daube (*HUCA* XXII, 1949, p. 239 ff.) entitled "Rabbinic Methods of Interpretation and Hellenic Rhetoric" reached me when this

However, we find this observation by Judah Hadassi[65] on the thirteen norms of interpretation: וגם מצאנו עוד לחכמי יון שיש להם בדיניהם ובחוקותיהם י"ב מדות וקוראים אותם באזנינו ארגשיאש קאיפכרימטא,[66] והם שש ושש הרי י"ב במספרם ובחננום ונסינום ונמצאו כאלה לנו "And we also found that the sages of Greece have twelve norms in their rules and laws. They are called ἐργασίας καὶ ἐπιχειρή-ματα.[67] They are *six and six*, together twelve. We examined them and we found them to be like those" (i. e. like the rabbinic rules). Comp. *Jubelschrift* etc. *Dr. L. Zunz*, p. 171.

Happily, we are in a position to verify the statement of the Karaite. We have no doubt that he refers to some mediaeval scholia to Hermogenes' περὶ εὑρέσεως (III. 7), i. e. to his chapter περὶ ἐργασίας ἐπιχειρημάτων. Hermogenes counts[68] six ἐπιχειρήματα (arguments): τόπος, χρόνος, τρόπος, πρόσωπον, αἰτία, πρᾶγμα,[69] "[On] place, time, way (manner) person,[70] cause, fact."[71] He further teaches (ibid., p. 148): ἐργάζεται δὲ πᾶν ἐπιχείρημα . . . ἀπὸ παραβολῆς, ἀπὸ παραδείγματος, ἀπὸ μικροτέρου, ἀπὸ μείζονος, ἀπὸ ἴσου, ἀπὸ ἐναντίου. "Every argu-

---

chapter was already ready for the press. However, we found no reason to change anything in this chapter, as will be self evident from the comparison of Dr. Daube's article with this paper.

[65] אשכל הכפר, 124b. He wrote his book in Constantinople in 1148.

[66] Cod. Leiden (according to J. Perles, see below) reads: קאיפיפיריומש, which appears to be a scribal error for קאיפיכירימט. Cod. Adler (in the Jewish Theological Seminary) No. 1650, f. 174b reads קַמִיפַּכְרִימָה, which is an obvious error for קאיפכרימטה.

[67] This correct transliteration was made by P. F. Frankel in *MGWJ* XXXIII, 1884, p. 457, but he suggested the change of the word ארגשיאש to אנששיש, ἐνστάσεις. J. Perles (*Byzantinische Zeitschrift* II, 1893, p. 576) proposes: ὀρέξεις καὶ ἀποχρήματα, or, as an alternative (according to cod. Leiden, see above n. 66), ἐργασίας καὶ ἐπιπειρισμάς. Both eminent scholars were entirely unaware of what the author is referring to. They contented themselves with the discussion of the two Greek words only without quoting the passage itself. We shall presently see that our text which is confirmed by two manuscripts must not be altered.

[68] Ibid. 5, ed. H. Rabe, p. 140.

[69] Comp. K. Lehrs, *de Aristarchi studiis Homericis*[3], p. 217.

[70] Comp. the style in *Mishnah Sanhedrin* V. 1 and *Tosefta* ibid. IX. 1, 428 15 ff.

[71] See R. Volkmann, *Rhetorik*, München 1901, p. 36.

ment is executed (or elaborated) . . . from a parable (an illustration), from an example,[72] from something smaller, from something bigger,[73] from something equal, from something opposite." Maximus Planudes[74] in his scholia to this chapter[75] mentions explicitly ἐξ ἐπιχειρήματα (six arguments) and ἐξ ἐργασίαι (six executions, exercises).[76] It is evident that these six ἐργασίαι and six ἐπιχειρήματα were well known in Constantinople in the time of Hadassi, and it is quite obvious that he refers to these rules (והם שש ושש).

The ἐπιχειρήματα have certainly nothing to do with the rabbinic rules; we therefore shall consider the ἐργασίαι only. A comparison between the ἐργασίαι and the thirteen hermeneutic rules of R. Ishmael will demonstrate that they have only the קל וחומר[77] and the analogy[78] in common.

---

[72] An anonymous author in προλεγόμενα τῆς ῥητορικῆς (Ch. Walz, *Rhetores Graeci* VI, p. 34) gives the following definition: τὸ μὲν παράδειγμα ἀπὸ προγεγονότων πραγμάτων παραλαμβάνεται· ἡ δὲ παραβολὴ ἐξ ἀορίστων καὶ ἐνδεχομένων γενέσθαι. "The example is taken from facts which [actually] happened before; the parable is taken from the indeterminate and possible things which may happen." See also O. Schissel, *Rheinisches Museum* LXXV, 1926, p. 312, and Stegeman in PW *RE* XV, s. v. Minukianos, p. 1987–8.

[73] See the anonymous scholiast to Hermogenes a. l., ed. Walz ibid. VII, p. 759.

[74] Flourished some two hundred years later than Hadassi, but he used earlier Byzantine scholia.

[75] 365, ed. Walz ibid. V, p. 402.

[76] Comp. also Joseph Rhacenditus, ed. Walz ibid. III, p. 479. He apparently flourished in Constantinople around the year 1300, see Walz ibid., p. 465.

[77] *A minori ad majus*, from the light — less important — to the grave — more important — and vice versa.

[78] Of R. Ishmael's rules the Karaite cited here only the first two, the קל וחומר and the גזירה שוה (analogy, see below), and added וגו' (etc.). Then he made his observation on the ἐργασίαι καὶ ἐπιχειρήματα. Perhaps Hadassi was struck by the *verbal* similarity of the ἐργασίαι with some of the norms contained in the so called thirty-two hermeneutic rules of the *Aggadah*, which he reproduced in his book (58b). They include: the analogy (No. 7); something important which is elucidated by something trivial (No. 14: דבר גדול שנתלה בקטן ממנו); the parable (No. 26) and (No. 27) the נגד (literally, the opposite). These respectively correspond to: ἀπὸ ἴσου, ἀπὸ μικροτέρου, ἀπὸ παραβολῆς and ἀπὸ ἐναντίου. But the similarity is only verbal, as can be seen from the

Hadassi has found his followers in modern scholars who were unaware of their early predecessor. A. Kaminka[79] asserts: "At least one of the seven rules by which Hillel explained the Torah seems to be identical with a philological method known at the Alexandrian school . . . in the Halakah it is known as גזרה שוה; in Greek δὶς λεγόμενα. I believe this system was *not* originally used by Hillel in connection with the juridical or ritual questions but when commenting on Biblical passages in general." It was pointed out[80] that the early Rabbis resorted to this simple system of comparison of parallel words and passages in their *Targumim* without making any mention of the term גזירה שוה. Moreover, etymologically this name has nothing to do with δὶς λεγόμενα (see below). The inference itself is so primitive that it could not escape any intelligent expounder of a text.

It goes without saying that any thinking person who was acquainted with Greek logic and who heard something of the nature of rabbinical exegesis of the Bible would be inclined to associate it in some way with the former. Indeed, Eusebius[81] remarks: Ναὶ μὴν καὶ τῶν πρώτων μαθημάτων δευτεροταί τινες ἦσαν αὐτοῖς· (οὕτω δὲ φίλον τοὺς ἐξηγητὰς τῶν παρ' αὐτοῖς γραφῶν ὀνομάζειν) οἳ τὰ δι' αἰνιγμῶν ἐπεσκιασμένα . . . δι' ἑρμηνείας καὶ σαφηνείας ἐξέφαινον. "Verily they (i. e. the Jews) have certain *deuterotai*[82] of primary studies (for so it pleases them to name the expounders of their Scriptures) who by interpretation and explanation . . . made clear what was obscurely rendered in riddles." Obviously, he is referring to the elementary-school *Tanna* who taught the children *Mishnah* and *Midrash*. He adduces them as examples of those who employ the method of logic in Hebrew philosophy,[83] a logic which pursues the

instances given in the Hebrew source, and quoted by Hadassi himself, to illustrate the rules.

[79] *Encyclopaedia Judaica* IV, p. 23 and *JQR*, N. S. XXX, 1939, p. 121. Comp. also Daube in *HUCA* XXII, p. 241, n. 7.

[80] See above, nn. 18 and 19.

[81] *Praep. Ev.*, 513c.

[82] This is the literal translation of the Hebrew מִשְׁנֶה, or the Aramaic מתניין — a teacher of *Mishnah*, see Bacher *Terminologie* I, p. 135, s. v. סופר I and n. 4 ibid.

[83] Ibid. 513a: τὸν λογικὸν δὲ τρόπον τῆς Ἑβραίων φιλοσοφίας.

truth, unlike the clever sophistries of the Greeks. Eusebius, of course, is noncommital. His words only suggest that the Jews had their system of logic, a declaration which aroused the anger of Julian the Emperor.[84]

So far so good. We can safely assert that the Jews possessed their rules of logic for the interpretation of the Bible in the second half of the first century B. C. E.[85] The question is when were these rules organized in a system with a nomenclature, specific numbers and definite categories. It will be demonstrated below that interpretation in general is older than the revelation of the Law at Mount Sinai. A very great number of hermeneutic rules existed in antiquity many of which could not be applied to the interpretation of the Torah. The hermeneutics of dreams and oracles could not as a rule be applied to the legal sections of the Bible. Generally Scripture does not express itself ambiguously but states the laws in clear language.[86]

A Rabbi who maintained that a certain law could be deduced from Scripture had to demonstrate that the words of the Bible really imply the ruling in question, although it does not state it explicitly. Apparent contradictions in the Bible had to be reconciled by more or less plausible, and not fanciful, means. New laws could be derived from Scripture by comparison, especially by comparison with something more important, with something less important and with something equal (see below). In this case the suggestion of Hadassi to compare the rabbinic hermeneutics to the ἐργασίαι of the rhetors deserves a closer analysis.

Let us first examine the terminology of the hermeneutic rules of the Rabbis. The strangest term among them is גזירה שוה. No convincing explanation of the etymology and the exact meaning of the name has been suggested until now.[87] The word

---

[84] *Contra Gal.* 222a.

[85] See above, n. 58.

[86] *Sifra* מצורע VII. V. 7, ed. Weiss 79a: לא בא [הכתוב] לנעול אלא לפתוח. Comp. Bacher, *Terminologie* I, s. v. סתום. There were, of course, not a few exceptions, see *Shemoth Rabba* XV.22 beginning.

[87] Blau (*REJ* XXXVI, 1898, p. 153) explains the expression גזירה שוה to mean "the same decision," "the same law." This is not exact. שוה does

גזירה in both Biblical and rabbinic Hebrew means: *decisio*,
decision, decree.[88] It corresponds to the Greek σύγκρισις, *decretum*, with which the Septuagint rendered the Hebrew משפט.[89]
σύγκρισις signifying *decretum*, decision, is already current in
the Egyptian papyri of the third century B. C. E.[90]

Thus it is evident that גזירה is σύγκρισις both etymologically
and logically. This word is also used in the sense of comparison
by Aristotle and the Septuagint.[91] By the second century C. E.,
at the latest, it served as a technical term in the works of the
Greek rhetors.[92] Aphtonius[93] defines this term:[94] Σύγκρισίς ἐστι
λόγος ἀντεξεταστικὸς ἐκ παραθέσεως συνάγων τῷ παραβαλλο-
μένῳ τὸ μεῖζον ἢ τὸ ἴσον. "*Syncrisis* is a comparative term which
by juxtaposition matches the greater or the equal with the thing
compared." Ioannes Sardianus[95] summarizes it: τριχῶς τὰς
συγκρίσεις ποιούμεθα, ἢ τὸ ἴσον πρὸς ἴσον ἢ πρὸς τὸ μεῖζον
ἢ πρὸς τὸ ἔλαττον. "We use *syncrisis* [comparison] in a threefold manner: the equal with the equal, [the smaller] with the
greater and [the greater] with the smaller." The term κατὰ τὸ
ἴσον σύγκρισις, "*syncrisis* with the equal," is also employed by
Hermogenes[96] who flourished in the second century C. E.

Hence we unhesitatingly translate the term גזירה שוה[97] σύγκρισις πρὸς ἴσον, a comparison with the equal. The beginning
of the *Baraitha* of R. Ishmael reads: בשלש עשרה מדות התורה

not mean "the same" but "equal". The result of *Gezerah Shawah* is that the
same law is applied to two situations. In rabbinic language we would expect
in this case גזירה אחת, and not גזירה שוה.

[88] גזר means to cut, *decidere*, κρίνειν.
[89] See Schleusner, *Lexicon in LXX*, s. v. συγκρίνω and σύγκρισις.
[90] See Liddell and Scott, s. v. σύγκρισις III. 2. Comp. also M. Schwabe
in ספר יוחנן לוי, p. 229.
[91] See Schleusner ibid.
[92] See Ioannes Sardianus, *in Aphtonii progym*. X, ed. Rabe, p. 180.
Comp. also F. Focke, *Hermes* LVIII, 1923, p. 331. However, its occurrence
in Aristotle's works establishes it as a logical term in use in the fourth century
B. C. E.
[93] Flourished in the fourth century.
[94] *Progymnasmata* X, in *Rhetores Graeci*, ed. Walz, I, p. 97.
[95] Ed. Rabe ibid., p. 184.
[96] *Progymn*. 8, ed. Rabe, p. 19.
[97] It is a contracted form. Comp. בניין אב instead of בנ[יין] ב[ית] אב.

נדרשת. מ ק ל וחומר[98] מ נ ז י ר ה שוה וכו'. This is certainly to be translated: The Torah is interpreted by thirteen hermeneutic rules: ἀπὸ μείζονος καὶ ἐλάττου, ἀπὸ συγκρίσεως πρὸς ἴσον κτλ. The Greek rhetors counted them as three rules,[99] while the Rabbis considered them two norms.

Thus, originally גזירה שוה was a simple analogy, a comparison of equals. In this sense it is employed by the School of Shammai:[100] [101]גזירה שוה חלה ומתנות מתנה לכהן ותרומה מתנה לכהן וכו' "It is an analogy (i. e. comparison of equals): Dough-offering and [Priests'] Dues are a gift to the priest, and the Heave-offering is a gift to the priest etc."[102]

We also find this term in the same meaning applied by R. Eliezer (of the School of Shammai). In *Sifre Zuta*[103] he is quoted as saying: אין דנין רשות מחובה ולא חובה מרשות אלא רשות מרשות לגזרה שוה וחובה מחובה לגזרה שוה "One does not compare a voluntary and an obligatory or vice versa, but one may compare two voluntary acts or two obligatory acts for the purpose of analogy," i. e. a σύγκρισις (an analogy) can be drawn between equal categories only.[104]

The Rabbis also employ another term for analogy, viz. היקש.[105] This word is the literal equivalent of the Greek παράθεσις,

[98] This seems to be the more original reading, see ed. Friedmann, p. 9 and the notes ibid.

[99] See above p. 55. Comp. Cicero, *Top.* IV. 23, and Daube in *HUCA* XXII, pp. 251–253. The superior cogency of קל וחומר over גזירה שוה is indicated in *Tosefta Sanhedrin* VII. 7, 42625. Both terms are frequently mentioned together (*Sifre* II, 313, ed. Finkelstein, p. 35511; ibid. 317, p. 35916; *TB Sukkah* 28a; *Temurah* 16a). Logically they may be characterized as one: σύγκρισις, comparison.

[100] Probably in the end of the first or beginning of the second century.

[101] *Mishnah Bezah* I. 6.

[102] See Geiger, *Wissensch. Zeitschrift f. jüd. Theologie* V. 1844, p. 67, n. 1; Bacher, *Terminologie* I, p. 14, n. 1; ibid. p. 13, n. 1.

[103] Ed. Horovitz, p. 25719. So far as is known to me this text was not noticed by the students who treated the problem of גזירה שוה.

[104] Comp. Bacher, *Terminologie* I, p. 23, s. v. דמה. When Paul wrote (I Cor. II.13): πνευματικοῖς πνευματικὰ συγκρίνοντες, "Comparing spiritual things to spiritual things," he used the legal terminology of the Jewish schools, i. e. you can apply the σύγκρισις to equal categories only.

[105] See Bacher ibid. s. v. הקש, p. 44 ff.; A. Schwarz, *Die hermeneutische Induktion*, p. 146 ff.

adpositio, vicinitas and comparison, juxtaposition, which is used in all these senses by Polybius.[106]

The school of R. Ishmael frequently employs the phrase:[107] מופנה להקיש ולדון ממנו גזירה שוה "The word [in the Torah] is vacant[108][for the purpose] of juxtaposing (= παρατιθέναι) it and deducing a *gezerah shawah* (= σύγκρισις) from it." Polybius[109] expresses himself in similar style:[110] ἐκ παραθέσεως συνθεωρουμένων καὶ συγκρινομένων, "Contemplated and compared by juxtaposition."[111] Again he employs the two terms together:[112] ἐκ τῆς παραθέσεως καὶ συγκρίσεως which means literally מהיקש ומגזירה שוה.

However in the official hermeneutic rules the term גזירה שוה was applied not to analogy of content but to identity of words (i. e. verbal congruities in the text), a manner of comparison which sometimes appears to be without logical basis. Rabbinic tradition therefore ruled[113] that אין אדם דן גזירה שוה מעצמו "No one may on his own authority draw an analogy from verbal congruities in the text," i. e. this method can be applied only where authorized by tradition. The Palestinian Talmud[114] demonstrated the absurd conclusions which might be reached if the method of גזירה שוה were utilized by anyone on his own initiative and not by tradition.

We have no ground to assume that the method itself of both logical and verbal analogy was borrowed by the Jews from the Greeks. However, the method and the definition of the method — the terminology — are two different things. Unfortunately we have no means to decide who among the Rabbis used this term first. The *Tosefta*[115] maintains that Hillel applied

---

[106] See J. Schweighaeuser, *Lexicon Polybianum* s. v. παράθεσις, p. 315 ff. and see below.

[107] See Bacher ibid., s. v. גזירה שוה, p. 15.

[108] Literally: emptied out, [λόγος] κεκενωμένος, comp. κενελογέω.

[109] Flourished in the second century B. C. E.

[110] III. 32. 5.

[111] Comp. Schweighaeuser ibid., p. 316.

[112] XVI. 29. 5.

[113] *TP Pesaḥim* VI. 1, 33a and parallels.

[114] Ibid.

[115] *Sanhedrin* VII, end, see above, n. 52.

the גזירה שוה in his discussion with the Bene Bathyra,[116] but it is very possible that this refers to the method alone and not to the term,[117] and it is the editor of the *Tosefta* who designated Hillel's arguments by the later terminology. The term גזירה שוה may thus be no older than the end of the first century C. E., or the beginning of the second,[118] the century when σύγκρισις πρòς ἴσον was already a favorite tool in the προγυμνάσματα (preparatory exercises) of the Greek rhetors in the Asiatic centers.

It has been pointed out that some of the hermeneutic rules found in the *Halakha* recur almost literally in the Roman legal classics (Sabinus, Celsus[119] and Gaius[120]). Hillel the Elder and the Rabbis of the following generations used to interpret not only the Torah but also secular legal documents.[121] Most likely general standards for the interpretation of legal texts were in vogue which dated back to high antiquity. But it was the Greeks who systematized, defined and gave definite form to the shapeless mass of interpretations.

The Rabbis were often confronted with the same problems as the Greek rhetors. The former sought to derive new laws from the Torah or to find support for old ones which were rooted in oral tradition. They were aware that in certain cases their interpretation is not borne out by the actual meaning of Scripture, and they accordingly termed such support זכר לדבר

---

[116] In the second half of the first century B. C. E.

[117] In *TP Pesaḥim* VI. 1, 33a, the term גזירה שוה is ascribed to the Bene Bathyra. But it is most likely the paraphrase of the editor, see *TB* ibid. 66a and *Tosefta* ibid. IV, p. 162. Our assumption is strengthened by the fact that *TP* ibid. ascribes to the Bene Bathyra the employment of the name היקש, a term which occurs neither in the rules of Hillel nor in those of R. Ishmael (i. e. in the *Baraitha* attached to the *Sifra*). Only קל וחומר appears to have been mentioned by name in this discussion (see *Tosefta* ibid.), but this norm (and perhaps also its name) is the oldest, and is intimated in the Bible itself, see Strack, *Introduction in the Talmud* etc., p. 285, n. 3.

[118] See above, n. 100.

[119] See David Daube, *Law Quarterly Review* LII, 1936, p. 265 ff.; idem, *Journal of Roman Studies* 1948, p. 115 ff.; idem, *HUCA* XXII, p. 252 ff.

[120] See M. Joël, *Blicke in die Religionsgeschichte* etc. I, p. 39, n. 1.

[121] See *Tosefta Kethuboth* IV, 9 ff., 264.30 ff. and parallels.

(allusion)[122] and אסמכתא (support).[123] They went so far as to lay down the rule:[124] כל מילא דלא מחוורה מסמכין לה מן אתרין סנין "For all laws which have no evident origin in Scripture support is adduced from *many* places [in the Bible].[125]

But rabbinic literature abounds in such artificial and forced interpretations. They were merely a literary conceit. Rab[126] maintained[127] that no one is to be appointed a member of the high court (*Sanhedrin*) unless he is able to prove from Biblical texts the ritual cleanliness of a reptile (although reptiles are definitely declared unclean in Lev. 11:29). The reason for this requirement can be inferred from the statement of a younger contemporary of our Rabbi. R. Johanan asserted[128] that a man who is not qualified to offer hundred arguments for declaring a reptile ritually clean or unclean will not know how to open [the trial of capital cases] with reasons for acquital.[129] The judge must thus be a rhetor who can *disputare in utramque partem* and prove at one and the same time the two opposite points of view.[130] But the example given by the Rabbis is selected from the interpretation of the ritual part of the Torah. The methods of the rhetor[131] and the grammarian must sometimes be identical.

In their schools the Greek rhetors taught the art of twisting the law according to the required aim and purpose. The jurist had to be equipped with all the methods of the γραμματικός. In Rome the early grammarians were the teachers of rhetoric,[132]

---

[122] See Bacher, *Terminologie* I, s. v. זכר, p. 51 ff. and s. v. סמך, p. 133 ff.

[123] See ibid. II, s. v. אסמכתא, p. 13 and סמך, p. 143.

[124] *TP Berakhoth* II. 3, 4c and parallel.

[125] Comp. also Bacher ibid. II, s. v. מחוור, p. 109.

[126] Flourished in the beginning of the third century.

[127] *TB Sanhedrin* 17a.   [128] *TP* ibid. IV. 1, 22a.

[129] Which is a *conditio sine qua non* in capital judicial procedure, see *Mishnah Sanhedrin* IV.1. Comp. also *TB* ibid. 17a (כולם שפתחו לחובה), according to the reading of Maimonides, *Hilkhoth Sanhedrin* IX.1; Me'iri a. l., p. 57. See the detailed evaluation of this reading in מלחמת מצוה by the RASHBASH, ed. pr., 33a.

[130] See *TP* ibid. and *TB ʿErubin* 13b.

[131] Comp. E. P. Parks, *The Roman Rhetorical Schools as a Preparation for the Courts under the Early Empire*, Baltimore 1945, p. 61 ff.; F. Schulz, *Principles of Roman Law*, p. 130, n. 3.

[132] Sueton., *de grammat.* IV: veteres grammatici et rhetoricam docebant.

and the dialectical jurisprudence of the Romans is known to be a Greek product.[133] The Jews with their love and devotion to παιδεία would be much more susceptible than the Romans[134] to the sound contribution of the Greeks to learning. They would certainly not hesitate to borrow from them methods and systems which they could convert into a mechanism for the clarification and definition of their own teachings. The instruction and the works of the rhetors were most suitable for application in the hermeneutics of the אסמכתא (support) type. For this purpose the τέχνη γραμματική and the τέχνη ῥητορική were combined and fused into one device.[135]

The two basic works of Greek theology, the books of Homer and of Hesiod abound in atrocities, immoralities and abominable vices which they report of the Olympian gods. As is well known the Greek philosophers eventually began to interpret the works of Homer allegorically. In the fifth century B. C. E. Stesimbrotus founded a school in Athens where he sought to find the ὑπόνοια (underlying, covert meaning) all through the works of Homer.[136] According to Greek tradition, Anaxagoras[137] was the first to teach that in his poems Homer treats of virtue and justice (περὶ ἀρετῆς καὶ δικαιοσύνης), a thesis which is developed at greater length by his friend Metrodorus of Lampsacus.[138] The Stoic philosophers exploited this method of allegoric interpretation of Homer even more.[139] The Alexandrian grammarians forced Homer to conform to the behavior and manners of the Ptolemaic court in Egypt,[140] or to the Greek customs and habits of their own time and place.[141]

K. Lehrs[142] has convincingly shown the two tendencies of

---

[133] See F. Schulz, *History of Legal Roman Science*, p. 62 ff.

[134] See Schulz ibid., p. 56 ff.

[135] Comp. above nn. 69 and 70. See Octave Navarre, *Essai sur la rhetor. grecque*, p. 40 ff.

[136] Comp. Laqueur in PW *RE* III², p. 2463 ff.

[137] Flourished in the fifth century B. C. E.

[138] Diog. Laert. II. 11.

[139] See C. Reinhardt, *De graecorum theologia capita duo*, 1910, p. 3 ff.

[140] See C. G. Cobet, *Miscellanea critica*, p. 228.

[141] See Athen. *Deipnos.* IV, 177b–f; ibid. 180c.

[142] *De Aristarchi Studiis homericis*³, p. 200, n. 122.

the grammarians with regard to Homer. One group, the so called ἐνστατικοί, indulged in charges (κατηγορίαι) against his writings, the others, named λυτικοί refuted the arguments of the accusers and came to his defence (ἀπολογία). The very terms of these grammarians prove their rhetorical methods.[143] We shall now consider one example of an ἀπολογία by one of the earliest Alexandrian grammarians, which is quite instructive. We read in the Iliad (XI. 636 ff.):

> ἄλλος μὲν μογέων ἀποκινήσασκε τραπέζης
> πλεῖον ἐόν, Νέστωρ δ᾽ ὁ γέρων ἀμογητὶ ἄειρεν

Another man would hardly move the cup from the table
When it was full, but Nestor, that old man, raised it easily.

Sosibius[144] the λυτικός[145] remarked:[146] Today the charge is brought against the Poet[147] that whereas he said all others raised the cup with difficulty, Nestor alone did it without difficulty. This statement of Homer seemed unreasonable (ἄλογος) to some of the grammarians. It appeared senseless to them that in the presence of Achilles, Diomedes and Ajax, Nestor should be represented as more vigorous than they, though he was more advanced in years. To this Sosibius replied: "Of these accusations then, we can absolve the Poet by resorting to the anastrophe."[148] He suggested that the word γέρων be transposed from line 637 to line 636 so that it will read:[149]

> ἄλλος μὲν γέρων μογέων ἀποκινήσασκε τραπέζης
> πλεῖον ἐόν, ὁ δὲ Νέστωρ ἀμογητὶ ἄειρεν

Another old man would hardly move the cup from the table
When it was full, but Nestor raised it easily.

---

[143] Lehrs ibid.

[144] Flourished under Ptolemy Philadelphus, i. e. in the first half of the third century B. C. E.

[145] See Lehrs ibid.

[146] Athen. deipn. XI, 493d.

[147] Νῦν τὸ μὲν ἐπιτιμώμενόν ἐστι τῷ ποιητῇ.

[148] τούτων τοίνυν οὕτως κατηγορουμένων τῇ ἀναστροφῇ χρησάμενοι ἀπολύομεν τὸν ποιητήν.

[149] I. e. mentally, but not literally, without destroying the meter.

The Poet is singling out Nestor from among the old men only. The difficulty is removed, and the Poet is acquitted of the charge of ἀλογία.

An exact parallel to this difficulty and solution is extant in rabbinic literature. It is stated in *Sifre*:[150] " *'And they came before Moses and before Aaron*[151] *on that day'* (Num. 9:6) R. Josiah said: If Moses did not know is it possible that Aaron would?[152] But the verse is to be *inverted* (סרסהו)[153] and expounded," i. e. the men first came to Aaron who did not know and then they came to Moses. See above note 149.

The Rabbis encountered the same difficulty in Num. 9:6, that the Alexandrian grammarians traced in Il. XI. 636 ff. It seemed unreasonable (ἄλογος) to them that the people whose question Moses failed to answer would consult Aaron on the same subject. They solved the problem by means of ἀναστροφή, rearrangement of the verse, just as Sosibius did.

However, from the anecdote related by Athenaeus[154] we learn that the solution proposed by Sosibius seemed strange and ridiculous to his contemporaries,[155] which indicates that in the third century B. C. E. this method was not yet fully accepted.

---

[150] I 68, ed. Horovitz, p. 63.

[151] I. e., they brought the problem before Moses and before Aaron.

[152] Comp. *Sifre* ibid. 133, p. 177, and the formulation in *TB Baba Bathra* 119b.

[153] The verb סרס means to turn upside down (Comp. *Mishnah Niddah* III. 5 and Rashi *TB* ibid. 28a, s. v. מסורס) which is the literal equivalent of ἀναστρέφειν. In our case it has *no* relation to τέμνειν, to castrate, to distinguish (See Daube, *HUCA* XXII, p. 261). The latter may have some connection with the interpretation of סריס (II Kings 25:19) by *Shir Rabba* (III. 7. Comp. *TP Sanhedrin* I. 2, 18c top). The *Midrash* states: סריס זה " *'Saris'* (II Kings 25:19) מופלא שבבית דין. ולמה קורא אותו סריס שמסרס את ההלכה refers to the *Mufla* (the head) of the court. Why is he called *Saris*, because he defines (literally: cuts) the *Halakha*." Comp. *Vay. Rabba* IV. 1: וישבו בשער התוך ששם חותכין את ההלכה. Some years after the first publication of my book Daube independently discovered his mistakes. Comp. his article in *Festschrift Hans Lewald* (Basel, 1953), p. 28. See also ibid., p. 29. Comp. also, p. 30 ibid. and our discussion below, pp. 79–80.

[154] Ibid. 494d.

[155] See K. Lehrs, *De Aristarchi studiis homericis*[3], p. 218.

In the time of R. Josiah[156] this means of interpretation was very common in the rabbinic schools.[157]

The rhetor Theon[158] writes:[159] τὴν δὲ ἀναστροφὴν τῆς τάξεως πολλαχῶς ποιησόμεθα. "We shall frequently make use of the inversion of the order." But he is really referring to the rhetoric scheme of ὕστερον πρότερον,[160] as is obvious from the examples he cites. This kind of ἀναστροφή is also utilized by the Rabbis,[161] but the more common rabbinic *anastrophe* is that employed by Sosibius the λυτικός.

The solutions (λύσεις) of the grammarians were not always complicated and artificial. They sometimes assumed much simpler forms. For instance, we read in the Iliad VIII. 555 ff. ὡς δ' ὅτ' ἐν οὐρανῷ ἄστρα φαεινὴν ἀμφὶ σελήνην φαίνετ' ἀριπρεπέα ("Even as in heaven around the gleaming moon the stars shine very bright"). "It was asked (ἐζήτησαν): How now could the moon be gleaming when the stars [around it] were shining bright. To which Aristarchus solving this says:[162] It does not mean that the moon was gleaming at that time, but that by its nature it is gleaming."[163]

This kind of interpretation is common in rabbinic literature. The sages rule[164] that a man who takes a vow to derive no benefit from creatures that are born is forbidden to benefit from the creatures that are yet to be born. Creatures that are born means creatures whose nature it is to be born,[165] and not only those that have already been born.[166]

Literary problems were solved in a similar way in the schools

---

[156] Flourished in the second century.

[157] See Bacher, *Terminologie* I, p. 136, s. v. סרס; ibid. II, p. 144.

[158] Flourished in the second century.

[159] προγυμνάσματα 193, ed. Spengel, p. 877.

[160] See Cicero, *Ad At.* I. 16, beginning.

[161] See *BR* LXX. 4, 800₆ and Bacher ibid.

[162] ὁ Ἀρίσταρχος τοῦτο λύων φησί.

[163] Ἀλλὰ τὴν φύσει λαμπράν (Apollonius Sophista, *Lexicon homericum*, ed. Bekker, Berlin 1833, p. 161).

[164] *Mishnah Nedarim* III. 9.

[165] שדרכן להיוולד. This is the reading of the majority of mss. See also מלאכת שלמה a. l.

[166] Comp. also ibid. 7; *TB Sotah* 25b passim.

of Alexandria and those of Palestine. The methods of the rhetors and their discussions had at least a stimulating effect on serious treatment of legal texts.[167] The following part of this chapter may shed more light on some aspects of text interpretation and its origin.

The Hermeneutic Rules of the *Aggadah*

Some of the hermeneutic rules used by the Rabbis to interpret the narrative parts of the Bible at first appear to us very artificial and far-fetched. These norms form part of the so called "thirty-two[168] hermeneutic rules of the *Aggadah*."[169] Let us consider a group of successive rules:

Rule 27. *Mashal*, i. e. parable or allegory or symbol. The *mashal* is already used in the Bible; as an allegory it is common in the *Midrash*.[170] Very often the interpretation by way of *mashal* is undoubtedly the only true explanation of the text. But some allegories are obviously far from the real meaning of the text.[171]

Rule 28. Paronomasia, amphiboly, i. e. playing with homonymous roots.[172]

---

[167] See F. Schulz, *Principles of Roman Law*, p. 130, n. 3 end.

[168] Some mediaeval authors quote "thirty-six rules" (See D. Cohen in *Tarbiz* II, 1931, p. 249). Joseph Rhacenditus (σύνοψις ῥητορικῆς, ed. Walz, *Rhetores Graeci* III, p. 479. See above, n. 76) repeats that the six ἐργασίαι. can be applied to each ἐπιχείρημα forming together thirty-six rules.

[169] The text is now available as an introduction to the *Midrash* ר' משנת אליעזר discovered and published by H. G. Enelow, New York 1933, p. 10 ff. An English translation of these rules can be found in Strack's *Introduction to the Talmud and Midrash*, p. 96. For the time of its compilation see ibid., p. 95; for the sources, translations and literature, see ibid., p. 289, nn. 2–3.

[170] See the abundant material collected by Einhorn in his מדרש תנאים II, Wilno 1838, 30d ff. See also I. Heinemann, *Altjüdische Allegoristik*, p. 15 ff.

[171] See Heinemann ibid., p. 33 ff.

[172] See Einhorn ibid. 33c; Bacher, *Terminologie* I, p. 111, s. v. מעל; Lieberman *GJP*, p. 22 ff. Comp. *BR* XXXI. 8, 2815 and Field, *Hexapla* (to Jer. 1:11), p. 573, n. 13. Comp. I. Heinemann, *The Methods of the Aggadah*, p. 257, n. 14.

Rule 29. *Gematria*,[173] ἰσόψηφα, i. e. computation of the numeric value of letters. Only a single instance is adduced in this *Midrash* to illustrate the *gematria*. The number 318 (servants of Abraham) in Gen. 14:14 has the numerical value of אליעזר, i. e. Abraham had only his servant Eliezer with him.[174] But rabbinic literature is replete with examples of *gematria*.[175]

Rule 30. Substitution of letters, the so called *Athbash* alphabet, i. e. א (the first letter) is written instead of ת (the last letter), ב (the second letter) instead of ש (the one before the last) etc. and vice versa. The *Midrash*[176] cites only one instance. לב קמי in Jer. 51:1 is nothing other than כשדים, according to the *Athbash* alphabet.[177] But this method is quite common in the *Midrash* and Talmud.[178]

Rule 31. Νοταρικόν,[179] i. e. the interpretation of every single letter (in a particular word) as the abbreviation of a series of words.[180] נמרצת (I Kings 2:8) is explained as signifying נואף, ממזר, רוצח, צורר, תועבה, i. e. נ' מ' ר' צ' ת'. The acrostic also belongs to this type, see below p. 79 ff.

Another kind of *notaricon* is the breaking of one word in two parts. Our *Midrash* cites as an illustration the word כרמל (Lev. 2:14) which is to be interpreted רך מל,[181] i. e. the word is

---

[173] I. e. γεωμετρία is used in the sense of manipulation with numbers. Comp. M. Cantor, *Vorlesungen über Geschichte der Mathematik* I³, p. 163.

[174] See *BR* XLII. 2, 4168 and parallels referred to in the notes ibid. Comp. F. Dornseiff, *Das Alphabet in Mystik und Magie*, Berlin 1922, p. 107 and n. 5 ibid.

[175] See Einhorn ibid. 34b; Bacher ibid. I, p. 127; II, p. 27 s. v. גימטריא and p. 69 s. v. חושבנא; Dornseiff ibid., p. 110 ff. Comp. below n. 211.

[176] Ed. Enelow, p. 38.

[177] Comp. the Septuagint (XXVIII. 1) and the Aramaic *Targum* a. l.; Field, *Hexapla* p. 728, n. 1; *Jahrbücher* of N. Brüll, I, 1874, p. 61, n. 2 and Rahmer in *Jubelschrift . . . Graetz*, p. 324. See also below, n. 213.

[178] See Bacher, *Terminologie* I, p. 127, n. 5; ibid. II, p. 27.

[179] Shorthand, i. e. written according to the use of the *notarii*. See Krauss, *Byzantinische Zeitschrift* II, 1893, p. 512 ff. Comp. W. Schubart, *Das Buch bei d. Griechen²* etc., pp. 78–80 and 180.

[180] This kind of *notaricon* is very common in the *Aggadah*, see Bacher *Terminologie* I, p. 126; ibid. II, p. 124 and especially rabbinic material adduced by Einhorn (see above n. 170) 34c ff.

[181] This is taken from *Sifra* a. l., ed. Weiss 12d, ed. Friedmann, p. 123.

broken in two parts, and the letters of the first part are transposed. The *notaricon* includes an *anagram* as well. The *Aggadah*[182] frequently resorts to the application of the anagram.[183]

Similarly אברך (Gen. 41:43) is interpreted by R. Judah[184] as אב רך. The name of the Patriarch ראובן is dissolved[185] into ראו בן.[186]

The artificiality of the last four hermeneutic rules is evident. An anonymous *Midrash* appended at the end of the thirty-two hermeneutic norms[187] remarks: הרי הוא אומר כי בא החלום ברוב עניין. והלא דברים קל וחומר ומה אם דברי חלומות שאינן לא מעלין ולא מורידין חלום אחד יוצא לכמה ענינים, דברי תורה החמורים על אחת כמה וכמה שמקרא אחד יוצא לכמה טעמים "Behold it says: '*A dream carries much implication*' (Eccl. 5:2). Now by using the method of *kal vaḥomer* (*a minori ad maius*) we reason: If the contents of dreams which have no effect may yield a multitude of interpretations, how much more then should the important contents of the Torah imply many interpretations in every verse."

The author of the anonymous *Midrash* possibly felt that some similarity exists between the methods of the interpretation of dreams and some of the hermeneutic rules of the *Aggadah*. Indeed, we shall demonstrate the striking fact that the hermeneutic rules mentioned above are also applied to the solution of dreams. In this realm they are quite understandable. It lies in the very nature of some dreams and most of the oracles to make their revelations in a concealed and disguised way. Dreams and oracles lend themselves to many and various kinds of interpretation. They are, of course, always right. The expounder will show by the remotest ways possible that they did

---

[182] And in this category we count the אסמכתא (see above p. 63) parts of the *Halakha* as well.

[183] See *TP Nazir* VII. 2, 56b; *TB Mo'ed Katan* 9b; *Tanḥuma*, beginning etc. etc.

[184] *Sifre* II. 1 (end), ed. Finkelstein, p. 8. See ibid. the strong objection raised by R. Jose of Damascus to this interpretation.

[185] *Pirkei R. Eliezer* ch. 36, ed. Rabbi David Luria, 84a, and comp. n. 36 ibid.

[186] Comp. *TB Berakhoth* 7b.

[187] *Midrash Haggadol Bereshith*, ed. Schechter, p. XXV, ed. Margulies, p. 39.

not lie. Necessity often compelled the priests and interpreters to invent the most clever devices for explaining the meanings of oracles and dreams. The cleverer the trick, the deeper the impression on the inquirer of the dreams and oracles. We shall now consider in order the application of the five above-mentioned rules to the elucidation of dreams and oracles.

1. Symbols[188] and allegories[189] are the most common means for the explanation of dreams.[190] We need not bring examples for it, the phenomenon being universally known.

2. Paronomasia, the playing with homonyms, is an important element in the interpretation of dreams. Artemidorus gives a number of instances[191] to this effect. Rabbinic literature[192] has preserved a lengthy catalogue of dream interpretations. H. Lewy[193] demonstrated the close parallel between Artemidorus' *Onirocriticon* and the dream interpretations of the Rabbis.[194] Paronomasia plays an important part in it.[195] In many places the style of the Talmudic passages (ibid.) makes the impression of being excerpts from a manual on dreams which contained general principles. The Rabbis frequently employ such general formulas[196] as חוץ ... כל, "All . . . except." For instance they say: כל מיני ירקות יפין לחלום חוץ וכו' "All kinds of vegetables are of good omen in a dream except etc."[197] Dream books from all over the world and of all times have utilized similar methods.

---

[188] See Bouché-Leclerck, *Histoire de la divination* I, pp. 116 ff. and 312.

[189] See Artemidorus, *Onirocriticon* I. 2; Bouché-Leclerck ibid., p. 302.

[190] See Rabbinowicz דקדוקי סופרים to *Berakhoth*, p. 315.

[191] Ibid. I. 68; II. 12, s. v. αἶγες; III. 28 passim. See Bouché-Leclerck ibid., p. 313 ff.

[192] *TP Ma'aser Sheni* IV. 9, 55b, *Ekha Rabba* I, ed. Buber 26a ff. and particularly *TB Berakhoth* 55a–57b.

[193] *Rheinisches Museum f. Philologie* N. F. 48 (1893), pp. 398–419.

[194] Comp. also I. Wiesner, *Scholien zum Babylonischen Talmud*, I, p. 124 ff.

[195] See A. Kristianpoller, "Traum un Traumdeutung im Talmud" (in *Monumenta Talmudica* IV), p. 46 ff., Nos. 139–153; H. Lewy ibid.

[196] *TB Berakhoth* 57b (many times).

[197] Comp. Artemidorus ibid. I. 68: τῶν ὀσπρίων πάντα μοχϑηρὰ πλὴν πίσον. "All pulses are of a bad omen except peas."

3. The *gematria*, ἰσόψηφα, the numerical value of letters, is one of the most important components of the *onirocritica*.[198]

To see the weasel in a dream is a bad portent, because the letters of γαλῆ (weasel) are of the same numerical value as δίκη (lawsuit or penalty).[199] Meeting a weasel on the way was believed in antiquity to be a bad portent,[200] and the Rabbis condemned this belief.[201] Nevertheless they saw in the weasel some sinister symbol. They said:[202] למה הוא מושל כל באי העולם בחולדה אלא מה החולדה הזאת גוררת ומנחת ואינה יודעת למי מנחת כך הן כל באי העולם גוררין ומניחין גוררין ומניחין ואינן יודעין למי הן מניחין. יצבר ולא ידע מי אוספם "Why does it[203] liken all inhabitants of the world to a weasel,[204] because just as this weasel drags and stores up and does not know for whom it stores, so the dwellers of the world drag and store, drag and store, not knowing for whom they store, [as it is written]:[205] '*He heapeth up riches, and knoweth not who shall gather them*'."[206]

Artemidorus[207] similarly explains that the vision of a weasel in a dream is a bad omen because it spoils whatever it takes.[208] The latter interpreted the dream of a weasel by means of *gematria* and a symbol; the Rabbis apply it in the *Aggadah* with the help of paronomasia.

Although there is no evidence in early rabbinic literature for the use of *gematria* (ἰσόψηφα) in the interpretation of dreams[209]

---

[198] See Artemidorus ibid., ed. Hercher, *Index rerum*, p. 303, s. v. ἰσόψηφα; Buché-Leclerck ibid. I, pp. 313 and 318 ff.

[199] Artem. III. 28: ἔστι γὰρ ἰσόψηφος δίκη καὶ γαλῆ.

[200] See H. Lewy, *Zeitschrift des Vereins f. Volkskunde* III, 1893, pp. 135–136. Comp. also Lieberman *GJP*, p. 98, n. 19.

[201] See Lieberman ibid.

[202] *TP Shabbath* XIV. 1, 14c.

[203] I. e. Scripture, Ps. 49:2.

[204] A play on חלד and חולדה.

[205] Ps. 39:7. Comp. ibid. 6.

[206] The Rabbis probably allude to the destruction of the weasel by the snake which then devours the food stored up by the former. See Arist. *Hist. anim.* IX. 1, 609b; ibid. 6, 612b.

[207] Ibid. III. 28.

[208] ὅ τι γὰρ ἂν λάβῃ, τοῦτο σήπει.

[209] Comp. A. Loewinger, *Der Traum in der jüdischen Literatur*, p. 27, n. 7 and p. 30. See below n. 211.

we can assume the Rabbis were not unaware of this method in the *onirocritica*. The wide use of the *gematria* in the magic and mystic literature[210] argues for its general application in all occult sciences of the time.[211]

4. Substitution of letters, *Athbash*[212] was widely practiced in antiquity.[213] No evidence is found for the application of *Athbash* in dream interpretations, but the common use of it suggests that the experts on dreams would not neglect this device when occasion arose. Rab[214] maintained[215] that Daniel had interpreted (Dan. 5:25) the oracle by the method of *Athbash*. This asserts its application in at least the interpretation of oracles.

5. *Notaricon* in all its forms and variations as it was employed by the Rabbis in the exposition of the *Aggadah*[216] is quite common in the interpretation of dreams among both Jews and Gentiles:

[210] See F. Dornseiff, *Das Alphabet* etc., pp. 91–118; Th. Hopfner, *Griechisch-Aegyptischer Offenbarungszauber*, p. 181; R. Eisler, *Weltenmantel*, p. 789, s. v. Isopsephie; idem, *Archiv f. Religionswissenschaft* XVI, 1913, p. 305, n. 2.

[211] The use of letters as numerals is apparently a Greek invention which was adopted by the Semites at a much later time, see Dornseiff, *Das Alphabet* etc., p. 11. (Comp. now H. L. Ginsberg, *Studies in Koheleth*, p. 32 ff.) At some time during the second commonwealth the Jews inscribed *α*, *β*, *γ* (signifying 1, 2, 3) on the several baskets in the temple of Jerusalem (See *Mishnah Shekalim* III. 2), i. e. the Jews availed themselves of the *Greek* alphabet to employ letters as numerals (In the *Mishnah* ibid. R. Ishmael is only explaining the statement of the first *Tanna*). Comp. however Tosefta *Ma'asser Sheni* V. 1.

The numerical value of *Greek* letters was also utilized in the rabbinic dream interpretations. R. Jose (*BR* ch. 68. 12, 785, see also the sources referred to above, n. 192) explains (the dream about the treasure in) Cappadocia to signify κάππα δοκοί, twenty beams. This is, of course, no ἰσόψηφον. The absence of the latter in early Jewish *onirocritica* may be quite indicative of its origin.

[212] See above n. 177.

[213] See Dornseiff, *Das Alphabet* etc., pp. 17 (and n. 2 ibid.), 125 and 136. Comp. also H. I. Marrou, *Histoire de l'éducation dans l'antiquité*, p. 212. For other ways of substitution of letters see Suetonius, *Jul.* LVI. 6 (A. Gelius, *Noct. Att.* XVII. 9. 1–5); idem, *Aug.* LXXXVIII. Comp. *TB Sukkah* 52b.

[214] Flourished at the beginning of the third century.

[215] *TB Sanhedrin* 22a.

[216] See above, nn. 180–185.

a. Every single letter is considered as an abbreviation of a word.[217] R. Joshua b. Levi said[218] that the vision of the letter ט״ת in a dream is a good omen. "Is it because ט״ת stands for טוב?"[219] Similarly, Artemidorus[220] relates that once a military commander saw the letters ι κ ϑ in a dream inscribed on his sword.[221] The Jewish war in Cyrene[222] broke out, and the man who saw the dream died a hero's death. Consequently, the explanation of the dream was that the ι stood for Ἰουδαίοις, the κ for Κυρηναίοις and the ϑ for ϑάνατος.

b. The anagram[223] was a common device in the onirocritica. The Rabbis say:[224] הרואה שעורים בחלום סרו עונותיו שנאמר וסר עונך וכו' "If a man sees barley in a dream it means that his sins were removed, as it is written (Isa. 6:7): 'And thine iniquity is taken away'." The letters שעורין (barley) are transposed and made to signify סר עון (sin is removed). It is a common procedure in the hermeneutic rules of the Midrash. TB[225] formulates it: גורעין ומוסיפין ודורשין "One may remove [a letter] and add [one] and then interpret." From Artemidorus[226] it is evident

---

[217] See above, n. 180. Comp. also the Onirocriticon of Rabbi Shlomoh Almoli פתרון חלומות, Gate I, ch. 1 end.

[218] TB Baba Kamma 55a, see דקדוקי סופרים ibid., p. 119.

[219] TB ibid. For ט״ת as an inauspicious sign, see Lieberman, GJP, p. 191. In the Midrash of the alphabet by the Samaritan Marqah (M. Heidenheim, Der Kommentar Marqah's des Samaritaners, p. XI, n. 2) this letter is the symbol of the snake which brought destruction into the world. Comp. however, Rettig, Memar Marqa, p. 23. Dornseiff (Das Alphabet etc.) who collected the material on the exegesis of the alphabet overlooked Marqah's Midrash. See H. Baneth, Des Samaritaners Marqah an die 22 Buchstaben, Berlin 1888, p. 50 ff.

[220] IV. 24.

[221] οἷον ἔδοξε στρατοπεδάρχης ἐπὶ τῇ μαχαίρᾳ αὐτοῦ γεγράφθαι ι κ ϑ. ἐγένετο πόλεμος ὁ Ἰουδαϊκὸς ἐν Κυρήνῃ, καὶ ἠρίστευσεν ἐν τῷ πολέμῳ ὁ ἰδὼν τὸν ὄνειρον, καὶ τοῦτο ἦ ὃ εἴπομεν, ἀπὸ μὲν τοῦ ι Ἰουδαίοις, ἀπὸ δὲ τοῦ κ Κυρηναίοις, ἀπὸ δὲ τοῦ ϑ ϑάνατος.

[222] The reference is probably to the Jewish war against Trajan, see Schürer, Geschichte I³, p. 665.

[223] See above n. 183.

[224] TB Berakhoth 57a.

[225] Yoma 48a; Baba Bathra 111b and parallels. Comp. TP Sota V. 1, 20a.

[226] IV. 23: μεταϑέντες . . . ἀφελόντες ἢ προσϑέντες γράμματα. "Changing . . . removing and adding letters." Comp. ibid. I. 11.

that this was the practice of the Greek interpreters of dreams. The anagram was also widely employed in mystic and magic literature.[227]

c. The dissolution of one word into two parts[228] was also generally practiced in the *onirocritica*. ישמעאל is there interpreted[229] as ישמע אל, "The Lord will hear [his prayers]," and לולב as לו לב "To Him is [his] heart."[230] During his siege of Tyre Alexander the Great is said to have seen a satyr in a dream who mocked him at a distance. "The diviners, dividing the word "satyros" in two parts (sa Tyros), said to him plausibly enough 'Tyre is to be thine'."[231]

We not only find the same methods employed in the *onirocritica* and in the *Aggadah*, but sometimes also come across the very same interpretations in both sources. The *Sifre*[232] playing on the word מורשה (Deut. 33:4), heritage, interprets it as if it were written מאורשה (betrothed), and, deriving from it that the Torah is betrothed to Israel, it draws certain conclusions.[233] The identical exegesis is used in the solution of a dream.[234] In the *onirocriticon* the betrothed girl symbolizes the Torah. In the *Aggadah* the Torah is betrothed to Israel.

The methods applied in the understanding of dreams were invented neither by the Jews nor by the Greeks. They go back to hoary antiquity. The ingenuity of the diviner or seer produced the most complicated solutions of dreams, oracles and magic, which lent themselves to similar ways of interpretations; they borrow from each other and supplement one another.

"Seventy years, as the period of its (i. e. Babylon's) desola-

---

[227] See L. Blau, *Das altjüdische Zauberwesen*, pp. 147–148; Dornseiff, *Das Alphabet* etc., p. 63.

[228] See above, nn. 181, 184–186.

[229] *TB Berakhoth* 56b.

[230] Ibid. 57a.

[231] Plut. *vit Alex.* XXIV. 5: οἱ δὲ μάντεις τοὔνομα διαιροῦντες οὐκ ἀπιϑάνως ἔφασαν αὐτῷ· Σὴ γενήσεται Τύρος. Artemidorus (IV. 24) ascribes this analysis to the famous seer Aristandros of Telmessus in Lycia. See on him Bouché-Leclerck, *Histoire de la divination* II, p. 76 ff.

[232] II, 345, ed. Finkelstein, p. 402. Comp. *Shemoth Rabba* XXXIII. 7.

[233] See also *TB Sanhedrin* 59a and *Pesaḥim* 49b.

[234] *TB Berakhoth* 57a.

tion, he (i. e. Marduk) wrote down (in the Book of Fate). But the merciful Marduk in a moment his heart was at rest (appeased) turned it upside down and for the eleventh year ordered its restoration."[235] The Babylonian numeral "70" turned upside down, or reversed, becomes "11", just as our printed "9" turned upside down becomes "6".[236]

Writing or reading letters upside down was probably not limited to oracular interpretation only, but was practiced in magic as well. More than a thousand years later Plinius Medicus prescribed[237] as a "remedy" for a persistent haemorrhage the writing of the patient's own name on his forehead in letters inverted upside down.[238] The methods were the same at different times among different nations.

The Rabbis knew this truth. R. Abbahu[239] was once involved in a controversy with non-Jews about the survival of children born after seven or eight months of pregnancy.[240] The

[235] The Black Stone of Esarhaddon of 680 B. C. E. (Luckenbill in *The American Journal of Semitic Languages* XLI, 1925, p. 242 ff.). Prof. H. L. Ginsberg has kindly drawn my attention to this inscription.

[236] Luckenbill ibid.

[237] I. 7, cited by Dornseiff, *Das Alphabet* etc., p. 56, n. 1.

[238] Nomen ipsius, inversis literis, apices deorsum.

[239] Died in the beginning of the fourth century.

[240] According to a tradition quoted from an unknown source in the Yemenite *Midrash Haggadol* on Ex 2:2 (p. 13): "All the prophets were born after only seven months of pregnancy." *Protev. Jacobi* (V. 2) asserts (according to two manuscripts and the Armenian version) that Anna gave birth to Mary after seven months of pregnancy. The same was said about Dionysus and Apollo, see Gaster, *The Joshua Bloch Memorial Volume*, p. 118, n. 4. Rabbi Simeon Duran in his book (composed at the beginning of the fifteenth century in Algiers) קשת ומגן relates: And they (i. e. the Gentiles) say that the reason a child born after eight months of pregnancy is not viable is that Jesus the Nazarene, who was born after eight months of pregnancy ordained that no child born after this period of pregnancy survive. Suspecting that the Rabbi drew his information from Moslem sources I inquired of Prof. Arthur Jeffery about this tradition in Arabic literature. Dr. Jeffery kindly supplied the following information: Ibrahim al-Tha'labi in his Ḳiṣaṣ al-Anbiā (i. e. *historiae prophetarum*), ed. Cairo 1921, p. 265 reports (The tradition goes back to Al-Kalbī): "The scholars differ as to the period of Mary's pregnancy and the time of her giving birth to Jesus. Some say that the measure of her

Rabbi remarked:[241] מדידכון אנא ממטי לכון זיטא איפטה איטה אכטו
"From your own [alphabet] I will prove it to you ζ ($\zeta\bar{\eta}\tau a$) =
$\dot{\epsilon}\pi\tau\dot{a}$, η ($\bar{\eta}\tau a$) = $\dot{o}\kappa\tau\dot{\omega}$."[242] The most plausible explanation was
suggested by O. Crusius:[243] Since ζ equals 7 and η 8 the
cryptogram has to be deciphered as: $\zeta\bar{\eta}$ $\tau\dot{a}$ $\dot{\epsilon}\pi\tau\dot{a}$ $<\mu\bar{a}\lambda\lambda o\nu>$
$\bar{\eta}$ $\tau\dot{a}$ $\dot{o}\kappa\tau\dot{\omega}$, i. e. "Infants of seven months are more likely to
survive than those of eight."[244] R. Abbahu resorted here to
the *notaricon*,[245] paronomasia and the numerical value of letters,
and combined them together[246] for the purpose of investing
letters of the Greek alphabet with mysterious significance. The
method was well understood by Jew and Gentile alike.

To sum up, numberless methods for the interpretations of
dreams, oracles and mystic writings existed in the ancient
world from times immemorial. Very often the same phenomenon lent itself to various and even contradictory explanations.[247]

pregnancy was the same as other women, namely nine months. Others say it
was *eight* months, and that that was an added miracle, since no eight months
child has ever lived save Jesus. Others say it was six months, others three
hours, and others, that it was a single hour." In this source, however, there is
no mention that it was Jesus who decreed that no child born after eight months
of pregnancy should survive. The Rabbi denied the claim, pointing out that
Hippocrate (See *de nutr.* XLII and the commentary of Sabinus quoted by
A. Gellius, *noctes Att.* III. 16) and Aristotle (See *hist. anim.* VII. 4 584b)
who lived hundreds of years before Jesus possessed knowledge of this rule.
Consequently, it cannot be ascribed to the decree of Jesus.

[241] *BR* XIV. 2, 1272 and parallels referred to by Theodor a. l.

[242] See A. Brüll, *Fremdsprachliche Redensarten*, Leipzig 1869, p. 16, n. 2;
S. Krauss LW I, p. 154.

[243] *Apud* L. Cohn in *MGWJ* XLIV, 1900, p. 569; see Lieberman *GJP*,
p. 23.

[244] Comp. Galen, *Phil. hist.*, ed. Kühn p. 333; Oribasius, *collect. med.*
XXII. 5, ed. Bussemaker et Daremberg III, p. 63. The latter remarks that
the theory according to which children born after eight months of pregnancy
are not able to live is false, for they do live ($\tau o\hat{v}\tau o$ $\delta\dot{\epsilon}$ $\dot{\epsilon}\sigma\tau\iota$ $\psi\epsilon\hat{v}\delta o\varsigma\cdot$ $\zeta\bar{\eta}$ $\gamma\acute{a}\rho$).
But the truth is that the number of surviving eight months infants is less
than that of seven months children ($\tilde{\eta}\tau\tau o\nu$ $\tau\hat{\omega}\nu$ $\dot{\epsilon}\pi\tau a\mu\acute{\eta}\nu\omega\nu$).

[245] I. e. breaking the names of the letters in two parts.

[246] It is the same device employed by R. Jose in his dream interpretation
where he dissolved Cappadocia in $K\acute{a}\pi\pi a$ $\delta o\kappa o\acute{\iota}$, twenty beams, see above
n. 211.

[247] See Cicero, *de divinat.* II. 70.

The Rabbis who flourished at the end of the first and the beginning of the second centuries (and among them we find R. 'Akiba,
the famous interpreter of the Torah) already employed the
shrewd and complicated methods of the *onirocritica* in their
dream interpretations.[248]

For the interpretation of sacred *legal* texts, which were not
as a rule formulated in an ambiguous language, different means
were undoubtedly in use among the priests. The Rabbis applied
comparatively few rules to the elaboration of the legal part of
the Torah. They were the result of choice, discrimination and
crystallization out of many ways for the exposition of texts.
In the *Aggadah* however and in the אסמכתות ("supports") for
the *Halakha*, the Rabbis resorted to well established devices
which were current in the literary world at that time. Had
the Rabbis themselves invented these artificial rules in their
interpretations, the "supports" from the Bible would be in-
effective and strange to the public. But as the utilization of
instruments accepted all over the civilized world of that time
their rules of interpretation of the *Aggadah* (and their "supports"
for the *Halakha* from Scripture) were a literary affectation which
was understood and appreciated by their contemporaries.[249]

However, although we possess no evidence that the Rabbis
borrowed their rules of interpretation from the Greeks, the
situation is quite different when we deal with formulation,
terms, categories and systematization of these rules. The latter
were mainly created by the Greeks, and the Jews most probably did not hesitate to take them over and adapt them to
their own rules and norms.

The name *Mekhilta, Mekhilata* (literally: measure, measures),
for the *Tannaitic* treatises which interpret the Bible[250] cor-

---

[248] *TP Ma'aser Sheni* IV, end, 55c.

[249] We have suggested that some of the artificial rules in *Aggadic* hermeneutics were derived from the *onirocritica* rather than from the realm of
oracles etc. because the former was in vogue among the Jews, whereas nothing
of the latter was used by them in the rabbinic period save the בת קול, see
Appendix I, below p. 194 ff.

[250] Or for collections of rabbinic law, see J. N. Epstein, *Tarbiz* VI. 3, p.
102 ff.

responds exactly to κανών, κανόνες,²⁵¹ the treatise, or treatises, of logic.²⁵² Again the term גזירה שוה appears to be the literal translation of the Greek σύγκρισις πρὸς ἴσον,²⁵³ which indicates the influence of Greek terminology.

Hence we may go a step further. Although the Rabbis cannot be definitely said to have adopted a certain method from the Greeks, they may nevertheless have learned from them the *application* of that method to a particular question. We shall cite one interesting instance.

It appears that the device of an acrostic in a composition to indicate the name of the author was already employed in the Orient in the second millenium B. C. E.²⁵⁴ According to Cicero²⁵⁵ Ennius Quintus wove into some of his verses the acrostic:²⁵⁶ Quae Q. Ennius fecit, "Quintus Ennius wrote it." In the view of modern scholars the Greek acrostic of this type²⁵⁷ is not earlier than the second century B. C. E.²⁵⁸

Perhaps we may venture the conjecture that even the early Alexandrian grammarians sought acrostics in Homer's books for the purpose of establishing the authorship of certain poems found in our Iliad and Odyssey.²⁵⁹ Athenaeus reports²⁶⁰ that Sosibius²⁶¹ was a recipient of a royal stipend from Ptolemy Philadelphus. The latter once commanded his stewards to refuse Sosibius his stipend and to tell him that he had already received it. The stewards obeyed the order of the king and, consequently, Sosibius went to him and complained of their action.

---

²⁵¹ See Hoffmann, *Zur Einleitung in die halachischen Midraschim*, p. 37 and Epstein ibid.

²⁵² Comp. ὁ 'Επικούρου κανών, see Diog. Laert. X. 30 ff.

²⁵³ See above, p. 59 ff.

²⁵⁴ See B. Landsberger, *Zeitschrift f. Assyriologie* 1936, p. 33; R. Marcus, *Journal of Near Eastern Studies* VI, 1947, p. 109 and notes ibid.

²⁵⁵ *De divin.* II. LIV. 111, referred to by Graf in PW *RE* I, p. 1200.

²⁵⁶ Quae ἀκροστιχίς dicitur.

²⁵⁷ Notwithstanding the report of A. Gellius (*Noct. Att.* XIV. 6. 4) that some authors tried to find acrostics in the poems of Homer (see Graf ibid.).

²⁵⁸ I. e. not earlier than the previously mentioned Latin acrostic, see Graf ibid. and Dornseiff, *Das Alphabet* etc., p. 147.

²⁵⁹ Comp. Seneca, *epist.* 88. 40.

²⁶⁰ *Deipn.* XI, 493f.   ²⁶¹ See above n. 144.

Ptolemy asked for the records and, upon examining them, affirmed that his stewards were right in their assertion that Sosibius had already received his stipend. The records had the following list of names of people who had already been paid their allowances: Soteros, Sosigenos, Bionos, Appolloniou. The king said: Take the *so* from Soteros, the *si* from Sosigenos, the first syllable from Bionos and the last letters from Appolloniou, and you have: So-si-bi-ou. "You will find that you yourself received your due according to your own devices,"[262] i. e. the way of your interpretation of Homer.

This anecdote makes good sense only if we suppose that Sosibius liked to look for acrostics in the poems of Homer which might contain the names (signatures) of their authors. Ptolemy argued that by Sosibius' own methods he could prove that the latter's name was found in his records indicating that he had already received his pay. If our conjecture is true, Sosibius was the first to introduce the search for an acrostic as a literary criterion for the establishment of the authorship of a given work. This innovation seemed ridiculous to his contemporaries, and he was accordingly given his own medicine.

In early rabbinic literature this kind of acrostic is not mentioned.[263] But the Rabbis were sometimes confronted with problems similar to the question of authorship in classic literature, and the possible discovery of an acrostic would be of some help.

For instance, the Rabbis differed as to the writer of the Second Tables. The Bible itself leaves room for doubt. Some verses imply (Ex. 34:1; Deut. 10:2, 4) that the Almighty wrote them (as He did the first ones). But other verses (Ex. 34:27, 28) indicate that Moses engraved the Second Tables. The prevalent rabbinic view is that both the First and the Second Tables were written by the Almighty Himself.[264] But some

---

[262] εὑρήσεις σαυτὸν ἀπειληφότα κατὰ τὰς σὰς ἐπινοίας.

[263] The only two instances are: *Pesikta Rabbathi* 46, ed. Friedmann, 187a which finds the acrostic למשה in מזמור שיר ליום השבת (Ps. 92:1) and *Tanḥuma* האזינו 5 where a *gematria* derived from an acrostic forms the name משה. In both cases we have apparently later interpolations.

[264] See *Tosefta Baba Kamma* VII, 3581 ff. and *Debarim Rabba* III. 17.

rabbinic sources suggest that the latter were the work of
Moses.[265] Rabbi Isaiah the Younger (of Trani) states explicitly:[266]
וכתבתי על הלוחות לאו דווקא שהרי אמר כתוב לך ולא היה מכתב אלקים
שתכתוב לך אצוה וכתבתי שאמר וזה הראשונים, אלא " 'And I will write'
(Ex. 34:1) is not meant in the literal sense, for it is said (ibid.
27): 'Write thou'. Only the First Tables were of the Lord's
own handwriting. The verse 'I will write' means I shall order
thee to write." Similarly Pseudo-Philo[267] records: Et dixit ei
Deus . . . rescribe in eis iusticias etc. "And the Lord said to
him . . . write upon them the laws etc."

Consequently the opinions of the Rabbis were divided as to
the handwriting of the Second Tables. Both parties found their
evidence in אנכי, the first word of the Tables, which they rated
as an acrostic. The prevalent opinion read it[268] to mean:
אנא נפשי כתבית יהבית "I Myself wrote [and] gave [them]." In
this view the first word of both the First and the Second Tables
indicates that they were both written by the Lord Himself.

However an anonymous statement preserved in the Yemenite
Midrash Haggadol[269] records: אנכי רבנן אמרי אנא נומיקה כתבית
יהבית "The Rabbis said אנכי is to be resolved into: I *nomico*
(νομικός) wrote [and] gave [them]." Here it is the νομικός
who wrote and gave the Tables. There can be no doubt that
the νομικός is none other than Moses. The Samaritan
Marqah,[270] in enumerating the titles of Moses, calls him מיסטה,[271]

---

[265] *Shemoth Rabba* XLVII. 9, end. Comp. ibid. 2 and *Tanḥuma* ibid., ed.
Buber 59a and n. 123 ibid.

[266] אוצר טוב, *Hebräische Beilage zum Magazin* of Berliner and Hoffmann,
1885, p. 16.

[267] XII. 10, ed. Kisch, p. 149.

[268] *TB Shabbath* 105a; *Pesikta Rabbathi* XXI, ed. Friedmann 105a;
Pesikta deR. Kahana XII, 109a.

[269] To Deut. 5:6 in הסגולה XVIII, p. 53; *Midrasch Tannaïm*, ed. Hoffman,
p. 20, note *.

[270] M. Heidenheim, *Bibliotheca Samaritana* III, p. 114; H. Baneth, *Des
Samaritaners Marqah an die 22 Buchstaben*, p. 48.

[271] This was the surname of Moses in the Jewish Hellenistic writings, see
W. Bauer, *Griechisch-deutsches Wörterbuch z. d. N. T.*, s. v. μεσίτης. Likewise
in *ascensio Mosis* (I. 14; III. 12) Moses is styled *arbiter*. The rabbinic writings
as well term Moses סרסור, see *TP Megillah* IV. 1, 77d; *Pesikta deR. Kahana*

μεσίτης, middleman, and נומיקה, νομικός, *iuris prudens*, or scribe, notarius.[272] The Samaritans[273] and the Palestinian *Targumim*[274] call Moses ספר. In the Greek of the Byzantine period νομικός was simply *tabellio*,[275] notary.[276] The Rabbis who maintained that the Second Tables were engraved by Moses explained that in these the נו"ן in אנכי stands not for נפשי (Myself) but for נומיקה, νομικός, Moses.

V, 45a (twice) and parallels; *Shemoth Rabba* III. 5; ibid. XXXIII. 1; *Debarim Rabba* III. 12 *passim*. Prof. Louis Finkelstein (*Tarbiz* XX, p. 96) discovered that Moses was also called ביניי, middleman. He is also termed שליח (*Sifra*, end, 115d), agent. See also *Pesikta Rabbathi* XV, ed. Friedmann 69a and *Shir Rabba* I. 4, ed. Rom 5a.

[272] And not law-giver, as translated by A. E. Cowley, *The Samaritan Liturgy* II, Glossary, p. LXII, s. v. נומיקה. *Aggadath Bereshith* (XXXVI, ed. Buber, Krakau, 1903, p. 72) in referring to איה סופר (Is. 33:18) renders it: איה הן הנמקין שלה "Where are her νομικοί" (Comp. S. J. Miller, *The Samaritan Molad Moshe*, p. 60₁₂, where the plural is spelled נומיקים).

[273] See Marqah, ed. Baneth ibid., p. 42.

[274] See ps.-Jonathan Num. 21:18 passim. He is also called ספרא רבה (*TB Sota* 13b, Onkelos Deut. 33:21, passim) which corresponds to כתבה רבה of the Samaritans, see Heidenheim, *op. c.* II, p. 138.

[275] See Goetz, *CGL* II, 149₃ and Preisigke, *Fachwörter d. öffentlichen Verwaltungsdienstens Ägyptens*, p. 130, s. v. νομικός.

[276] Comp. also Payne Smith, *Thesaurus Syriacus*, p. 2232.

THE PUBLICATION OF THE *MISHNAH*

In addition to the canonical Hebrew Scripture[1] the Jews of the second commonwealth possessed a compilation of laws, customs and ethical sayings known as *Mishnah*.[2] This is the main source of the earlier statements of the *Halakha*[3] which

---

[1] And other books such as the *Targumim* etc.

[2] In this chapter the term *Mishnah* is employed in the sense given to it by the ancient and mediaeval Rabbis. The *Baraithoth* are also included under this name. See J. N. Epstein, מבוא לנוסח המשנה, pp. 805, 811 ff.

[3] The origin of this word is not definitely established. Leopold Wenger (*Canon in den römischen Rechtsquellen und in den Papyri*) undertakes to prove that canon as *regula iuris* (see pp. 47–71) derived its meaning from canon, rent annually paid by the tenant to the land owner (κανὼν ἐμφυτευτικός) and canon, land tax paid to the government. "The characteristic features of the economic and financial *canon* are that its amount is fixed beforehand as a regular, annual payment which, on principle, is unchangeable. These features are the bridge which connects the two meanings of the term. *Canon* as synonymous with *regula* shows the same traits as the various payments covered by the term: stability, regularity and fixedness, although moderation is not excluded." (A. Berger, *Seminar* VII, 1944, p. 96). Although Wenger's study covers a later period (*canon* as land tax is not attested by sources earlier than the fourth century C. E.) his research and reasoning may perhaps elucidate our term. In Ezra (4:13 passim) the tax הלך is mentioned. It has been identified (see Gesenius-Buhl, s. v. הלך) with the Babylonian *ilku* (tax) which is already extant in the laws of Hammurabi. From the Aramaic Indorsements on the Documents of the Murašû Sons (A. T. Clay in *Old Testament and Semitic Studies in Memory of W. R. Harper* I, p. 308, No. 26; p. 316, No. 48) we learn that a land tax was called הלכא. Hence it is possible that the term הלכה, *regula*, fixed rule (הלכה קצובה), has its origin in the name of the fixed land tax.

In practice הלכה has the same meaning as ὅρος (literally "boundary") which means *regula*, and especially a statement of the law, a juristic principle, in antithesis to case law (מעשה), see F. Schulz, *History of Roman Legal Science*, p. 137, n. 4. The Rabbis (*Sifre* II 188, ed. Finkelstein, p. 227) interpreted the verse (Deut. 19:14) "*Thou shalt not remove thy neighbor's boundary*" (גבול). The Septuagint and Symmachus render it ὅρια) as a reference to the deliber-

forms the bulk of Jewish oral law. The word משנה, *Mishnah*, in its broader sense signifies the whole body of the early Jewish oral transmission (including the *Halakhic Midrashim*, see n. 2) and was rendered δευτέρωσις by the Christian Church fathers.[4] We now have the oral law in the form of books, but there is a persistent tradition (see below) that once upon a time there was an injunction against putting the oral Law in writing.[5]

Mediaeval scholars disagree as to the time when the *Mishnah* was indited. Some assert[6] that every scholar wrote the *Mishnah* for his private use, whereas others maintain[7] that the *Mishnah* and the Talmud were not reduced to writing until the post-Talmudic period. Modern scholars are divided in the same two camps.[8] As for the rabbinic sources themselves, they state clearly[9] that the oral Law is not to be put down in writing. At the same time there is abundant evidence indicating that the Rabbis were in possession of written *Halakhoth*.[10]

Upon a closer analysis of the rabbinic sources, however, we shall see that Rab Sa'adiah Gaon and his followers were undoubtedly right in their view regarding the writing of the *Mishnah*. Modern scholars have failed to treat the whole

ate change of the traditional *halakha* (See Lieberman, *Tosefeth Rishonim* IV, p. 52). Comp. also Dionysius of Alexandria quoted by Eusebius, *Historia Eccles*. VII. 7. 5 and A. Rahlfs, *Septuaginta Studien* I, 1904, p. 76.

The הלכות רופאים mentioned in *Sifre* (II. 247, ed. Finkelstein, p. 276 and parallel) have no relation with the ὅροι ἰατρικοί of Pseudo-Galen (ed. Kühn XIX, p. 446 ff.). The latter are only definitions.

[4] See Bacher, *Terminologie* I, p. 122 ff.; Juster, *Les Juifs dans l'empire Romain* I, p. 372, n. 6.

[5] See Strack, *Introduction to the Talmud* etc., pp. 12 ff., 243 ff. and see below.

[6] Rab Sa'adiah Gaon (ספר הגלוי) in A. Harkavy's זכרון לראשונים V, p. 194. See also Schechter, *Saadyana*, p. 5), R. Samuel b. Hofni (מבוא התלמוד ed. B. M. Lewin, p. 1) and many others (See the long list compiled by J. N. Epstein, מבוא לנוסח המשנה, p. 693).

[7] Rashi on *Baba Mezi'a* 33b, '*Erubin* 62b. See Epstein ibid.

[8] See the list drawn by Epstein ibid.

[9] *TP Pe'ah* II. 6, 17a and parallels; ibid. *Megillah* IV. 1, 74d; *Tanḥuma* וירא 5; ibid. כי תשא 34; *TB Gittin* 60b and *Temurah* 14b passim.

[10] See Strack ibid., pp. 16, 245; Epstein ibid., pp. 693 and 699 ff.

problem properly, because they missed the basic point at issue.

Let us begin with this question: Was the *Mishnah* published? Publication in antiquity was achieved in two ways. Books which had, or were expected to have, a large circulation were handled by special publishers. They employed many professional copyists to whom the text was dictated, and thousands of copies would be produced in a short time.[11] The Bible could not be published in this way, for every scroll had to be copied from another scroll and could not be written by dictation.[12] The particularly sacred character of the Jewish writings and the minute care required from the Scribe would not encourage a large production of books.[13]

But there was a second way of publication in antiquity. The authentic original copy would be deposited in a temple, a library or the archives. Such an act guarded the book against possible forgeries. In case of doubts or controversies regarding readings in the given book, the copy placed in the archives would be decisive.[14] Such deposition was designated by various verbs such as ἀποτιθέναι (to store away, to deposit, see below), εἰσφέρειν (to enter, to bring in),[15] *referre*[16] and others.[17]

According to rabbinic tradition, some Jewish books were

---

[11] See Th. Birt, *Das antike Buchwesen*, p. 118; W. Schubart, *Das Buch bei den Griechen etc.*[2], p. 151 ff.; E. Bickerman, *JBL* LXIII, 1944, p. 341, n. 13; H. L. Pinner, *The World of Books in Classical Antiquity*, p. 32 ff. and nn. ibid., p. 61.

[12] See *TP Megillah* IV. 1, 74d; *TB* ibid. 18b and parallels.

[13] Comp. *TB Pesaḥim* 50b. It appears there that the copyists of Jewish sacred books were not counted among the rich. See also *Koheleth Rabba* II 17; *TB Baba Bathra* 155b and comp. *Gittin* 45b.

[14] See on the deposition of a copy in the archives or libraries, E. Peterson, Εἷς ϑεός, pp. 217–220 (The correct explanation of Ignat. *ad Philad.* VIII. 2 was already suggested by S. Reinach; see *Anatolian Studies Presented to Sir W. M. Ramsay*, 1923, p. 339 ff. and p. 340, n. 1 ibid.); E. Bickerman, *JBL* LXIII, 1944, p. 352 ff.

[15] See Bickerman, ibid. p. 345, n. 37. Comp. below, n. 49.

[16] Tacit. *Dial.* XXI. 6: *fecerunt enim et carmina et in Bybliothecas rettulerunt*. "For they (i. e. Caesar and Brutus) did write poems and deposited them in the libraries."

[17] See Peterson and Bickerman ibid.

published in this second way. In the *Midrash*[18] it is stated:[19]
[משה] כתב שלש עשרה תורות י"ב לי"ב שבטים וא' ה נ י ח באר ון שאם
יבקשו לזייף דבר שיהיו מוציאי' אותה שבארון "[Moses] wrote thirteen
Scrolls, twelve for the twelve tribes and one which he *deposited
in the ark*,[20] so that if one wished to forge something they would
produce the Scroll deposited in the ark," i. e. and thereby prove
the authentic reading. A book which was laid away in the
temple was thereby published;[21] no forgeries could be made in
the other copies. The Rabbis relate that the Palestinian Jews
had hesitated to adopt the Purim festival, because they feared
the consequences of making the contents of the Esther scroll
known. But Mordecai and Esther reassured them that the
story related in it was written and *entered* in the archives[22]
(כתובה ומעלה בארכיים), i. e. it was already published.

כתוב ומונח, written and deposited,[23] is equivalent to "it is
published." The *Sefer Gezeratha* of the Zadokites was כתוב ומונח,
written and deposited, and whenever a question was encountered the book decided it.[24] This law book, in other words, was
published. The *Megillath Ta'anith* (the Scroll of Fasting) was
written and deposited (כתיבא ומנחא),[25] i. e. published. In the
post-Talmudic period they wrote down and deposited (כתבין
ומנחין) the *Halakhoth*,[26] i. e. they published them. In case of
doubts and controversies these books could be consulted.

---

[18] *Debarim Rabba* IX.9; *Midrash Tehillim* XC. 3, ed. Buber, p. 386;
Pesikta deR. Kahana XXVI, 197b; interpolation in *Sifre* II. 1, ed. Finkelstein,
p. 1 (See variants and notes ibid.). See Appendix II, below p. 200 ff.

[19] I copy from *Debarim Rabba*, ed. prin.

[20] Comp. Berthelot, *Alchim Gr.*, p. 320 (quoted by Peterson ibid., p. 219):
ὃν ἀπέθεντο εἰς ἕκαστον ἱερόν.

[21] Comp. I Sam. 10:25.

[22] *TP Megillah* I. 7, 70d. In mss. of *TB* (ibid. 7a): כתובה אני ומונחת על
ספר וכו'. See *Aggadath Esther* IX, ed. Buber, p. 80, n. 108.

[23] See above, n. 21.

[24] *Megillath Ta'anith* IV, ed. H. Lichtenstein, p. 75.

[25] *TB 'Erubin* 62b; see ibid. *Shabbath* 13b.

[26] See *TB Temurah* 14b and שיטה מקובצת ibid. n. 4; Lewin, Introduction
to the *Epistle of Rav Scherira*, p. LII, n. 4; Epstein, מבוא לנוסח המשנה, p. 696.
This passage is a later interpolation in the Talmud, for the *Gaon* records it
(*Festschrift z. 50 jährigen Bestehen d. Franz-Josef-Landesrabbiner-Schule in
Budapest*, 1927, Hebrew part, p. 96) as his own comment. See Epstein ibid.

Since in the entire Talmudic literature we do not find that a book of the *Mishnah* was ever consulted in case of controversies or doubt concerning a particular reading[27] we may safely conclude that the compilation was *not published in writing*, that a written ἔκδοσις of the *Mishnah* did not exist. On the other hand it is well known that the Rabbis possessed written *Halakhoth* and comments.[28] Those *Halakhoth* were written in מגילות סתרים (secret, i. e. private rolls),[29] or on πίνακες, writing tablets.[30] The decisions and comments of the masters were put down by their pupils on πίνακες[31] or on the *wall*.[32] Since all those writings had the character of private notes they had very little legal authority. If in the course of an argument a Rabbi had produced his notes they would have had no more authority than his oral assertion. The character of the notes recorded on the writing tablets, or the wall,[33] makes it obvious that we have to do with private ὑπομνήματα (notes) put down only for the use of their writer.

Ὑπομνήματα as a rule were not suitable material for publication,[34] and very often their reliability was highly questionable. When disciples of a great master issued an edition (ἔκδοσις) of their notes, the result sometime was that the teacher felt compelled to publish his work in order to correct the errors and blunders in the edition of his pupils.[35] The pupils of Galen also issued their notes behind the back of their teacher

---

[27] On *TP Ma'aser Sheni* V. 1, 55d see below, n. 107.

[28] See Epstein ibid., p. 700 ff.

[29] *TB Shabbath* 6b; ibid. *Baba Mezi'a* 92a.

[30] *TP Ma'aseroth* II. 4, 49d; *Menahoth* 70a.

[31] *TB Shabbath* 156a, *TP Kila'im* I. 1, 27a. See Appendix III, below p. 203.

[32] *TP* ibid.   [33] See *TP Kila'im* ibid.

[34] See T. W. Allen, *Homer*, p. 307 ff. G. Zuntz, *Byzantion* XIV, 1939, p. 560.

[35] Quintilianus relates (*Inst.* I, praef. 7–8) that two books of his art of rhetoric were issued by his pupils on the basis of lecture-notes which they had jotted down hastily. He says that the intention of the good pupils was noble, for they desired to glorify their teacher, but the master was compelled to reedit the books with many alterations, still more additions, better system and more elaboration (multa mutata, plurima adiecta, omnia vero compositora et, quantum nos poterimus, elaborata).

and distorted his views.[36] When a Babylonian Rabbi produced in evidence a list of Mar b. Rabina concerning relatives among whom intermarriage is forbidden, his colleagues disregarded it. It was argued. "Mar b. Rabina did not sign it" (לאו מר בריה דרבינא חתים עלייהו).[37] The list was prepared by the pupils of that great master, but he was not responsible for it.

Thus, the written notes of the Rabbis had no more value than the oral statements of their owners, and carried no weight as written documents.

We have now arrived at the conclusion that the *Mishnah* was not published in writing. But we have good evidence to establish that it was published in a different way. A regular oral ἔκδοσις, edition, of the *Mishnah* was in existence, a fixed text recited by the *Tannaim* of the college. The *Tanna* ("repeater", reciter) committed to memory the text of certain portions of the *Mishnah* which he subsequently recited in the college in the presence of the great masters of the Law. Those *Tannaim* were pupils chosen for their extraordinary memory, although they were not always endowed with due intelligence. The Rabbis characterized these reciters as follows:[38] רטין מגושא ולא ידע מאי אמר. תני תנא ולא ידע מאי אמר "The magian mumbles and understands not what he says. [Similarly] the *Tanna* recites and he understands not what he says." Indeed the stupider the *Tanna*, the more reliable his text; he was not suspected of "doctoring" it.[39]

When the *Mishnah* was committed to memory and the *Tannaim* recited it in the college it was thereby published and possessed all the traits and features of a written ἔκδοσις. When Rabbi Judah the Prince, the מתקן (the διορθωτής, editor, see below) of the *Mishnah*, changed his mind regarding a law in the *Mishnah*, and wanted to alter it, his son refused to accept

---

[36] Galen, *de libris propriis*, praef. 10.

[37] *TB Yebamoth* 22a.

[38] *TB Sotah* 22a.

[39] There were, of course, notable exceptions of great scholars who fulfilled the function of college-*Tanna*. The name *Tanna* for the college reciter was apparently introduced in the time of R. 'Akiba (the first half of the second century), as correctly indicated by J. N. Epstein, מבוא לנוסח המשנה, p. 674.

the modification. He preferred to adhere to the law as preserved in the first edition.[40] Some printed texts and some manuscripts of the *Mishnah* have preserved the reading of the first
edition. In his recension of the *Mishnah* Rabbi Judah the
Prince often left the *old* text unrevised, although the law was
subsequently repealed. משנה לא זזה ממקומה "The *Mishnah* was
not removed from its place."[41] Once the *Mishnah* was accepted
among the college *Tannaim* (reciters) it was difficult to cancel it.

Jerome[42] complains that once he has written something he
is not able to correct it, for his letters are immediately published. In this connection he quotes the words of Horace:[43]
Delere licebit quod non edideris; nescit vox missa reverti. "You
can delete what you did not publish. The word that is sent
abroad you can never revoke."[44] As an established text in the
mouths of the *Tannaim* the *Mishnah* was a *vox missa.*

The authority of the college-*Tanna* was that of a published
book. In case of doubt he was consulted as to the sequence or
the arrangement of the several clauses in the *Mishnah.*[45] The
Midrash Yelamdenu[46] states that there were various *Tannaim*
who respectively recited the different collections of the *Mishnah.*
"One recites [the *Mishnayoth*] of Bar Kappara, the other those
of R. Hiyya, and the third those of our sainted teacher" (i. e.
R. Judah the Prince). And the *Midrash* remarks: כולן נכנסין
לחבורה. כלם נתנו מרועה אחד "All of them[47] *enter the college,* all of

<hr>

[40] *TP Baba Mezi'a* IV. 1, 9c. Comp. *TB* ibid. 44a; *TP 'Abodah Zarah*
IV. 4, 44a, *TB* ibid. 52b. For the later period comp. Lieberman הירושלמי
כפשוטו, p. 400.

[41] *TB Abodah Zarah* 35b and parallels.

[42] *Epist.* 49, to Pammachius.   [43] *Ars poetica* 389.

[44] In asking his publisher to erase the name of L. Corfidius, Cicero (*ad
Att.* XIII. 44) mentions three copyists whom he wants to undertake the job
of deleting this name from all the copies. The fact that three men were required for the removal of one word indicates that most of the copies were still
in the publishing house and were not sent abroad. The correction was therefore
possible.

[45] *TB Baba Mezi'a* 34a; *Niddah* 43b.

[46] *Yalkut* Num. 771; Grünhut ספר הלקוטים IV, 72a. Comp. also ps.-Jonathan
to Num. 24:6.

[47] I. e. all of the mentioned collections of *Mishnayoth.*

them *'are given from one shepherd'*."[48] Thus it is obvious that
the phrase "all of them enter the college" means all of them
are authoritative (for all of them are given from one shepherd).
To "enter the college" seems to be a technical term like
εἰσφέρειν εἰς τὴν βιβλιοθήκην,[49] to bring in (to deposit) into
the library, thereby to give authority to the copy deposited, to
publish it. This is firmly corroborated by the statement in *TP*:[50]
כל משנה שלא נכנסה לחבורה אין סומכין עליה "Any *Mishnah* which
did not enter the college is not trustworthy." Similarly *TB*[51]
formulates the rule: כל מתניתא דלא מיתניא בי ר' חייא ור' אושעיא
משבשתא היא "Any *Mishnah* which was not taught in the college
of R. Hiyya or R. Hoshaia is faulty."[52] Hence the prerequisite
for making a *Mishnah* trustworthy is to bring it (εἰσφέρειν)
into the college and recite it there,[53] i. e. to publish it.

Evidently the *Tanna* was a living book, or, as TB[54] charac-
terizes him, a basket full of books (צנא דמלי סיפרי). But the
question is: What was the nature of that book? How was the
mass of diverse material arranged and systematized before it
was delivered to the Tanna, before he memorized it?

We shall first consider the technical terms used by the
Rabbis to denote the edition of the *Mishnah*. They are סדר[55]
and תקן.[56] The two verbs are synonymous;[57] they signify to bring
in order, to arrange, to systematize. But the Aramaic תקן
translates the Hebrew יַשֵּׁר,[58] διορθοῦν, which has the same
technical meaning in Greek, viz., to edit. Having spoken of
the rabbinic technical terms for systemizing and editing, we

---

[48] Eccl. 12:11. The allusion is to בעלי אסופות ibid.

[49] See above n. 15.   [50] *'Erubin* I. 6, 19b.

[51] *Ḥullin* 141a, bot.   [52] Comp. also *TB Gittin* 73a.

[53] After it was approved by the masters of the school.

[54] *Megillah* 28b.

[55] See Bacher *Terminologie* II, p. 133.

[56] *TB Yebamoth* 64b. Comp. also סדר תנאים ואמוראים (ed. K. Kahan, 1935,
p. 8): ולא תקנו מהלל ושמאי אלא ששה סדרים. See also B. M. Lewin, *Epistle of
Rav Scherira Gaon*, Introduction, p. XIV.

[57] See Bacher ibid. I, p. 204, s. v. תקן.

[58] ויישרם in II Chr. 32:30 is translated by the *Targum* ותקננון. See also
Jastrow, *Dictionary* etc., p. 1690, s. v. תקין 2. Both the Aramaic and the
Greek verbs signify: to correct.

shall now consider the work of those Rabbis whom tradition counts among the first editors of the *Mishnah*. We read in *TP*[59]:

זה ר' עקיבא שהתקין מדרש הלכות ואגדות, ויש אומרים אלו אנשי כנסת הגדולה.
מה שהתקין זה כללין ופרטין "It is R. 'Akiba who systemized (or: edited) the *Midrash*, the *Halakhoth* (*Mishnah*) and the *Aggadoth*. Some say this was done by the men of the Great Synagogue, what R. 'Akiba instituted[60] were general and specific rules."[61]

Thus the Palestinian Talmud credits R. 'Akiba with editing the *Midrash* and the *Mishnah*.[62] The *Tosefta*[63] portrays a part of his editorial work more fully. It is reported there: כשהיה
ר' עקיבא מסדר הלכות לתלמידים אמר כל מי ששמע טעם על חבירו יבוא ויאמר "When R. 'Akiba systematized *Mishnayoth* for his pupils he said: If anyone has heard some reasonable argument against his fellow student[64] let him come forth and tell it." A series of traditions is recorded there[65] which were delivered to R. 'Akiba by his pupils.[66] In many cases the Rabbi accepted the versions of his pupils in preference of his own.[67]

What R. 'Akiba actually did was to consult the ὑπομνήματα, the notes,[68] of his pupils as well as those of R. Ishmael. The character of pupils' notes was outlined above (p. 87). Pupils are not always exact in their notes. They sometimes mix the tradition of one teacher with that of another. It also happens that the master has changed his mind: some pupils have heard the older version, others the revised version and still others

[59] *Shekalim* V. 1, 48d.

[60] The word התקן means also to institute. But even here it may signify to edit, to systematize, see below.

[61] See below.

[62] Comp. also *TB Sanhedrin* 86a. See Frankel, דרכי המשנה, 1923, p. 221.

[63] *Zabim* I. 5, 676 33 ff.

[64] *RASH* a. l. reads: מחבירו, "From his fellow student," see Lieberman, *Tosefeth Rishonim* IV, p. 120.

[65] Ibid. I. 5-8.

[66] At least one pupil of another school (of R. Ishmael) participated in the discussion (ibid. 8).

[67] Ibid. 6; *Mishnah Ta'anith* IV. 4; *Tosefta Shebi'ith* II. 13, 63 17; *'Ukatzin* III. 2, 688 31. Comp. *Sifre* I, 4, ed. Horovitz, 7 21; *Sifre Zuta* ibid. 232 8; *TP Abodah Zarah* II. 4, 41b.

[68] Retained either in writing or orally.

have heard both, situations which are attested in both the Palestinian and Babylonian Talmuds.[69]

The *Tosefta*[70] remarks: משרבו תלמידי שמיי והלל שלא שימשו כל צרכן הרבו מחלוקות בישראל ונעשו שתי תורות "When the disciples of Shammai and Hillel, who did not wait upon their masters[71] sufficiently increased in number, controversies multiplied in Israel, and [the Torah] became [like] two *Toroth*."[72] Thus the growth of divergences of opinions among the pupils is blamed on their unsatisfactory attendance of their masters' instruction.

We find exactly the same phenomenon in Greek classic literature. K. Lehrs[73] remarks that the constant revision by Aristarchus of his "edition" of Homer accounted for the many contradictory opinions in the notes of his pupils. Some of the pupils put down his former views not knowing that he subsequently revised them. Hence the frequent quarrels among his pupils and successors concerning his Homeric readings.[74] E. Ludwich[75] correctly assumes that the pupils of Aristarchus were guided by their notes which they wrote for themselves; they jotted down there the items in which they were particularly interested. They sometimes added what they heard from other teachers as well as their own interpretation etc.

We further learn from the *Tosefta*[76] that the discussion of R. 'Akiba and his pupils involved the *Mishnah* of the two schools of Shammai and Hillel. At the time of that great master the body of the *Mishnah* comprised only the opinions of the

---

[69] *TP Baba Kamma* II, end, 3a; *TB Bezah* 24b.

[70] *Ḥagigah* II. 9, 235 14 (Cod. Vienna) and parallels; *TP Sanhedrin* I, 19c; *TB* ibid. 88b.

[71] I. e. were not in permanent personal contact with their masters, and may have sometimes missed their explanations. See *TB Berakhoth* 47b; ibid. 7b; *Sotah* 22b.

[72] On the controversies of pupils regarding the opinions of their teachers, see J. N. Epstein, מבוא לנוסח המשנה pp. 5–7.

[73] *De Aristarchi studiis homericis*[3], p. 16.

[74] See T. W. Allen, *Homer*, p. 308, n. 1, who remarks that among doctors also doubts existed about the views of Erasistratus and Chrysippus (Galen XI, ed. Kühn, 151).

[75] *Aristarchs homerische Textkritik* I, p. 25 ff.

[76] Ibid., see above, n. 63.

representatives of these two schools and their predecessors. This *Mishnah* was "published" and taught. But in the course of time a mass of interpretations had accumulated. The interpretations were not published, but were rather taught by the teachers themselves. The pupils would put down the explanations of their masters in their private notes, which had all the characteristics of the ὑπομνήματα mentioned above. The task which fell to R. 'Akiba was to sift through that *mixtum compositum* and to crystallize it in an exact and definite shape. His work resulted in the compilation of a new *Mishnah*.

Then the procedure adopted by the master was probably something like the following. He taught the new *Mishnah* to the first *Tanna*; afterwards he taught it to the second *Tanna* (in the presence of the first), then to the third etc. Subsequently the first *Tanna* repeated the *Mishnah* to the second, to the third etc. Then the second *Tanna* recited it to the third, to the fourth etc.[77] *TB* (ibid.) reports an anecdote according to which one Rabbi repeated the *Mishnah* to his pupil four hundred times! After the *Mishnah* was systematized,[78] and the *Tannaim* knew it thoroughly by heart, they repeated it in the college in the presence of the master who supervised its recitation, corrected it (תני תנא קמי דר' פלוני . . . א'ל)[79] and gave it its final form.

Thus, the old *Mishnah* was augmented by a new stratum formed of the later interpretations. The new material was incorporated in the old version, the compilation was systematized and edited, committed to the memory of a group of *Tannaim*, and finally "entered the college."[80] The new *Mishnah* was thus published in a number of "copies" (ἴσα) in the form of living books, which subsequently spread and multiplied.

However the editorial performance of R. 'Akiba was not limited merely to the introduction of some of the later inter-

[77] The picture (*TB* '*Erubin* 54b) of Moses reciting the *Mishnah* to Aaron, to his children, to the elders etc. was most likely taken from the practice of the academies.

[78] סדורה, see *TB ibid.* and comp. *Ta'anith* 8a.

[79] See Epstein מבוא לנוסח המשנה, p. 676 and n. 1 ibid.

[80] נכנסה לחבורה, see above nn. 49–50.

pretations into the body of the *Mishnah*. As an editor, he undoubtedly contributed to the systematization of the material. It was stated above[81] that some version in the Palestinian Talmud attributes to him the introduction of general and specific rules.[82] But general rules had been formulated in the *Mishnah* before the time of R. 'Akiba.[83] R. Joshua's share in this formulation[84] and in the edition of the old *Mishnah*[85] is quite evident. The entire tractate save for a few additions of *Kinnim* ("Bird-offerings") which is preserved in our edition of the *Mishnah* is supposed to be the work of R. Joshua.[86] The greater part of this tractate contains such complicated hypothetical cases that it would do honor to the most brilliant προγυμνάσματα of the rhetors. A *Mishnah* of the same character by R. Joshua is also preserved in our edition of the tractate *Niddah*.[87] In the Babylonian Talmud[88] it is reported that when R. Joshua visited Alexandria the people of that city posed twelve puzzling questions before him. All those riddles were in the typical spirit of the Alexandrian schools of that time. At least one of these questions pleased R. Joshua definitely and won his praise.[89] The contact of R. Joshua with this particular branch of Alexandrian "exercises" is thus well established; it

---

[81] See above n. 59.   [82] מה שהתקין זה כללין ופרטין.

[83] The greater part of the material was collected and analyzed by Rabbi Opfenheim in his article "The general rules in the *Mishnah* and the *Tosefta*" in כנסת ישראל ed. S. P. Rabbinowicz, I, 1886, p. 351 ff.

[84] See *Mishnah Ḥullin* II. 4; *Me'ila* I. 1; ibid. IV. 3; *Zabim* V. 1. Comp. Frankel דרכי המשנה 1923, p. 88 ff.

[85] See *Pesaḥim* IX. 6; *Yebamoth* VIII. 4; *Parah* I. 2.

[86] See *TB Zebaḥim* 67b–68a.

[87] VI. 14. Comp. *TB* ibid. 54a. It appears that there were opponents to this kind of complicated προγυμνάσματα by R. Joshua. This is probably the import of R. Eleazar Ḥisma's remark (*Aboth* III, end): קינין ופתחי נדה הן הן גופי הלכות "[The rules about] Bird-offerings and the calculations about the onset of menstruation — these are the essentials of the *Halakhoth*." The reference is probably to the above mentioned teachings of R. Joshua, which R. Eleazar defended.

[88] *Niddah* 69b.

[89] *Tosefta Nega'im* end. See in detail on this and similar passages of the "Alexandrian Talmud" in the "Response" by Lieberman, *Proceedings of the Rabbinical Assembly of America* XII, 1948, pp. 273–276.

can be therefore safely assumed that he was acquainted with the methods and practices prevalent in the rhetorical schools of Alexandria at that time.

However, R. 'Akiba is explicitly credited with an edition of the *Mishnah* as well as with introducing general and specific rules, and this tradition cannot be disregarded. We also read in *Aboth deR. Nathan*:[90] למה ר' עקיבא דומה לפועל שנטל קופתו ויצא לחוץ מצא חטים מניח בה. מצא שעורים מניח בה. כוסמין[91] מניח בה עדשים מניח בה כיון שנכנס לביתו מברר חטים בפני עצמן שעורין בפני עצמן פולין בפני עצמן כך עשה ר' עקיבא, ועשה כל התורה טבעות טבעות "To whom may R. 'Akiba be likened? To a laborer who took his basket and went out; he found wheat and put it in, he found barley and put it in, he found spelt[92] and put it in, he found lentils and put it in. When he came home he assorted the wheat by itself, the barley by itself, the beans by themselves, the lentils by themselves. R. 'Akiba acted similarly, and he converted the whole Torah into rings."[93] These rings seem to signify general rules,[94] i. e. R. 'Akiba used to convert case law into abstract general rules.[95] At any rate the part played by R. 'Akiba as a systemizer of the Mishnah[96] is quite evident from the tradition reported in *Aboth deR. Nathan*.

---

[90] I, ch. 18, ed. Schechter 34a.

[91] Ms. of *collectanea* on *Aboth* (see Schechter ibid. 73a) reads: פולין.

[92] Variant reading: beans, see above, n. 91, and see below.

[93] Κύκλα? Comp. *TB Shabbath* 138a top and *'Abodah Zarah* 42b where Abaye and R. Shesheth are credited with collecting the rings of the *Mishnayoth* (מנקיט אביי חומרי מתנייתא) [and forming it into a chain]. *Catenae* in this sense is used only in mediaeval Christian literature.

[94] See *Rashi Shabbath* ibid. s. v. חומרי. Comp. also *Sifre* II, 306, ed. Finkelstein, p. 336₁₄, 338₁₀, *TB Shabbath* 75b and the remarks of Rabbi Joseph Engel in his גליוני הש"ס ibid.

[95] For the introduction of abstract general rules in Roman law, see F. Schulz, *Principles of Roman Law*, p. 49 ff. The rabbinic attitude to the import of general rules is reflected in the statement of R. Johanan (*TB 'Erubin* 27a and parallels): "No inference may be drawn from general rules even when the exceptions were specified." Comp. also *TP Terumoth* I. 2, 40c and parallels.

[96] The general rules of R. 'Akiba are frequently mentioned in the *Mishnah*, see *Shebi'ith* VI. 2; *Shabbath* XIX. 1 passim. Comp. also *Sifra* קדושים IV. 12, ed. Weiss 89b (*TP Nedarim* IX. 4, 41c) and J. Bernays, *Gesammelte Abhandlungen* I, p. 275.

The disciples of R. 'Akiba[97] continued their teacher's work;
they added the comments of R. 'Akiba and his contemporaries
to the body of the new *Mishnah*. A large number of different
versions of the *Mishnah* was created by R. 'Akiba's disciples
around the middle of the second century. The various *Tannaim*
in the different colleges memorized divergent superpositions on
R. 'Akiba's *Mishnah*. The multiplication of such different versions of the latter would eventually result in multiplying and
deepening controversies in Israel. For this reason R. Judah the
Prince undertook a new edition of the *Mishnah* around the end
of the second or the beginning of the third century C. E. His
Mishnah was virtually canonized; the rest of the *Mishnayoth*
were declared "external," *Baraithoth*, which had only a second-
ary authority in comparison with the *Mishnah* of R. Judah the
Prince.

We do not know exactly what part Rabbi Judah the Prince
played in the systematization of the *Mishnah*.[98] It is a well
established tradition that he adopted the *Mishnah* of R. Meir
as the basis of his edition,[99] eliminated those parts of it which
were unacceptable to him and added the rulings of other rabbinic sages. In his youth R. Judah the Prince would attend
the school of R. Eleazar b. Shammu'a for the purpose of discovering the teachings[100] of that master.[101] Once R. Eleazar's
pupils refused to reveal to him certain specific details of a law
laid down by their teacher.[102] For this reason R. Judah the
Prince was compelled, in his edition of the *Mishnah*, to limit
the scope of that rule to one specific case only.[103] Subsequently
when he became Patriarch he was probably granted access to
the traditions of the different colleges and was thus able to

[97] R. Meir, R. Judah, R. Simeon, R. Nehemiah, R. Jose etc.

[98] See Frankel, דרכי המשנה 1923, p. 224 ff.; J. N. Epstein מבוא לנוסח המשנה,
p. 7 ff. Comp. *TP Kiddushin* III. 6, 64b.

[99] *TP Yebamoth* IV. 11, 6b; *TB 'Erubin* 96b and parallels.

[100] למצות מדוחיו, literally to "drain" his canons.

[101] See *TB Menaḥoth* 18a; *Tosefta Zebaḥim* II. 17, 483₅.

[102] *TP Yebamoth* VIII end, 9d.

[103] On the relation among the several rabbinic colleges see *TP Kiddushin*
II. 8, 63a; *TB* ibid. 52b and *Nazir* 49b. On the relation between the Cassiani
and Proculiani see Schulz, *History of Roman Legal Science*, p. 120 ff.

superpose and incorporate the comments and traditions of
R. 'Akiba's pupils into the old *Mishnah*, in other words, to edit
a new corpus of *Mishnayoth*. The new collection was committed
to memory by the *Tannaim* of the colleges, and the *Mishnah*
was published.

This oral publication possessed all the traits and features of
the written publications of that time.[104] The *Tannaim* were dis-
tinguished by all the qualities and characteristics of books in
circulation. The most valuable copies were, of course, those
which were revised by a learned grammarian or by the author
himself. Such texts were known as ἐξητασμένα[105] which is the
literal equivalent of the Hebrew בחונות,[106] tested, revised. R.
Judah the Prince, the editor of our *Mishnah*, testified that to
the *Tanna* of his school, R. Isaac the Great, the whole *Mishnah*
was בחנת,[107] i. e. ἐξητασμένα. R. Ze'ira censured his elders for
not having revised (דלא בחנון) the *Mishnah* in accordance with
the tradition of their contemporary, R. Isaac.

Many *Tannaim* were known as being דווקני,[108] i. e. they were
like the ἠκριβωμένα,[109] accurate copies. Their accuracy consisted in the fact that they sometimes noted (סיים) that the
particular *Mishnah* was based on the opinion of one particular
Rabbi only and consequently had no authority.[110] Such
Tannaim did not incorporate their short notes in the body of
the *Mishnah*, they only added it as a kind of oral marks.[111]
They are similar to the χαριέστερα copies[112] which contained
the critical marks,[113] but not many deliberate changes of the
text. Some *Tannaim* did sometimes deliberately incorporate the
comments of the masters in the body of the *Mishnah*,[114] but as

---

[104] See above p. 88 ff.
[105] See A. Ludwich, *Aristarchs homerische Textkritik* I, p. 19.
[106] בחן in Ps. 11:4, 5 is translated by the Septuagint ἐξετάζειν.
[107] *TP Ma'aser Sheni* V. 1, 55d: דבחנת ליה כל מתניתא. In Hebrew it would
be: שכל המשנה בחונה לו.
[108] *TB Yebamoth* 43a.   [109] See Ludwich ibid. p. 24 ff.
[110] זו אינה משנה, "This is not a [n authoritative] *Mishnah*."
[111] See Epstein, מבוא לנוסח המשנה, p. 680.
[112] See Ludwich ibid. (above n. 105), p. 46.
[113] See T. W. Allen, *Homer*, p. 307.
[114] See *TB Zebaḥim* 114b.

a rule the early *Tannaim* did not correct the reading of the *Mishnah*[115] on account of difficulties of the text. From the time of Resh Lakish,[116] however, the Rabbis began to alter the text of the *Mishnah* because of difficulties. Resh Lakish corrected the reading of the *Mishnah*,[117] because it seemed unreasonable (i. e. ἄλογος) to him that "a holy mouth should have said such a thing."[118]

The corrections and the emendations of the *Tannaim* and the masters of the rabbinic academies affected our text of the *Mishnah* to a certain degree,[119] but the great majority of alterations remained outside of the text. These emendations influenced our texts approximately as much as the corrections of Aristarchus affected the texts of Homer[120] and those of Galen our books of Hippocrates.[121]

We must not lose sight of the fact that the *Mishnah* is not only a literary work; it is also a law book. Some *Tannaim* changed the text of the *Mishnah* in order to have it correspond to authoritative law,[122] but this never attained such dimensions as the alterations in the Roman law books.[123] Some Babylonian Rabbis attempted to epitomize certain *Mishnayoth*,[124] but it is highly doubtful that such pure epitomes existed independently. We have probably cases of commenting epitomes, i. e. a kind of commentary in which the *Mishnayoth* are condensed for the purpose of elucidating them. This was widely practiced in connection with the works of the classical Roman jurists.[125] Paraphrases and epitomes of the *Mishnah* were particularly common in quotations from the *Mishnah* in the Talmud;[126] in such quota-

---

[115] See Epstein ibid., pp. 245, 350 ff.

[116] Flourished in the middle of the third century.

[117] *TB Sanhedrin* 23a.

[118] The reference is to R. Meir.

[119] See Epstein, מבוא לנוסח המשנה, pp. 168 ff., 180, 201 and 352.

[120] See T. W. Allen, *Homer*, pp. 304 ff., 309 ff.

[121] Ibid., p. 311 ff.

[122] See *TP Mo'ed Katan* III. 1, 81d; J. N. Epstein ibid., p. 680.

[123] See F. Schulz, *History of Roman Legal Science*, p. 142 ff.

[124] *TB Shabbath* 138a; *'Abodah Zarah* 42b.

[125] See Schulz ibid., p. 185 ff.

[126] See Epstein ibid., p. 782 ff.

tions *Mishnayoth* and *Baraithoth* were fused together[127] as if they are drawn from a single source. We find exactly the same phenomenon in Roman juristic works.[128]

We have included this chapter in our essay as illustrating some features in the formal aspects of literary transmission which were common to the Mediterranean civilized world.

[127] Ibid., p. 797 ff.

[128] Schulz ibid., pp. 185–186. When rabbinic literature was committed to writing, it was affected with the same fusion and confusion of the lemmata with the commenting text (See Lieberman, *Tosefeth Rishonim* I, pp. 61, 96 passim). Moreover, the *Mishnaic* lemma sometimes represents a different text from that which the commentator had before his eyes (See Epstein ibid., p. 923 ff.), a phenomenon which is paralleled in Greek texts (See T. W. Allen, *Homer*, p. 312). In our manuscripts of the Talmud, the *Mishnayoth* which are commented upon are sometimes written outside the text (ἔκθεσις) either in the margin or preceding the commentary (See Epstein ibid., p. 922). The original Talmudic manuscripts comprised a continuous commentary with small lemmata of the *Mishnah* (Epstein ibid., p. 927). Exactly the same practice was employed by the Greek and Roman commentators of literary and juristic texts. See Schulz ibid., p. 183 ff.; H. Lewy *apud* Zuntz in *Byzantion* XIV, 1939, p. 580 ff.

THE ALLEGED BAN ON GREEK WISDOM

It is universally accepted that the Rabbis imposed a ban on the study of Greek Wisdom. However, upon a closer examination of the sources this well rooted opinion seems to have no basis whatever.

We read in *TB*:[1] שאל בן דמה בן אחותו של ר' ישמעאל את ר' ישמעאל
כגון אני שלמדתי כל התורה כולה מהו ללמוד חכמת יונית קרא עליו המקרא
הזה . . . והגית בו יומם ולילה צא ובדוק שעה שאינה לא מן היום ולא מן הלילה
ולמוד בה חכמה יונית "Ben Dama the son of R. Ishmael's sister asked R. Ishmael: Is a man like myself who has mastered the whole Torah allowed to study Greek Wisdom? R. Ishmael applied the verse in Joshua (1:8) to him: . . .'*Thou shalt meditate therein* (i. e. in the Torah) *day and night,*' go and find a time when it is neither day nor night and study Greek wisdom."

Thus, it is clearly stated that the study of Greek Wisdom is not forbidden *per se* but only because it leads to the neglect of the study of the Torah.[2]

Tosafoth (a. l.) observe: "The question of Ben Damah is surprising: did he not know that there was a ban on the study of Greek Wisdom?"[3] However, no source is known to me which forbids the study of Greek Wisdom. A famous *Baraitha*[4] records that in the course of the war between Hyrcanus and Aristobulus it was decreed: cursed be the man who *teaches his son* Greek Wisdom. Later on the ban was extended to the teaching of the language as well. So we read in the *Mishnah*:[5] בפולמוס של

---

[1] *Menaḥoth* 99b.

[2] Comp. also *Sifre* Deut. 34, ed. Finkelstein 61 and my remarks in *Kiryath Sefer* XIV, p. 333.

[3] See *Tosafoth* ibid. 64b and the commentary of Rabbi Samson Sens on *Pe'ah* I. 1.

[4] *TB Sotah* 49b; *Baba Kamma* 82b and *Menaḥoth* 64b.

[5] *Sotah*, end.

קיטוס[6] גזרו . . . שלא ילמד אדם בנו יונית "During the war of Quietus[7] they decreed . . . that no man should *teach his son* Greek."[8] TP[9] inquiring into the reason for this injunction quotes the *Tosefta*[10] which states: R. Joshua[11] was asked whether one is allowed to *teach his son* Greek[12] and he replied: "Let him teach him Greek at a time when it is neither day nor night, for it is written *'Thou shalt meditate therein day and night'* " (Josh. 1:8). *TP* rejected it as a valid reason for the ban, since its only objection is that it leads to the neglect of the study of Torah. If a man, it argues, wants his son to take up Greek as a possible profession he should be allowed to teach him, just as he is permitted to teach his son any trade. The Talmud therefore concludes that the ban on Greek was aimed at the *delatores*, informers (מפני המסורות).[13]

In all the above-mentioned sources there is no hint of a ban on the *study* of Greek Wisdom or the Greek language;[14] the

[6] So codd. Cambridge and Parma.

[7] Governor of Judea in 117.

[8] See *Tosafoth Baba Kamma* 82b and שיטה מקובצת ibid. But from *TP* (see below) it is clear that at the time of Quietus the ban included the language as well as Greek Wisdom. *TB* follows a different tradition, according to which instruction in Greek language was never forbidden, see ibid. 83a and below n. 13.

[9] *Sotah* a. 1. and *Pe'ah* I. 1, 15c.   [10] *'Abodah Zarah* I. 20, 461 29.

[11] Flourished at the end of the first and the beginning of the second centuries.

[12] The reading in the *Tosefta* ibid. is ספר יוני, a Greek book. Some mediaeval authorities quoted from *TP* חכמת יונית, Greek Wisdom (See Ratner אהבת ציון וירושלים on *Pe'ah*, p. 6–7 and below, n. 23). It is an obvious interpolation from *Midrash Tehillim* (I. 17, ed. Buber, p. 16, which is a combination of *TB Menaḥoth* 99b and the *Tosefta*) and has no basis whatever in the manuscripts of *TP*.

[13] The study of Greek may induce young people to become *rhetores*, and wittingly or unwittingly betray the interests of the group and the private individuals. This danger, of course, was real in Palestine only (where Greek was spoken in government offices) but not in the Persian empire. Accordingly *TB* (*Baba Kamma* 83a) ruled that the teaching of only Greek Wisdom was forbidden, but not the language.

[14] The question in *TB* (*Baba Kamma* 82b) "why was Greek Wisdom forbidden", coming as it does after R. Judah the Prince's praise of Greek, means why was it prohibited to *teach children* Greek Wisdom.

injunction involves only the *teaching of children*. The fear that
the teaching of Greek may produce or give aid to future informers could be entertained only with regard to children whose
development was not yet certain, but not to mature people who
seek self-instruction.[15]

Again we read in the *Tosefta*:[16] התירו להם לבית רבן גמליאל
ללמד בניהן יונית מפני שהן קרובין למלכות[17] "Permission was granted
to the House of Rabban Gamaliel to teach the children[18] Greek
owing to its relation with the (Roman) government." Hence we
may summarize. None of the early rabbinic sources mentions
the direct prohibition of the study of either the Greek language
or Greek Wisdom. An old ban was in force on the teaching of
Greek Wisdom to children. In the time of Quietus (117 C. E.)
it was extended to the teaching of Greek in general. But even
this involved only instruction and only to children. Study was
not enjoined.

This conclusion altogether unnoticed by modern scholars was
already reached by at least one mediaeval authority. The
prominent Talmudist and scholar, Rabbi Israel of Toledo,[19]
writes in his commentary to *Aboth*:[20] אמרו ארור שילמד את בנו חכמת

---

[15] In the late *Midrash Pirka deRabbi*, ed. Grünhut, p. 58 (See Lieberman
שקיעין (1939), p. 17 and p. 98 on the time of its compilation) we read: אמר ר'
יוחנן... ולא ילמד אדם את בתו יונית ואסור לו שילמד יונית "R. Johanan said ... a
man should not teach his daughter Greek *and he himself is forbidden to study
Greek*". This is, of course, the individual opinion of the late compiler of the
Midrash who combined the statement of *TP* with R. Ishmael's statement in
TB Menaḥoth 99b. See Lieberman *GJP*, p. 24, n. 56.

[16] *Sotah* XV. 8. Comp. *TP Shabbath* VI. 1 and parallels.

[17] So ed. pr. and cod. Vienna and *TP* ibid.

[18] In *Tosefta* cod. Erfurt the word בניהן "their children" is missing, but it
does not alter the sense, for ללמד means to teach and not to study. *TB*
(*Sotah*, end, and *Baba Kamma* 83a. See Rabbinovicz, *variae lectiones* ibid.,
p. 187, n. 2) records: של בית רבן גמליאל התירו להן חכמת יוונית "Greek Wisdom was
permitted to the House of Rabban Gamaliel", which means that they were
allowed to *teach their children* Greek, as is obvious from the context ibid.,
from the codices of the *Tosefta* and from *TP*.

[19] Flourished in the thirteenth century. See S. Sachs' catalogue of Baron
Ginzburg's mss., col. 26 ff. (Only 48 columns were printed.)

[20] II. 14, as quoted by Rabbi Isaac b. Solomon; see Sachs ibid. col. 31.
Part of the quotation is also available in מדרש שמואל by Rabbi Samuel of

יונית ולא אמ' שילמוד חכמת יונית . . . ועוד אמרו שאלו את ר' יהושע מהו
שילמ(ו)ד אדם את בנו חכמת יונית אמ' להם ילמדנו בשעה שאינה לא מן היום
ולא מן הלילה, גם כאן לא הזכירו רק בנו "They said:[21] 'Cursed be
the man who teaches his son Greek Wisdom,' [they said 'who
teaches his son'] but did not say [cursed be the man] who
studies for himself . . . They further said:[22] R. Joshua was asked
whether a man is allowed to teach his son Greek Wisdom[23] etc.
Here again they mentioned the son only." R. Israel clearly dis-
criminates between the education of children and self-instruction
which he allows without qualifications, unlike some other
mediaeval authorities who permitted the pursuit of secular
studies only after a man has reached a certain age.[24] The Rabbi
further quoted the statement of R. Eliezer the Great:[25] מנעו
בניכם מן ההגיון "Prevent your children from [engaging in] the
science of logic"[26] (or dialectics and sophistry).[27] In this connection he again draws a difference between the education of
children and self-education.[28]

Uceda a. 1., Venice 1579. Fragments of his commentary in Arabic are available
in the Bodleiana, Oxford; see the catalogue of Neubauer-Cowley II, No.
2859.17.

[21] *TB Sotah* 49b and parallels.

[22] *TP Pe'ah* I. 1, 15c.

[23] See above, n. 12.

[24] Twenty five years; see, for instance, מנחת קנאות 70, p. 141 ff.

[25] *TB Berakhoth* 28b. Comp. II *Aboth deR. Nathan* XXXI, ed. Schechter,
p. 67. See Brüll's *Jahrbücher* etc. IX, p. 137. G. Allon's ingenious explanation
(*Tarbiz* XXI, p. 106 ff.) is not acceptable to me.

[26] See *Otzar Hageonim* a. 1. I. 2, p. 39 bot.

[27] See R. Joseph 'Aknin's explanation in the *Jubilee Volume in honor of
N. Socolov*, p. 382, bot. Comp. below n. 62.

[28] Comp. also 'Aknin ibid.; the preface to מלמד התלמידים; *Menorath Hamaor*
by Abohab, Light IV, 3.3.1 and יוחסין השלם 124b. The reading ומנעו עצמכם
quoted in the *Geonic responsa* ed. Harkavy 302, p. 144 is a scribal error; see
the editor's note 14 a. 1.

Cato the Elder whose hatred for Greek rhetoric is well known (Plin.,
nat. hist. VII. 30, 112; Plut. *Cato mai.* XXII) undertook in his old age the
study of Demosthenes (Plut. ibid. II). His instructions to his son in this
respect are therefore quite instructive. He warned him (Plin. ibid. XXIX. 7.
14): "It is a good plan to become acquainted with their literature, but
not to learn it thoroughly" (bonum sit illorum litteras inspicere, non

Evidently Rabbi Israel realized clearly that the rabbinic injunction against Greek Wisdom covered only the education of children. As regards self instruction the early Rabbis no more objected to the study of Greek Wisdom than they did to the learning of a trade.

The special permission which was granted to the House of the Patriarch to give the children a Greek education was not only theoretical. *TB*[29] records in the name of R. Simeon[30] son of Rabban Gamaliel: עיני עוללה לנפשי מכל בנות עירי. אלף ילדים היו בבית אבא חמש מאות למדו תורה וחמש מאות למדו חכמת יונית ולא נשתייר מהם אלא אני ובן אחי אבא בעסיא "[The verse] '*My eye [has been left like] a gleaning-grape*[31] *alone of all the daughters of my city*'[32] [could be applied to the] thousand young men in my father's house; five hundred of them studied Torah while the other five hundred studied Greek Wisdom and out of all of them only I have remained here and the son of my father's brother in Asia."[33]

We have no reason to disbelieve this statement. Nobody would have invented this kind of a tradition, for there is no possible ground for such an invention by the Babylonian Rabbis. A rabbinic statement which is not in harmony with the general

---

perdiscere). See H. I. Marrou, *Histoire de l'éducation dans l'antiquité*, p. 333 ff. Comp. below, n. 63.

[29] *Baba Kamma* 83a and parallel.

[30] Flourished in the middle of the second century.

[31] This is how the Rabbi interpreted the verse, as the following context shows. Comp. LXX: ἐπιφυλλιεῖ. The commentaries explain it differently.

[32] Lam. 3:51.

[33] A similar passage is available in *TB Gittin* 58a, *TP Ta'anith* IV. 8, 69a and *Ekha Rabba* III. 51, ed. Buber, p. 138. Greek Wisdom is not mentioned there. But these sources bear an obviously legendary stamp, as is evident from the exaggerated numbers mentioned there (sixty four million students according to the Babylonian source; more than a quarter of a million according to the Palestinian source). Moreover, the teaching of Greek Wisdom is not essential to the thread of the story there, and it may have been deliberately eliminated by the *Aggadist*. The passage quoted by us in the text is recorded in *TB* in a *Halakhic* context and has all the marks of reliability as we shall presently see. It is also noteworthy that the number of sixty four million drops to one thousand in our text!

attitude of the Rabbis[34] is, as a rule, quite trustworthy. We have here explicit testimony to the effect that the young men belonging to the House of the Patriarch who studied Greek Wisdom were numerically at least approximately equal to those who studied Torah, and whose number must have been considerable.

Although we do not know exactly what the Rabbis designated by the term חכמה יונית, Greek Wisdom,[35] it is obvious that in our case it comprised information which could help the individual in his association with the educated Hellenistic circles of Palestine.[36] The Rabbis had therefore a Jewish channel through which Hellenistic culture could be conveyed to them if they wanted to avail themselves of it.

The question now arises: What material does Talmudic literature contain which may indicate rabbinic acquaintance with Greek literary sources that do not have a direct bearing on the practical life?

The only Greek author whom the Rabbis mention by his name is Homer. The pertinent passages have been dealt with

[34] As, for example, their objection to teaching children Greek Wisdom. On the Greek education of the children of the later Patriarchs see M. Schwabe לתולדות טבריה, Jerusalem 1949, p. 36 and n. 91 ibid.

[35] See Maimonides' commentary on Mishnah Sotah, end; Me'iri ibid. and שיטה מקובצת on TB Baba Kamma 82b; Responsa of R. Isaac b. Shesheth, 45, and Rabbi Simeon Duran's commentary on Aboth II. 14 passim.

[36] In the beginning of the third century C. E. the law school of Berytus was already a famous center. In a speech pronounced around 240 C. E., Gregorious Thaumaturgus (PG X, 1065 b ff.) relates that he studied the Latin language and Roman law in order to be prepared to go from Cappadocia to Berytus. See Paul Collinet, Histoire de l'école de droit de Beyrouth, p. 26 ff. The young men belonging to the House of the Patriarch certainly did not study in the law school of Berytus (even if we accept the early foundation of the school, see Collinet ibid. p. 17 ff.). At that time the language of instruction of the school was Latin and not Greek and, furthermore, only Roman and not the provincial law was studied there (See Collinet ibid., p. 211 ff. and p. 209, n. 1). Hence the House of the Patriarch had no particular interest to attend the school of Berytus, and their knowledge of Greek would not qualify them for the studies in that school. On the children of the later patriarchs, see M. Schwabe ibid. (see above, n. 34).

by many Jewish and non-Jewish scholars,[37] but it is advisable
for our purpose to review all the material and explain it. We
read in the *Mishnah*:[38] אומרין צדוקין קובלין אנו עליכם פרושין שאתם
אומרים כתבי קדש מטמין את הידים ספרי ה מ י ר ס [39] אינן מטמאין את
הידים. אמ' רבן יוחנן בן זכיי וכי אין לנו על הפרושים אלא זו בלבד, והרי
הן אום' עצמות חמור טהורים ועצמות יוחנן כהן גדול טמאים . . . כתבי הקדש
לפי חיבתן היא טומאתן (שלא יעשה אדם)[40] ספרי ה מ י ר ס שאינן חביבין
אינן מטמאין את הידים.

J. Derenbourg[41] and especially N. Brüll[42] realized that the
language of our *Mishnah* is in the *polemical* style of the academies, and our passage should accordingly be translated: "The
Sadducees say: 'We complain against you, O ye Pharisees, for
according to you[43] the Holy Scriptures defile the hands [whereas]
the writings of המירס *would not*[44] defile the hands.' Rabban

[37] See Krauss LW II, p. 230, s. v. המירס. Add: M. Friedmann in *Haggoren*
III, 33, n. 1 and 35, n. 1; L. Ginzberg in *JBL* XLI, 1922, 127 ff.; A. M. Honey-
man *JQR* XXXVIII, 1947, 151 ff.; R. Gordis ibid. 1948, 359 ff. and others
whom we shall mention below.

[38] *Yadaim* IV. 6. I quote from edition Lowe IV. 14.

[39] המירס is also the reading of cod. Parma. *Tosefta* ibid. 684², cod. Vienna:
המורים. The anonymous Gaon (*Der Gaonäische Kommentar*, ed. J. N. Epstein,
p. 136): המירוס. Cod. Munich and early editions read: המירם which is almost
the same as המירס (For in some Hebrew mss. it is hard to discriminate between
ם and ס.). The word was corrupted (cod. Kauffmann and '*Arukh*) into מירון.
Some read here, as well as in parallel passages: מירום, מירוס, מרון, all of which
are, of course, corruptions or emendations of ה[ם]ירום, ה[ם]ירוס and ה[ם]ירון.
The ה', of המירום was taken by the scribes as the definitive article preceding
a proper noun, and following correct usage they dropped it. The reading
המינים can be dismissed without further discussion. See below.

[40] A dittography from the previous line, and it is missing in the other
editions and mss.

[41] *Essai* etc., p. 133.

[42] *Beth Talmud*, ed. Weiss, II, p. 319.

[43] Derenbourg ibid. translates: *selon vous* etc. We may add that this is
the usual polemical style of the academy. In *Tosefta Sotah* VI. 1, *Shebu'oth*
I. 7 אמרת means "You will admit" (אמרת, אומר in the sense of "it follows"
is very frequent in the *Halakhic Midrashim*).

[44] See Derenbourg and Brüll ibid. The correctness of this translation is
assured by the second clause of the *Mishnah*: הן אומרין . . . עצמות יוחנן כה'נ וכו.
The Rabbis certainly never explicitly stated that the bones of Johanan the
High Priest are unclean. Nobody doubted it.

Johanan b. Zakkai said: 'Have we naught against the Pharisees save this! According to them, the bones of an ass are clean and the bones of Johanan the High Priest are unclean'. . . . Even so the Holy Scriptures: as is our love for them so is their uncleanliness; the writings of המירס which are worthless[45] do not defile the hands'."

Let us first examine the second half of the discussion. The Rabbi ironically remarked that the bones of an ass are clean whereas the bones of Johanan the High Priest are unclean; of course he chose two extremes.[46] However, the retorts of the Rabbis are usually very pointed, and we deem it not impossible that the Rabbi had the flute in mind when he referred to the bones of the ass. Flutes made from such bones were quite common,[47] and they were preferred to those made of any other bones.[48] It is therefore plausible to assume that when the Rabbi argued that bones of an ass do not defile the hands he was thinking of the common handling of such bones converted into flutes. This contrast between the flute and the bones of Johanan

---

[45] Literally: "not dear". אינן חביבין is used in contrast to חביבין in the first part of the clause.

[46] See Brüll ibid., p. 319, n. 4. Comp. Geiger *Jüdische Zeitschrift* II, p. 21 ff.

[47] Plinius, *nat. hist.* XVI. 66 end; Philostratus, *Vita Apoll.* XXI.

[48] Plin. ibid. XI. 87: asinorum ad tibias canora. "[The bones] of asses are resonant enough to use as flutes". Plutarch (*sept. sap. conv.* 5, 150e) puts in the mouth of Aesop: τοὺς νῦν αὐλοποιοὺς ὡς προέμενοι τὰ νεβρεῖα, χρώμενοι τοῖς ὀνείοις, βέλτιον ἠχεῖν λέγουσιν. "The modern flute-makers have given up the use of bones from fawns, and use bones from asses, asserting that the latter have a better sound". The Jews used pipes made not only of reeds (κάλαμος, βόμβιξ) and metals (See *Tosefta 'Arakhin* II. 3 and parallels), but also of the bones of animals (*Mishnah Kinnim* III. 6, *Midrash* ק'ברוה זו היא שנאמרה, ed. Mann [*The Bible as Read* etc., p. 67] and *Midrash Haggadol Bereshith*, ed. Mordecai Margulies, p. 356).

It is noteworthy that R. Joshua quotes (*Kinnim* ibid.) a (popular?) saying: "While [the animal] lives it has but one voice, after it is dead it has seven voices, viz. its two horns become two trumpets, its two leg-bones become two flutes etc." It is similar to the remark of Plutarch who said (ibid.): So we may well be astonished that the ass, which otherwise is most gross and unmelodious, yet provides us with a bone which is most fine and melodious. (This translation as well as the previous one is from the Loeb Class. Library).

the High Priest, in the second clause of our *Mishnah*, will be a harmonious parallel to the first clause, if we grant that the latter sets the books of Homer ("The Prophet of All"),[49] the Greek Bible,[50] versus Scripture.[51]

That the ספרי המירס are books of heretics or books of Christian sects is completely ruled out by the following rabbinic sources. We read in *TP*:[52] ר' עקיבא אומר אף הקורא בספרים החיצונים כגון ספרי בן סירא וספרי בן לְעֲנָא[53] אבל ספרי ה מ י ר ס[54] וכל ספרים שנכתבו מכן והילך הקורא בהן כקורא באיגרת[55] מאי טעמא ויותר מהמה בני היזהר וגו' להגיון ניתנו ניתנו ליגיעה לא נתנו "*R. 'Akiba says: Also he who reads*[56]

---

[49] ὁ τοῦ Πάντος προφήτης, see above, p. 20, n. 2.

[50] A very interesting illustration of similarity of the attitude on the part of the Jews and Greeks towards the Scripture and the books of Homer respectively is available in the ancient sources. The Jewish rule is that the king must always wear the Scroll on his person (See Deut. 17:19). *TB (Sanhedrin* 21b and 22a) remarks to this effect: אותה שיוצאה ונכנסת עמו עושה אותה ברועו קמיע ותולה כמין "That [Scroll] which is to go in and out with him he shall make in the form of an amulet and fasten it to his arm". This is exactly what the Roman Emperor Julian reports about his treatment of Homer and Plato (Letter to his uncle Julian, ed. Bidez, No. 80): καὶ ταῦτα δὲ αὐτὰ τοῖς περιάπτοις ἔοικε καὶ φυλακτηρίοις· δέδεται γὰρ ἀεί. "And these (i. e. Homer and Plato) are like amulets and talismans, for they are always fastened [on me]." Comp. also Plut. *Alex.* VIII and the spurious letter ascribed to Julian (Sp. 383a, Bidez, No. 190).

[51] We want to make it clear that we do not use this argument to establish the identity of המירס; that will come later. We try only to explain the *Mishnah* in the light of our subsequent conclusions.

[52] *Sanhedrin* X. 1, 28a.

[53] That is the reading and vocalization of the *Yerushalmi Fragments from the Genizah* (ed. L. Ginzberg, p. 262, l. 18). I copy from the photostats of the manuscripts. The editions read לענה; Duran (in his commentary to *Aboth* II. 14, ed. prin. 33a) quotes יענה; *Koheleth Rabba* XII. 12 reads תגלא. We are not able to identify the man, nor can we accept the various emendations of modern scholars.

[54] This is the reading of our editions and Duran ibid. The *Fragments* read הַזְמִירָם (or הַזְמִירַס). The vocalization eliminates the ז.

[55] This is also the reading of the *Fragments*. Duran reads: באנדות, "In [books of] legends". Our reading is probably the correct one, see *TP Berakhoth* IV. 3, 8a.

[56] N. Krochmal in his מורה נבוכי הזמן, Lemberg 1851, p. 101, explains it to mean reading them aloud in the synagogue, and treating them like Scripture. This interpretation disagrees with *TB Sanhedrin* 100b and *Pesikta Rabbathi*

the extra-canonical[57] books[58] such as the books of Ben Sira and the books of Ben La'aga[59] [has no share in the world to come], but he who reads the books of Homer and all other books that were written beyond that[60] is considered like one who is reading a secular document,[61] for [it is written]: *'And furthermore, my son, beware of making many books, and much study[62] [of them] is a weariness of flesh'* (Eccl. 12:12). Hence casual reading[63] is permissible but intensive study is forbidden,"

III, ed. Friedmann, 9a. Rabbi David Frankel, in שי"ק a. l., explains that the prohibition of the reading of Ben Sira was based on the assumption that the reader may mistake this book for Scripture, owing to its arrangement and style.

[57] Krochmal ibid. compares the expression החיצונים to *Baraitha* (in relation to the *Mishnah*). Comp. also (Swete, *Introduction to the Old Testament in Greek*, 1914, p. 281) τὰ ἔξω.

[58] The words הקורא אף אומר עקיבא ר' are a quotation from the *Mishnah* (פיסקא). The rest is a later comment. Comp. *TB Sanhedrin* 100b.

[59] See above n. 53.

[60] I. e. beyond Scripture, comp. the references by Lieberman in *Tosefeth Rishonim* IV, p. 157. This meaning of מכאן והילך is common in *TP*, see *Kethuboth* II. 1, 26a, bot.; ibid. IV. 14, 29b passim.

[61] This is usually the meaning of איגרת in *TP*. See *Terumoth* X. 7, 47b; *Kethuboth* II. 3, 26b. Comp. also *Mishnah Gittin* VI. 5; *Mekhilta deRashbi*, ed. Hoffmann, p. 86; Mann, *The Bible as Read and Preached in the Old Synagogue*, Hebrew section, p. 56.

[62] The Septuagint translates ולהג הרבה καὶ μελέτη πολλή. It renders both להג and הגיון, as well as שיחה and שעשועים, μελέτη. μελετᾶν had a special connotation among the Jews. See Blondheim, *Les parlers Judeo-Romans* etc., pp. 76 ff. and 167. Hesychius defines μελετάω as = ἀσκέω, ἐπιμελέομαι, γυμνάζομαι, i. e. "exercise one self in". It is therefore very near to the Hebrew עסוק, "to engage in". להגות means both to pronounce, to recite, to engage in the study of the Torah as well as to derive, to deduce (see Jastrow, *Dictionary* etc. s. v. הגי). Both Sophocles (Lexicon, s. v. μελετάω) and Blondheim omitted the latter meaning of μελετᾶν which follows from a passage in Irenaeus (*Contra Haer.* I. 9. 4, *PG* VII, 544b): ἔπειτα πειρωμένοις ἐκ τῶν Ὁμήρου ποιημάτων μελετᾶν αὐτάς. "And then try to *derive* them from the poems of Homer". The expression תורה הגיון frequently occurs in the *Mishnah of* R. *Eliezer*, ed. Enelow. See ibid. pp. 255, 367.

The explanation of הגיון as dialectics, sophistry, *progymnasmata* and even logic (see above nn. 27, 26) is therefore plausible.

[63] See the preceding note. Comp. the instruction of Cato to his son, above, n. 28.

(for only *much study* is a weariness of flesh, but not casual reading).[64]

The permission of the Rabbis to read the books of המירס shows that those works could not be heretical or Christian, but innocuous writings.[65] We are therefore justified in accepting the *Geonic* interpretation that ספרי המירס are the books of Homer.

Again we read:[66] אמר ר' שמעון בן לקיש הרבה מקראות שראויין לישרוף כספרי מ י ר ו ס [67] והן הן גופי תורה העוים היושבים בחצרים עד עזה מאי נפקא לן מינה וכו' "R. Simeon b. Lakish said: There are many [single] verses which [one might think] may be[68] burnt like the books of מירוס, but [in reality] they are essentials of the Torah. [It is written, for instance]: '*And the Avvim that dwelt in villages as far as Gaza*' (Deut. 2:23); so what of it, etc.'' The comparison of these verses with the books of מירוס suggests that one might think that they are of the same character: descriptions of the past and stories. This again favors the explanation that המירוס is Homer.[69]

Likewise it is stated in *Midrash Tehillim*:[70] ולא יהו קורין בהם כקורין בספרי מ י ר ם [71] אלא יהו קורין בהן ונוטלין שכר עליהם כנגעים ואהלות "[David prayed] that men shall not read his words as they read the books of מירס, but shall read them [and engage in their study][72] so that they receive reward for doing it as they

---

[64] Comp. *TB Shabbath* 31b, *Koheleth Rabba* VII. 17. The reading of the *Genizah Fragments* ליניעה נתנו "they were given for intensive study" is undoubtedly a scribal error (See *JBL* XLI, 1922, p. 131, n. 40), for it is not only against the reading of the editions, the quotation by R. Simeon Duran (see above n. 53) and *Koheleth Rabba*, but also necessitates a very forced interpretation of the verse. The explanation of the latter by Rabbi Moses Almosnino in ידי משה on Eccl. a. l. (53a) is untenable. The *Targum* (Eccl. 12:12) is based on *Bemidbar Rabba* XIV. 4. It has nothing to do with our tradition in *TP* and *Koheleth Rabba* which explains the "many books" to refer to profane literature (but not to the Oral Law).

[65] As correctly observed by Rabbi Samuel Jaffe in his יפה מראה a. l.

[66] *TB Hullin* 60b.

[67] See Rabbinovicz, *variae lectiones* 80b, n. 4. Add: Rabbenu Nissim חבור יפה מהישועה (Amsterdam 1746, 35a, bot.: בספר מדוון) and *Midrash Haggadol Bereshith*, ed. Schechter, p. 695, ed. Margulies, p. 791.

[68] Literally: fit.

[69] See L. Ginzberg in *JBL* XLI, 1922, p. 128, n. 32.

[70] I, ed. Buber 5a. I quote from ed. pr.

[71] So ed. pr. Buber has in his text מירס, and in his note he quotes מירוס.

[72] See ed. Buber. See above n. 62.

would for studying *Nega'im* and *Ahiloth*."[73] The contrast between *Nega'im* and *Ahiloth* and the books of מירוס and the distinction between the hymns of David and the latter again suits the identification of מירוס with Homer. This identification was already made by the *Gaon* in his comment[74] to the *Mishnah* under discussion.[75] The majority of modern rabbinic scholars adopt his view.

A serious objection to this opinion was raised by M. Friedmann.[76] He contends that it is impossible that the Rabbis can have permitted the reading of Homer's books which are replete with the names of idols. It is, he maintains, a transgression of the law (Ex. 23:13): *"And make no mention of the name of other gods, neither let it be heard out of thy mouth."*

As a matter of record Friedmann's objection was already raised by an ancient author. Tertullian[77] protested against the Christians who taught pagan literature and he referred to the same Scriptural verse.[78] However, even Tertullian censured only its teaching, but explicitly permitted its study;[79] he asserted that while teaching heathen literature one involuntarily commends and affirms the praises of the idols. This distinction obviates Friedmann's objection as well, as we shall presently see. Indeed, the *Tannaitic* sources interpret the "mention of the names of idols" to mean not to swear by them, not to praise them[80] and not to designate the pagan temples and their vicinity as meeting places.[81]

---

[73] These laws were regarded as the most abstruse parts of the Torah. See *TP Mo'ed Katan* II. 5, 81b; *TB Baba Mezi'a* 59a. In *TB* (*Ḥagigah* 14a, *Sanhedrin* 38b, 67b) these parts are contrasted with אגדה, legends.

[74] *Der Gaonäische Kommentar*, ed. Epstein, p. 136.

[75] See above n. 38.

[76] *Haggoren* III, p. 33, n. 1.

[77] *De idolat.* X, *CSEL*, vol. XX, p. 40.

[78] Si fidelis litteras doceat . . . cum lex prohibeat, ut diximus, deos pronuntiari. "If a believer teach literature . . . whereas the Law, as we have said, prohibits the names of gods to be pronounced".

[79] Comp. also *Const. Apost.* I. 6.

[80] See *Mekhilta* a. l., ed. Horovitz, p. 332, ed. Lauterbach III, p. 181, l. 24; *Sifre* Deut. 61, ed. Finkelstein, p. 127.

[81] See *Mekhilta* ibid. *Tosefta 'Abodah Zarah* VI. 11, 470₁₅ and parallels. Comp. also H. A. Wolfson, *Philo* I, p. 174 seq.

Some Rabbis seem to go as far as prohibiting the mere mention of the names of idols. We read in the *Mekhilta*:[82] ושם אלהים
אחרים לא תזכירו . . . ולא תאמר לו היכן אתה שרוי במקום ע"ז פלונית
'אתה ממתין לי אצל עבודה זרה פלונית וכו' " '*And make no mention of
the name of other gods*' (Ex. 23:13). This means . . . do not say
to any one: Where do you live? In the place of such and such
an idol. [Nor say] wait for me at the place of such and such
an idol."[83] But the later Rabbis understood that this injunction
applies only to cases where the mention of the idol could be
avoided, when the given place could be designated by another
appellation; otherwise it was not prohibited to mention places
which bear the names of idols, for the *Mishnah* and the Talmud
incidentally do mention such places.[84]

The early Christians adopted the same attitude. Tertullian
maintains:[85] deos nationum nominari lex prohibet non utique
nomina eorum pronuntiemus, quae nobis ut dicamus conver-
satio extorquet. nam id plerumque dicendum est: in templo
Aesculapii illum habes, et in vico Isidis habito. "The Law
prohibits to name the gods of the nations, not, of course, that
we are not to pronounce their names, the mention of which is
required by conversation. For this must frequently be said:
You find him in the temple of Aesculapius and I live in the
Isis street."

Furthermore, there was no prohibition to mention the names
of idols in derision and mockery.[86] While they studied — and
possibly taught — Homer the Jews enjoyed the charm of his
style and plots, but certainly saw Homer's mythology as mere
fairy tales and as a good occasion of making fun of idol worship.
The Christians of the fourth century followed the Jewish tradition. It was not in vain that the emperor Julian issued his
famous decree forbidding Christians to teach classic literature.
He demanded: "Let them first really persuade their pupils that

[82] Ibid.
[83] See also *TB Sanhedrin* 63b where 'Ula is criticized for having said that
he had spent the night at *Kalnebo*. Comp. *Meiri* a. l. p. 239.
[84] See שו"ת חות יאיר, resp. 1, ed. princ. 5b–6a.
[85] *De idolatria* XX, *CSEL* ibid., p. 54.
[86] See *Tosefta Abodah Zarah* VI. 4, 46924 and parallels; *TB Sanhedrin* 63b.

neither Homer nor Hesiod nor any of these writers whom they expounded, and have declared to be guilty of impiety, folly and error in regard to the gods etc.''[87] The Christian school teacher made fun of Homer's treatment of the gods, as the church fathers did (see below). Thus the reading and teaching of Homer could be performed by both Jews and Christians without the formal violation of the verse in Ex. 23:13.

The books of Homer were not probably included in the category of חכמה יונית (Greek Wisdom), and they were employed as exercises for those children who in any case did not study Torah. It is likely that the Greek book — ספר יוני — whose use for the instruction of the young was a topic of discussion[88] was a Homeric epic, the text from which the children got their first education in Greek literature. Moreover, in all likelihood, there were in Palestine many Jews who did not live up to the high religious standards of the Rabbis, and they studied the Greek epics as well as "Greek Wisdom." Hence we can safely assume that the contents of Homer's books were well known in certain Jewish circles of Palestine.[89]

However it is very hard to prove that the Rabbis made direct use of the Odyssey or the Iliad. Homer was so popular that all the ancient Greek speaking world quoted from him; many of his phrases became mere commonplaces. His myths were known even to the half educated masses who never read Homer. It is, of course, natural that traces of Homeric myths and phrases can also be discovered in rabbinic literature. The Rabbis, for instance, mention the siren[90] by name; they know of the monster Centaurs[91] etc. It was not necessary to read Homer in order to be acquainted with the popular Greek myths.

As for Homeric phrases which occur in rabbinic literature we shall content ourselves with the following example. In the *Midrash*[92] the swiftness of Asahel is described as follows: שהיה

---

[87] Letter 36, 423b.   [88] See above, n. 12.

[89] See the Greek epigram published by M. Schwabe in the *Bulletin of the Palest. Explor. Soc.* VI, 1939, p. 107 ff.; ibid. 159 ff.

[90] As a human being dwelling in the water, see below, p. 183, n. 29.

[91] *Bereshith Rabba* XXIII. 6, ed. Theodor, p. 227.

[92] *Koheleth Rabba* IX. 11.

רץ על סאסי שיבלייא ואינן משתברין "He used to run on the ears of corn and they were not broken."[93] This phrase occurs in Homer verbatim. He says[94] about the half-divine horses of Erichtonius: ἄκρον ἐπ' ἀνθερίκων καρπὸν θέον οὐδὲ κατέκλων. "They would run over the topmost ears of ripened corn and did not break them."[95] Virgil,[96] for instance, says the same about Camilla: Illa vel intactae segetis per summa volaret gramina nec teneras cursu laesisset aristas etc. "She might either fly over the topmost blades of an unreaped cornfield and not have bruised in her course the tender ears etc."[97] The Rabbis may have heard this figure from some orator, or have read it in some Jewish apocryphon[98] composed by a Hellenistic Jew.[99]

Nevertheless, although rabbinic acquaintance with the Homeric epics cannot be proved, the ensemble of all the above mentioned sources gives the impression that some of the Rabbis who knew Greek most likely did read Homer. Now one may ask: Why did they not utilize the contents of the Odyssey and the Iliad for the purpose of ridiculing idol worship, as some of the ancient Greeks and church fathers did? In order better to resolve this difficulty it is in place to analyze rabbinic polemics against idolatry in general.

[93] See also *Yalkut Shime'oni* on Jer. sect. 285. An anonymous *Midrash* quoted by Rabbi David Hanagid (in his Arabic commentary on *Abboth* IV. 4) ascribes this quality to king Asa. *Sefer Hayashar* on ויגש credits the Patriarch Naphtali with the same skill.

[94] *Il.* XX. 227. Comp. Dio Chrysostomus, *or.* 33, 21, and the editor's note in the Loeb Classical Libr. Vol. III, p. 293, n. 7.

[95] See also Oppian, *Cynegetica* I, 231.

[96] *Aen.* VII, 808 ff.

[97] He borrowed the picture from Homer, as observed by Macrobius, *Saturn.* V. 8. 4.

[98] See above n. 93, end.

[99] The Rabbis were exceedingly fond of utilizing famous sayings for the illustration of the Bible. The well known utterance ascribed to Archimedes (Pappus Alexandrinus, *collect.* VIII. 11. 10) δός μοι ποῦ στῶ καὶ κινῶ τὴν γῆν (or: πᾶ βῶ καὶ κινῶ τὰν γᾶν. Simplicius *in Arist. Phys.* VII. 5, ed. Diels, p. 1110₅) found its way into rabbinic literature. The anonymous *Midrash* quoted in *Yalkut Shime'oni* and by Rabbi David Hanagid (see above, n. 93) contends that Abner used to say: אלולי היה לארץ מקום לאחוז בו הייתי מזעזעה "If the earth had a place where one could get hold of it I would shake it."

RABBINIC POLEMICS AGAINST IDOLATRY

The Rabbis had a fair knowledge of the rites and practices of idol worshippers and of the various regulations bearing on heathen divinities;[1] they were aware of their wide ramifications. In a text which abuses the idols a Rabbi of the second century remarked:[2] אלו נפרט שמה של עבודה זרה לא ספקו להם כל עיירות[3] שבעולם "If the name of every idol were to be specifically mentioned, all donkeys in the world would not suffice [to carry them]." In a similar context it was observed by Clement of Alexandria:[4] ἀλλὰ γὰρ ἐπιόντι μοι τοὺς προσκυνουμένους ὑμῖν τάφους, ἐμοὶ μὲν οὐδ' ὁ πᾶς ἂν ἀρκέσαι χρόνος. "If I were to go through [the names of] all the tombs worshipped by you, the whole of time would not suffice." Both the Jews and the Christians engaged in polemics against idol worship. The rabbinic sources frequently contain material which they call[5] ליצנותא דעבודה זרה, "Ridiculing of idols." The Iliad and the Odyssey provide the richest collection for this purpose. Many of the ancient Greek philosophers attacked these fables.[6] The Christian church fathers made ample use of them to demonstrate the absurdity of heathen beliefs.[7] Unlike the church

[1] See below. Comp. I. Lévy, *REJ* XLIII, 1901, p. 183 ff.; Lieberman, *JQR* XXXVII, 1946, p. 44 ff.

[2] *Sifre* II, 43, ed. Finkelstein, p. 97. Comp. also *Mekhilta Baḥodesh* VI, ed. Horovitz, p. 224; Lauterbach II, p. 240.

[3] This is the correct reading; see J. N. Epstein in לשוננו XV, 1947, p. 104. I now accept the interpretation of the latter. For the use of the phrase, see Lieberman, *JQR* XXXVI, 1946 p. 346, n. 122.

[4] *Protrept.* III, end. Comp. John XXI. 25.

[5] *TB Megillah* 25b and parallel.

[6] See Geffcken, *Zwei griechischen Apologeten*, Einleitung, p. XVIII ff.; Ch. Clerc, *Les théories relatives au cultes des images*, p. 89 ff.

[7] See Clement of Alexandria, *Protrept.* II, *PG* VIII, 100c ff. 108a ff.; ibid. VII, 185a; Athenagoras, *Apol.* XVIII; ibid. XXIX and many others; see below.

fathers the Rabbis never allude to the ridiculous tales about the gods contained in the writings of Homer.

However, a perusal of the ליצנותא דעבודה זרה (ridiculing of idols) found in early Talmudic sources will convince us that there is a great difference between the rabbinic and Christian attacks on idolatry. In rabbinic writings we possess only comparatively few scattered passages on this topic. The whole tractate of 'Abodah Zarah which deals with idol worship and worshippers almost ignores this subject. It only records and discusses laws and precepts, but does not engage in refutations of the principles of idol worship.[8] We may say that the kind of polemics against idol worship in which men like Clement of Alexandria, Athenagoras, Theophilus of Antioch, Tertullian, Arnobius, Lactantius and others indulge is almost not to be found in rabbinic literature.

The Rabbis occasionally dramatize the abuse of the idols available in the Prophets, relatively in the same spirit which is predominant in the Epistle of Jeremy. A typical example of it is contained in *Debarim Rabba*.[9] The rabbis portray a poor man ordering a wooden idol from the artisan. The latter tells him: "Not every tree is suitable for this. If you utilize a tree which grows in a field watered by rain[10] it is good; if you use another kind of tree you achieve nothing,[11] as it is written (Is. 44:14):

---

[8] The polemics in Rome between the Rabbis and the philosophers (*Mishnah 'Abodah Zarah* IV. 7; *Tosefta* ibid. VI. 7, 469₃₁ and parallels) as well as the disputation of the philosopher and Rabban Gamaliel (*TB* ibid. 54b and parallel, see Lieberman *GJP*, p. 126 ff.) lack the specific features of ליצנותא דעבודה זרה, the derision of idol worship, or the refutation of its principles.

[9] Ed. Lieberman, p. 56; *Midrash Hallel* in *Beth Hamidrash* ed. Jellinek V, p. 98 ff. The earlier parallels are referred to in Lieberman's note a. l.

[10] I. e. not by artificial irrigation.

[11] An interesting statement in regard to the material of wooden images is made by the Rabbis in *Mekhilta deRashbi* (ed. Hoffmann, p. 2). In explaining why the Almighty appeared to Moses on the bush and not on any other tree, they declare: מפני שהוא טהור ואין אומות העולם עושין אותו ע"ז "Because it (i. e. the bush) is clean, and the Gentiles do not make it an idol". The Hebrew is ambiguous and can also be translated: "and the gentiles do not worship it" (like any other tree). But the mediaeval authorities who drew on this source had a more explicit reading: ואין יכולת לחרוט בו פרצוף צלם, "And it is impossible to carve from it a face of an image" (*Ḥiskuni* a. l., ed. prin. 53c. Comp. also Kasher,

'He heweth him down cedars [and taketh the ilex and the oak, and strengtheneth for himself one among the trees of the forest; He planteth a bay-tree, and the rain doth nourish it].'[12] And if he makes a standing idol it cannot sit, and if he makes a sitting idol it cannot stand, as it is said (ibid. 46:7): '[And set in his place and he standeth, from his place he doeth not remove]. Yea, though one cry unto him, he cannot answer'."[13] The Midrash goes on further to depict the plight of a poor man who replaces his gold idol with one of silver, of copper, of wood until the final denouement. "The man had nothing to eat; he had to [bake] a fourth of a kab of flour which he had in his house. Outside it was raining and he could not go to the field on account of the rain. Meanwhile turning to the corner of the house he stumbled over the idol, and he said: 'What is this doing in the house?' He took the axe, cleft the idol, built a fire with one half of it and worshipped the other half, as it is said (Is. 44:16–17): 'He burneth the half thereof in the fire . . . And the residue thereof he maketh a god'."

Clement of Alexandria made fun of the idols in a similar way. He quoted the famous anecdote of Diagoras.[14] "Taking an image of Heracles made of wood (for he happened most likely to be cooking something at home) he said: 'Come, Heracles, now is your time to undertake for us this thirteenth labor, as you did the twelve for Eurystheus, and prepare the food for Diagoras!' Then he put it into the fire like a log of wood."

The rabbinic satire is only a literary elaboration of the Bible;[15]

Torah Shelemah VIII, p. 119, n. 40). This is undoubtedly the correct reading as appears from Theodoret. (PG LXXX, 229c): φασὶ δέ τινες, ἐν βάτῳ φανῆναι τὸν θεὸν, καὶ οὐκ ἐν ἄλλῳ φυτῷ διὰ τὸ μὴ δύνασθαί τινα ἐκ βάτου γλίψαι θεόν, which is literally the same as recorded by the above-mentioned Hebrew source. This passage was also used in mediaeval Judeo-Christian polemics; see Berliner פליטת סופרים, p. 29 and Z. Kahn in Festschrift . . . A. Berliner, Hebrew part, p. 82. On the kind of wood out of which men of old made images, see Frazer on Pausanias IV, p. 245 ff.

[12] Comp. Frazer ibid.   [13] Comp. also the Epistle of Jeremy 26.

[14] Protrept. II, PG VIII, 93a. Comp. schol. Aristoph. Nubes 830.

[15] See also Debarim Rabba ibid., p. 53 and the parallels referred to in the notes; ibid. p. 56, top, and comp. Geffcken ibid. (see above, n. 6), p. 23.

the sarcasm of the Christian church father is based on an anecdote about the notorious atheist drawn from the classics. In preparing their attacks against idolatry both parties had different listeners and readers in mind. The arguments were seasoned for the consumption of the audiences according to their background and taste. Instances from the classics convinced the Greeks; illustrations from the Bible appealed to the Jews. The Rabbis were mainly interested in elucidating the Bible. The latter combats the worship of idols, but ignores pagan mythology. The Jewish sages who commented on the narrative portions of the Bible had no suitable opportunity to take Homer's mythology to task. The Rabbis failed to utilize the latter in their scoffs at idolatry (independently of Scripture) not on account of ignorance, but because they probably knew that their gentile neighbors themselves treated them as mere fairy tales.[16] As for the church fathers, as correctly noted by many scholars,[17] they simply used pagan literary sources which ridiculed the old tales; it was only a literary genre which they adopted for the purpose of combatting idolatry.

Here we may go a step further and consider the character of the rabbinic attacks on idolatry in general. The Hellenistic Jews had concentrated their attacks on the gods of their new environment,[18] on the divinities of the Greeks and the Egyptians. The same practice was adopted by the Christian church fathers. The Rabbis, on the other hand, assail the idols mentioned in the Bible and idolatry in general, but they do not denounce the Greek gods specifically. They do not stigmatize the heathen mystery cults, although they certainly knew some-

[16] The *pantomimi Caesareae* in Palestine of the fourth century were the most famous in Syria (see Schürer, *Geschichte* etc. II⁴, p. 51 and p. 49, n. 90; comp. Lieberman *GJP*, p. 33, n. 24); certain performances of such *pantomimi* could not fail to impart to the spectators the impression that the pagans themselves did not take their myths too seriously. Comp. Lucian, *de saltatione*, 37–40.

[17] See the references above, n. 6, and J. Bidez, *Vie de Porphyre*, p. 143. Comp. Clerc, *Les théories relatives au culte des images*, p. 89 ff. See also Arnobius, *adversus nationes* III. 7, regarding the suppression of certain books of Cicero.

[18] See H. A. Wolfson, *Philo* I, p. 14 ff.

thing about them. The Greek word μυστήριον frequently occurs in rabbinic literature,[19] and it sometimes means mystery in its religious connotation.

The Rabbis seem to have known certain rites of the mysteries which are not explicitly mentioned in any other source. The Mishnah[20] rules that it is forbidden to derive any benefit from hides pierced at the heart, from the so called עורות לבובים[21], for the cut indicates that the animal was used for idol worship. R. Simeon b. Gamaliel explains[22] that they are forbidden only when the incision is circular. TP (a. l.) comments that the round shape of the hole shows that the incision was made when the animal was still alive, and the skin was able to corrugate. The Rabbis, it appears, had in mind rites of the mysteries of Demeter, Attis and Cybele. The information which we glean from them may shed light on a description by Clement of Alexandria. Among the mysteries of these divinities he numbers:[23] καὶ πόμα χολῆς, καὶ καρδιουλκίαι, καὶ ἀρρητουργίαι. "The drink of bile, the extraction of the hearts [of the victims] and unspeakable obscenities." It is evident from the context that the καρδιουλκία was as repulsive to him as the drinking of bile and the unspeakable obscenities; it points to an operation which was performed upon the animal while it was going through the death struggle, before it was skinned.[24]

---

[19] Although it often means merely "a secret" (see Krauss LW II, p. 346), the Rabbis also used it as a technical term. So, for instance, circumcision is the mystery of God (Tanḥuma I, Buber 40a and parallels, see notes ibid.). Similarly, the Mishnah, the oral law (in contradistinction to the Scriptures which were translated into Greek), was termed the mystery of the Lord. (Pesikta Rabbati V, ed. Friedmann 14b and parallels; comp. TP Pe'ah II. 6, 17a, where the term mystery is not mentioned). Comp. also Bereshith Rabba L. 9, p. 524, and see H. A. Wolfson, Philo I, p. 43 ff., p. 92, n. 33.

[20] Nedarim II. 1; 'Abodah Zarah II. 3.

[21] The literal translation can be rendered in German: entherzte Tierfelle.

[22] 'Abodah Zarah ibid.   [23] Protrept. I. 2, PG VIII, 76a.

[24] It appears from Lucian (de sacr. 13) that the καρδιουλκία was performed after the animal was cut to pieces. But Lucian is not talking about the rites of the mysteries. Moreover, it is possible that he did not intend to describe the acts of the priest in their consecutive order, but to recall several rites which stained the priest with blood. K. J. Popma, Luciani de sacrificiis, Amsterdam 1931, p. 35, overlooked the passage of Clement.

This extraction of the living heart from the sacrifice is not known to have been practiced in the regular rites of idolatry.[25] It was most probably connected with the oriental mystery-worship.

As a matter of fact documentary evidence is hardly necessary to prove that the Rabbis knew something about the heathen mysteries. It is inadmissible that religious rites which excited the curiosity of the multitudes, practices which were constantly talked about, praised and attacked, can have entirely escaped the notice of the Jews. Yet, not the slightest allusion is extant in rabbinic literature to the symbols and formulas of the heathen mysteries, to their phallic rites[26] and licentiousness.

The Rabbis of the third century mention the shameless practices of the heathen in illustration of Amos (6:1-7),[27] and the maiouma ($\mu\alpha\iota o\tilde{\upsilon}\mu\alpha s$) festivals served them as a good example of these verses.[28] The obscene rites of idolatry are cited by them when dealing with Num. 25:1-5[29] and other Biblical passages.[30] But the Rabbis never directly and explicitly assailed the heathen rites of mysteries. They simply had no reason to engage in such attacks. Unlike the earlier Hellenistic Jews the Rabbis were no longer struggling with gentile paganism. They mostly preached to Jews. To Judaism the mysteries represented no danger. A Jew had to become an idol worshipper before he could be initiated into the mysteries. In the first centuries C. E.

---

[25] In his *Sepher Haschoraschim* (ed. Bacher, p. 238, s. v. לבב) Rabbi Jonah Ibn Gânaḥ (born towards the end of the tenth century) remarks on our *Mishnah*: "And this was the custom of some nations, and particularly the Greeks, who used to pull out the heart of the beast while it was still alive; they split the breast of the animal, extract its heart and sacrifice it to the idol, according to what we have found written in the history of the Greeks and in their literature". The source (or sources) of the Rabbi is not known to me.

[26] See below, n. 30.

[27] See *TB Kiddushin* 71b; *Vayyikra Rabba* V. 3, passim.

[28] See the excellent article of A. Büchler in *REJ* XLII, 1901, p. 125 ff.

[29] See *Sifre* I, sect. 131, ed. Horovitz, 170 ff. and parallels.

[30] See *TB Sanhedrin* 63b passim. The Biblical בעל, *Ba'al*, according to the Rabbis, was a phallos of the [shape and] size of a *bean* (*TP Shabbath* IX. 1, 11d and parallel). Comp. Diogenes Laert. VII. 34; Lucian., *vit. auct.* 6; A. B. Cook, *Zeus* III, p. 1032o.

the Jews were so far removed from clear-cut idolatry that there was not the slightest need to argue and to preach against it.

The bulk of rabbinic sources which have come down to us is of the third and fourth centuries, and by that time the Rabbis had already abandoned the effort to win proselytes.[31] Those few Jews who worshipped idols in order to identify themselves with the gentiles did it for lucrative reasons, and there was, of course, little hope of reclaiming this type of apostate with moral tracts. The problem of idolatry and its *raison d'être* no longer had any practical significance for the Rabbis. They were concerned with the heathen rites only in so far as they affected the social and commercial contact of the Jew with the gentile, and they occasionally utilized contemporary idol worship to illustrate Biblical passages. Although they repeatedly emphasized that idolatry is one of the gravest abominations (like murder and incest), they did it in order to deter Jews from falling victims to it under duress or for lucrative reasons. Their derision of the idols consisted in distorting the appellations of the divinities,[32] in stressing that the heathen gods are lifeless matter,[33] and in dramatizing the pertinent passages of the Scriptures.[34] Their mockery lacks the pathos of the Jewish Hellenistic and Christian literature. It is sometimes no more malicious than the famous satire of Horace.[35]

Furthermore, there is a basic difference between the apologetics of the Hellenistic Jews[36] and the Christians on the one

[31] See *TP Kiddushin* IV. 1, 65b; *TB Yebamoth* 47b.

[32] *Tosefta 'Abodah Zarah* VI. 4, 469₂₄ and parallels.

[33] It appears from the earlier non-rabbinic Jewish sources that the Jews believed demonic spirits to lurk behind the dead images. See W. A. L. Elmslie, *The Mishna On Idolatry*, pp. 42–43. On this belief of the gentiles comp. E. Bevan, *Holy Images*, London 1940, p. 90 ff. See also *Corp. Herm. Asclep.* 24 and 37, ed. Nock-Festugière, pp. 326, 347 and nn. ibid.; A. D. Nock, *Harvard Theological Review* XXVII, 1934, p. 92. Even the Jews of the second century were of the belief that daimons governed the idols. See *Sifre* I, sect. 131, ed. Horovitz, p. 171₁₂ ff. and parallels. On the later Jewish belief in the efficacy of incubation in pagan temples, see Lieberman, *Debarim Rabba*, p. 75, n. 1.

[34] See above, n. 9.

[35] *Sat.* I. 8. 1 ff.

[36] See H. A. Wolfson, *Philo* I, p. 14 ff.

hand and the preaching of the Rabbis on the other. These Jews had argued along the lines of a certain literary genre, drawing from Greek literary sources,[37] interpreting and presenting them in a good literary form. The Christian church fathers had before them a well established pattern. Christians such as Athenagoras, Theophilus of Antioch, Clement of Alexandria, Arnobius and others were pagans converted to Christianity; they wanted to convince others as well as themselves; their fierce attacks on heathenism are very understandable. They utilized Greek and Jewish criticism of idolatry and entered the fray[38] in the accepted literary way. The Rabbis, on the other hand, drew most of their material from personal contact and oral information. They often applied their knowledge towards the elucidation of the Bible, and they were not interested in utilizing it for an impassioned derision of idolatry which presented no practical problem to them.

We shall finish with a very instructive illustration. Herodotus relates an amusing tale about king Amasis:[39] "At first, the Egyptians contemned Amasis and held him in but little esteem, as being a former commoner and of a house that was not illustrious. But afterwards Amasis won them over, by cleverness, not by arrogance. He had among his countless

---

[37] See Geffcken, *Zwei griechischen Apologeten*, Einleitung, pp. XVIII, XXIII.

[38] See Geffcken ibid., p. XXII and E. Bevan, *Holy Images*, London, 1940, p. 64 ff.

[39] II. 172: τὰ μὲν δὴ πρῶτα κατώνοντο τὸν Ἄμασιν Αἰγύπτιοι καὶ ἐν οὐδεμιῇ μοίρῃ μεγάλῃ ἦγον ἅτε δὴ δημότην τὸ πρὶν ἐόντα καὶ οἰκίης οὐκ ἐπιφανέος· μετὰ δὲ σοφίῃ αὐτοὺς ὁ Ἄμασις οὐκ ἀγνωμοσύνῃ προσηγάγετο· ἦν οἱ ἄλλα τε ἀγαθὰ μυρία ἐν δὲ καὶ ποδανιπτὴρ χρύσεος, ἐν τῷ αὐτός τε ὁ Ἄμασις καὶ οἱ δαιτυμόνες οἱ πάντες τοὺς πόδας ἑκάστοτε ἐναπενίζοντο· τοῦτον κατ' ὧν κόψας ἄγαλμα δαίμονος ἐξ αὐτοῦ ἐποιήσατο, καὶ ἵδρυσε τῆς πόλιος ὅκου ἦν ἐπιτηδεότατον· οἱ δὲ Αἰγύπτιοι φοιτέοντες πρὸς τὤγαλμα ἐσέβοντο μεγάλως. μαθὼν δὲ ὁ Ἄμασις τὸ ἐκ τῶν ἀστῶν ποιεύμενον, συγκαλέσας Αἰγυπτίους ἐξέφηνε φὰς ἐκ τοῦ ποδανιπτῆρος τὤγαλμα γεγονέναι, ἐς τὸν πρότερον μὲν τοὺς Αἰγυπτίους ἐνεμέειν τε καὶ ἐνουρέειν καὶ πόδας ἐναπονίζεσθαι, τότε δὲ μεγάλως σέβεσθαι. ἤδη ὧν ἔφη λέγων ὁμοίως αὐτὸς τῷ ποδανιπτῆρι πεπηγέναι· εἰ γὰρ πρότερον εἶναι δημότης, ἀλλ' ἐν τῷ παρεόντι εἶναι αὐτῶν βασιλεύς· καὶ τιμᾶν τε καὶ προμηθέεσθαι ἑωυτοῦ ἐκέλευε.

possessions a golden footbath, in which both Amasis himself and all his banquet guests always had their feet washed. This he broke in pieces and made thereof a god's image, which he set in the most suitable part of the city. And the Egyptians resorted to the image and reverenced it greatly. When Amasis learned what was being done by the townsmen, he called the Egyptians together and disclosed that the image had been made out of the footbath, into which, before that, the Egyptians had been wont to vomit, to pass water and to have their feet washed, but which now they greatly revered. Now, then, he said, he himself had fared even as the footbath. For if before he was a commoner, now he was their king. And he ordered them to honor and show regard for him."

The Christians were fond of alluding to this story[40] as an example of gods made of base material. We can prove that the Rabbis also availed themselves of that tale, but in an amazingly different way.

We find the first allusion to it in *Bereshith Rabba*,[41] in connection with the account of the Almighty's consultation with the angels regarding the creation of Adam. A Rabbi of the third century objected:[42] "There is no [question of] taking counsel here. But it may be likened to a king who was strolling at the door of the palace and saw a nugget ($\beta\omega\lambda\acute{\alpha}\rho\iota\sigma\nu$) lying about. Said he: 'What shall we do with it'? Some said: 'Public baths' ($\delta\eta\mu\acute{\sigma}\sigma\iota\alpha$) and some said: 'Private baths' ($\pi\rho\iota\beta\tilde{\alpha}\tau\alpha$). 'I will make a statue of it', said the king, 'Who can interfere'?" Whoever is familiar with the keen parables of the rabbis will agree that this one is pointless. It makes sense only if we assume that the Rabbi alluded here to the well known story.

The advisers of the king suggested that a public or a private bath-tub be prepared from the nugget, but the king decided to

---

[40] The material was collected by Klette in his note on the *Acta Apollonii* 17 and by Geffcken ibid. XXI, n. 1. See M. J. Milne, *American Journal of Archaeology* XLVIII, 1944, p. 32, n. 44.

[41] VIII. 8, p. 62.

[42] לית הכא מלכו. אלא למלך שהיה מטייל פתח פלטין וראה בולרין אחת מושלכת אמר מה נעשה בה. מהן אומרים דימוסיות ומהן אומרים פרבטיות. אמר המלך אדריינטיס אני עושה אותה מי מעכב.

make a statue of it. The parable will be better understood if we take into consideration that according to a certain Jewish tradition Adam was lying around as a lump, as a shapeless mass, for six days.[43] The angels objected to the creation of a man from the lump,[44] but the Lord did not listen to them. The Rabbis applied the tale of Herodotus to the creation of man who was shaped in the image of the king from a lump of earth.

The second instance is much more instructive. We read in the *Midrash*:[45]

משל לעץ נאה שהיה נתון בתוך המרחץ נכנס פרופסיטוס[46]
לרחוץ הוא וכל עבדיו ודשו את העץ וכל הפגאנין וכן כל אחד ואחד מהן
(מתאוים לכרוע לפניו)[47]. לאחר ימים שלח פרוטומו שלו לאותה מדינה שיעשו[48]
לו איקונין ולא מצאו[49] עץ חוץ מאותו שהיה במרחץ. אמרו האומנין לשלטון אם
מבקש אתה להעמיד האיקונין הבא את העץ שיש במרחץ שאין לך טוב ממנו
הביאוהו ותקנו אותו כראוי והביא[50] צייר וצייר את האיקונין עליו והעמידה
בתוך הפלטין. בא השלטון וכרע לפניה וכן דוכוס ואפרכוס וכן הפרופוסיטון[51]
וכן הלגיונות וכן דימוס וכן כלם.[52] אמרו להן אותן האומנין אתמול הייתם
מדיישין את העץ הזה במרחץ ועכשיו אתם משתחוים לפניו. אמרו להם אין אנו
כורעים לפניו בשבילו אלא בשביל פרוטומו של מלך שהיא חקוקה עליו. כך
אומ' המלכים[53] עד עכשיו היינו עושים בישראל מה שאי אפשר, שנ' לבזה נפש
למתעב גוי ועכשיו לישראל אנו משתחוים. אמר להם הקב"ה הן בשביל שמי

---

[43] A passage to this effect from a manuscript of Yalkut תלמוד תורה (citing *Midrash Ruth* VII as its source) was published in הצופה מארץ הגר IV, p. 35. The learned author observed that this *Midrash* is not found in our *Midrash Ruth* nor in any other *Midrash*. However, the whole passage has been available for some four hundred years in the אות אמת to *Midrash Ruth* VII. 2 on the authority of נ'א, (אחת נוסחא=) א'נ, "An exact text".

[44] See L. Ginzberg, *Legends of the Jews* V, p. 79.

[45] *Shemoth Rabba* XV. 17. I copy from ed. prin. and cod. Oxford, Hebr. 147, f. 192b.

[46] So cod. Oxf. Ed. prin.: פרוספיטוס. *Yalkut Hamakhiri* on Is., p. 176: פרוכסיטוס, which is probably a misprint for פרופסיטוס, πραιπόσιτος, praepositus.

[47] The words in parentheses are an obvious dittography from the previous lines in the *Midrash*; they were correctly deleted by אות אמת. The reading of the modern editions follows a correction of מתנות כהונה, which has no basis.

[48] So cod. Oxf. and *Makhiri*.

[49] So *Makhiri*.

[50] So cod. Oxf. and *Makhiri*. Ed. pr. ביד.

[51] So cod. Oxf.

[52] So cod. Oxf. and modern editions. Ed. pr. and *Makhiri*: בולי, βουλή.

[53] So ed. pr., cod. Oxf. and *Makhiri*.

שכתוב עליהם שנ' למען ה' אשר נאמן "It may be likened to a choice [piece of] wood which lay in the bathhouse. When the prefect (πραιπόσιτος, praepositus) and his attendants came in to bathe they trod on it and similarly all the commoners (παγανοί) and everyone else. By and by [the king] sent his bust (προτομή) for the purpose of having an image (εἰκόνιον) of himself made. The only suitable [piece of] wood they found was the one in the bathhouse. Accordingly, the artisans said to the governor: 'If you want to set up the image (εἰκόνιον), bring hither the [piece of] wood that is in the bathhouse, for there is none better than it.' It was fetched and properly prepared for the purpose. And he (i. e. the governor) brought an artist (literally: a painter) who designed the image on it and set it up in the palace. The governor came and knelt before it; and the dux, the *eparchos*,[54] the prefect (praepositus), the legionaries, the people (δῆμος) and everybody else did likewise.[55] Then did those artisans say unto them: 'Yesterday you were trampling this [piece of] wood in the bathhouse, and now you prostrate yourselves before it'! But they replied: 'It is not for its own sake that we kneel before it, but for the sake of the king's bust (προτομή) which is engraved upon it'. So the kings will say: until now we have been treating Israel in an unspeakable manner, as it is written (Is. 49:7): '*To him that is despised of soul, detested of nations*', and shall we now prostrate ourselves before Israel? But the Holy One blessed is He will answer them: Yes, for the sake of My name which is inscribed upon them,[56]

[54] The last word appears here by attraction as part of the standard combination דוכסין ואפרכין, a *lapsus* designated *ashgarah*, which is very frequent in rabbinic literature. See S. H. Margulies, *L'Ashgara nella letteratura talmudica*, in *Rivista Israelitica* I, 1904, p. 3 ff.

[55] See Alföldi, *Mitteilungen d. deutschen archaeol. Inst.*, Roemische Abteil., 49, 1934, p. 70 ff.

[56] Comp. Jos. *Ant*. XI. 8. 5 (333): οὐ τοῦτον, εἶπεν, προσεκύνησα, τὸν δὲ θεόν, οὗ τὴν ἀρχιερωσύνην οὗτος τετίμηται. " 'I did not prostrate myself before him', he said (i. e. Alexander the Great), 'but before God by Whom he was honored with the high-priesthood'." According to Josephus Alexander added that he saw the high-priest in a dream urging him to conquer Asia. Rabbinic literature (*Megillath Ta'anith*, ed. Lichtenstein, p. 340; *Vayyikra Rabba* 13, end; *TB Yoma* 69a, *Pesikta deR. Kahana*, 41a. Comp. also *TP Berakhoth* VI. 1, 9a) stressed only the detail about the dream, but

as it is written (Isa. ibid.): *'For the sake of the Lord Who is faithful, [of the Holy One of Israel who has chosen thee]'.*"[57]

The rabbis here state clearly that it is not to the piece of wood from the bathhouse that the Romans were kneeling, but to the symbol behind it, to the emperor. The gentile kings, required to prostrate themselves before Israel, will be persuaded by the argument that they are really asked to kneel before the Lord whose name is inscribed on Israel. The Rabbis employed the tale of Herodotus not, like Philo and the church fathers,[58] for an attack on idolatry but for the purpose of elucidating the Bible. Their understanding of the tale is worthy of the Greeks of the time. The statues are only symbols! We would expect the argument from some one like Maximus Tyrius or Dio Chrysostomus, but not from the Rabbis.

However, the truth is that to the Rabbis symbols[59] are the same idols as mere fetishes. Although the Rabbis were not so naive as to think their heathen contemporaries to be mere fetishists,[60] this distinction did not in their eyes lessen the idolatrous character of their worship.

To summarize. Some of the Jews probably read Homer in their childhood. We have no definite traces of his mythology in rabbinic literature, because the Rabbis had no occasion to mention it. If the Bible had contained material about the mythology of the heathen gods we might have expected to find in rabbinic sources some material drawn from Homer's books.

Josephus emphasized (ibid. 331) that the high-priest was dressed in the golden plate on which God's name was inscribed ($\tilde{\wp}$ τὸ θεοῦ ἐγγέγραπτο ὄνομα). It goes without saying that the existence of this Alexander legend does not affect our conclusions about the general character of our rabbinic parable.

[57] The text is anonymous. From the abundance of the Greek words and from its general style it seems to be a Hebrew translation from an Aramaic *Yelamdenu Midrash*, i. e. a source of the third or fourth century.

[58] See above n. 40.

[59] As they were understood at that time, see A. Harnack, *Lehrbuch der Dogmengeschichte* I⁴, p. 228. The Jews did not deny the heathen belief that demons are lurking behind the idols, see above, n. 33. Comp. also Maimonides הלכות ע"ז III. 6.

[60] Even the ancient Philistines, according to the Rabbis, worshipped not the statue of *Dagon*, but the Genius who dwelt in (or behind) it. See *TB* '*Abodah Zarah* 41b. Comp. also Maimonides, *Guide* III, ch. 46.

But since the Bible contains no such references, the Rabbis found no occasion to utilize Homer. They composed no theoretical treatises on idolatry for gentile consumption; hence no evidence is available that the Rabbis were acquainted with the literary works of the Greeks which either condemned idolatry or commended it. The Jewish teachers were primarily concerned with the practical rites of idolatry in so far as they might affect the behavior of the Jews, and they composed a whole tractate (*'Abodah Zarah*) on this subject. The material contained therein is taken not from literature but from personal contact[61] and oral information, and is consequently of precious value for the understanding of the religious rites and practices of the heathens. We shall therefore devote the following chapters to this subject.

[61] See *Mishnah 'Abodah Zarah* and the sources referred to above n. 8. See also Bacher, *Die Agada d. Tannaiten* I, p. 83 ff.

HEATHEN IDOLATROUS RITES IN
RABBINIC LITERATURE

We have maintained in the previous chapter that the Rabbis did not deem it necessary to engage in theoretical discussions against "Alien Worship." The Jews of that time had no need of such arguments. Instead, the Rabbis enacted a series of laws for their co-religionists restricting their association and negotiations with the heathen during the latter's religious festivals. They prohibited all action by the Jews which may result in conferring any benefit on idols (or a heathen temple) or in deriving any profit from them. In these laws pagan rites and practices are naturally mentioned very frequently. A long tractate devoted to such legislation forms part of the Talmud. It is the well known treatise *'Abodah Zarah*, "Alien Worship," which consists of *Mishnah, Tosefta*, Palestinian and Babylonian Talmuds.[1] In addition, the Rabbis left us a long catalogue of the so called "Amorite Practices," i. e. popular heathen superstitions.[2] Many isolated items on idolatry and idol worshippers are scattered all over rabbinic literature. It would require a large volume to treat this topic and it would have to include a full translation of the greater part of *'Abodah Zarah.*

In the following chapters we shall confine ourselves to a comparative study of pagan pre-sacrificial rites and the parallel Jewish practices[3] which are not explicitly mentioned in the Bible. This subject too cannot be handled exhaustively without the translation of a great part of *Seder Kodashim*. However, a few remarks may be sufficient to demonstrate how much his-

---

[1] On the translation of these sources into Latin and modern languages, see H. L. Strack, *Introduction to the Talmud and Midrash*, Philadelphia 1931, p. 142 ff.; ibid. pp. 157–158. Add: *Mishnah and Tosefta* translated into Russian by H. Perefferkovitz, St. Petersbourg, 1902–1906.

[2] *Tosefta Shabbath* chps. VI–VII, 173 ff.

[3] We omit here the bloodless sacrifices.

torians of religion can learn from the rabbinic knowledge of sacrifices and how greatly Talmudists can benefit from a study of the *leges sacrae* of the pagans.

We may safely assume that the overwhelming majority of defects and blemishes which disqualify an animal from sacrifice according to the *leges sacrae* of the heathen also obtained among the Jews. On the basis of the verse (Mal. 1:8): *"And when ye offer the lame and sick, it is no evil! Present it now unto thy governor"* (הקריבהו נא לפחתך) the Rabbis would disqualify any animal which the gentiles consider unworthy of being offered to their divinity.[4] They would consequently apply many of the limitations set by the gentiles on animals to be offered in addition to their own restrictions.[5]

With these introductory remarks we shall now dwell on certain phases of Jewish sacrificial procedure and compare it with the general practice of the time, as described by Jewish and non-Jewish sources. The Jewish oral tradition relating to sacrifices is undoubtedly very old, but we have explicit testimony in our sources that some unessential changes were subsequently introduced in the ceremonial. Such modifications, according to the Rabbis stemmed from a desire to differ from the heathen. Nevertheless well rooted and firmly established ancient rites could not be relinquished merely because "the ways of the heathen should not be followed," for in such cases the Jews could maintain that the heathen were following Jewish practices and not vice versa.[6] Moreover it is safe to assume that the tendency to avoid pagan customs was not always strictly followed in practice. In matters of external decorum the Jews

---

[4] See *TB Sukkah* 51a and parallels. On the basis of the same verse it was forbidden to make the sacred vessels of the Jerusalem Temple of base material; see *TB Sotah* 14b. The same verse is offered by some of the mediaeval rabbinic authorities as the reason for the disqualification of some sacrifices, although in the Talmud it was based on an allusion in the Pentateuch. See Maimonides, הלכות איסורי מזבח II. 10, and *Tosafoth Zebaḥim* 35b, s. v. אלא.

[5] See *TB Gittin* 56a; comp. also *Mishnah 'Abodah Zarah* I. 5 and *Sifra Nedabah* VI. 3, ed. Weiss 8b (and parallels). According to *TP 'Abodah Zarah* (I. 5. 39d) the heathen [sometimes] offered maimed animals to their divinities. Comp. P. Stengel, *Die griechischen Kultusaltertümer*[3], p. 121, nn. 10–12.

[6] See *TB 'Abodah Zarah* 11a and commentaries ibid.

might imitate the gentiles without any feeling that they are breaking the law; after all it was commendable "to adorn a religious act" (הדור מצוה). Similarly, as is generally known, the Temple of Herod, although built in close conformity with the ancient plan of the Sanctuary, was marked by some details which are not known from the description in the Bible. In matters of external beauty various adornments were gradually introduced in the Temple, and the sacred vessels were continually improved.[7] There was a general pattern in the ancient world of temples and sacrifices with which the Jews shared.

Since we shall have to discuss the heathen rites and practices which are cited in rabbinic literature, we must say a few words about the several foreign cults reflected in it. We find there a record of most of the well known objects of pagan worships: Astral bodies,[8] mountains and hills,[9] seas, rivers and wildernesses,[10] marshes,[11] sources of rivers,[12] bricks,[13] the dust of the feet,[14] heaps of grain,[15] standing corn,[16] houses,[17] fire,[18] water,[19]

---

[7] See *Mishnah Yoma* III. 9–10.

[8] *Mishnah 'Abodah Zarah* IV. 7; *Tosefta Hullin* II. 18, passim. The Rabbis were more lenient towards the worshippers of these bodies than to those who adored other objects (*Sifre* II, 318, ed. Finkelstein, p. 364). This is also the view of the author of the Wisdom of Solomon XIII. 6. See also Deut. 4:19 and Field *Hexapla* ibid. n. 29. Comp. Just. Mart. *Dial.* LV; Clement of Alexandria, *Strom.* VI. 14; Julian the emperor, Letter 20 (63) end, 454b. See also *Mekhilta Bahodesh* XIV, ed. Horovitz 512; Lauterbach I, p. 112; *TB 'Abodah Zarah* 55a.

[9] The worship of the latter seems to have been very common in the time of the Rabbis. See *Mishnah 'Abodah Zarah* III. 5; *Tosefta* ibid. VI. 8, 470₅; *TB Hullin* 40a; *Sanhedrin* 61a; *'Abodah Zarah* 46a passim. Lactantius, *de mort. pers.* XI (*CSEL* XXVII. 1, p. 185), reports that the mother of Galerius was: *deorum montium cultrix*, "A worshipper of the gods of the mountains". The reading *gentium* instead of *montium* (see variants ibid.) is to be dismissed. *TB Hullin* ibid. mentions the Genius (נדא τύχη) of the mountains.

[10] *Mishnah Hullin* II. 8.

[11] λειμῶνες? *TP 'Abodah Zarah* III. 6, 43a.

[12] See *JQR* XXXVI, 1946, p. 321.

[13] *TB 'Abodah Zarah* 46a; *Sanhedrin* 107b (in the uncensored editions).

[14] *TB Baba Mezi'a* 86b.   [15] *TP Pesahim* II. 3, 29a.

[16] *TB 'Ab. Zar.* 46b.   [17] *Mishnah* ibid. III. 7.

[18] *Bereshith Rabba* XI. 13, p. 363; *TB Ta'anith* 5b, *Nedarim* 62b passim.

[19] *BR* and *Ta'anith* ibid.

vapors,[20] winds and clouds,[21] trees,[22] eggs,[23] doves,[24] small worms,[25] all kinds of animals,[26] reflections,[27] angels,[28] altars[29] and all kinds of statues and images.[30]

According to the Rabbis the heathen of their time did homage to Pe'or by uncovering themselves, by purging themselves and by similar indecencies.[31] It is related[32] that a certain governor (שלטון) resented this manner of worship, and the idol attendants were beaten by his order.[33] In TB[34] it is recorded that a sick heathen woman refused to adore Pe'or in this ugly way, declaring that she would rather remain sick than perform such ritual. The Rabbis assert[35] that hair was offered to Kemosh[36] and that as late as the third century human sacrifices

---

[20] Mephitic? *Sifre* II. 320, ed. Finkelstein, p. 367: "They worship the vapor arising from a [boiling] pot".

[21] *BR* ibid. On sacrifices to winds, see Frazer's commentary on Pausanias, vol. III, p. 74 ff., and P. Stengel, *Opferbräuche der Griechen*, p. 146 ff. On sacrifices to clouds, see Cook, *Zeus* III, p. 69 ff.

[22] *Mishnah 'Abodah Zarah* III. 7, passim.

[23] *TP* ibid. III. 6, 43a; *TB* ibid. 48a. Comp. Cook, *Zeus* II, 1033 ff. Frazer's commentary on Pausanias, III, p. 339.

[24] *TP 'Abodah Zar.* V. 4, 44b; *TB Ḥullin* 6a.

[25] *Tosefta Ḥullin* II. 18. Comp. *Mekhilta Jethro* VI, ed. Horovitz, p. 225.

[26] See below.

[27] *Sifre* II, 320, ed. Finkelstein, p. 367; *TB 'Ab. Zar.* 47a, *Ḥullin* 41b, and the sources referred to in my *Tosefeth Rishonim* II, p. 226, bot. Comp. also *Mekhilta* ibid.

[28] *Tosefta Ḥullin* II. 18. Comp. *Mekhilta* ibid.

[29] See *JQR* XXXV, 1944, p. 32, n. 201; *REJ* XLIII, 1901, p. 203.

[30] *Mishnah 'Ab. Zar.* III. 1–3, passim.

[31] *Sifre* I, 131, ed. Horovitz, p. 171, *TP Sanhedrin* X, 28d passim.

[32] Ibid.

[33] A similar story is told by Herodot. (III. 29). The Egyptian priests were flogged by order of Cambyses after they brought Apis into his presence and declared the bull to be their god. He rebuked them in much the same manner that the governor employed with the attendants of Pe'or, according to the Rabbis.

[34] *Sanhedrin* 64a.

[35] *Mekhilta deRashbi* to Ex. XX. 5, ed. Hoffmann, p. 105.

[36] See D. Künstlinger in *Hakedem* III, German part, p. 18 ff. This should not be confused with Greco-Roman customs; see *Mishnah 'Ab. Zar.* I. 3 and Elmslie in his edition, p. 24.

were offered to an idol (Prince of rain?), for the purpose of
bringing rain.[37]

The representative idol of the Greco-Roman Pantheon in
rabbinic literature is Mercurius or Merkulis, as they call it;[38]
the names of other Greco-Roman divinities occur only rarely.
The *Mishnah*[39] records that Rabban Gamaliel[40] was washing in
the bathhouse of Aphrodite in Akko (Ptolemais), which was
adorned by [a statue of] Aphrodite.[41]

We also read in *TP*:[42] ר' שמעון בן לקיש הוה בבוצרה חמתון מזלפין
להדא אפרודיטי אמר לון לית לית אסיר. אתא שאל לר' יוחנן אמר ליה . . . אין
דבר של רבים נאסר "R. Simeon b. Lakish was in Bostra and he
saw that they (i. e. Gentiles) were pouring [water] to Aphrodite.
He asked them (i. e. the Jews): 'Do not [the waters] become
forbidden?' He[43] came and asked R. Johanan. The latter replied:
'A public object does not become prohibited through use in
idol worship'." A commentary ascribed to Rabbi Elijah of
Wilna explains it to mean that they offered water libations to
Aphrodite, and that the Rabbi wanted to prohibit the use of
the river (from which the water was taken) to the Jews. If this
were so we should have to assume that we have here a case of
Ἀφροδίτη Οὐρανία to whom wineless libations (νηφάλια) were
offered.[44]

But it is very difficult to understand the *halakhic* problem
according to this interpretation; nor does it fit the whole context in *TP* ibid. The text of Rabbi Shelomo Siriliu reads בהדה
אפרודיטי instead of להדא אפרודיטי, and it has been shown elsewhere[45] that *TP* very frequently uses the preposition ל instead

[37] *TB* ibid. 55a. See A. Lewy, *Philologus* LXXXIV (1928–29), pp. 377–78;
Grégoire-Kugener, *Vie de Porphyre*, p. 127.

[38] The Greek Ἑρμῆς never occurs in rabbinic literature. See Lieberman
JQR XXXVII, 1946, p. 42 ff.

[39] *'Ab. Zar.* III. 4.

[40] Flourished at the end of the first and the beginning of the second
centuries.

[41] See *JQR* ibid., p. 45 and nn. 32, 33 ibid.

[42] *Shebi'ith* VIII end, 38b–c.   [43] I. e. R. Simeon b. Lakish.

[44] Polemon in schol. on Soph. *Oed.* col. 100. See Frazer, *Pausanias*, vol.
III, p. 583; Stengel, *Opferbräuche der Griechen*, pp. 181, 180, n. 2, 36 ff.

[45] *Ginze Kedem*, ed. Lewin V, p. 180 ff.

of ב.⁴⁶ Hence we ought to translate our text: "R. Simeon b. Lakish was in Bostra and he saw them (i. e. the Jews) sprinkling water [over themselves] in that [Bath of] Aphrodite.⁴⁷ He asked them: 'Is not this forbidden?' "⁴⁸ But R. Johanan ruled that the waters are public property and could not be forbidden by virtue of its being a pagan sanctum.⁴⁹

Similarly it is stated in *TP*:⁵⁰ ר' אחא בר יצחק עאל מיסחי עם ⁵³
[ר'] בא בר ממל בטרים בר יטסס⁵¹ חמא חד בר נש מזלף על גרמיה וכו'
"R. Aha b. Isaac accompanied by R. Abba b. Memmel came to wash in [the Bath of] the Three Graces (τρεῖς χάριτες), and he saw a man sprinkling water on himself etc."

Likewise we read in the *Midrash*:⁵² למה הוא דומה לנמפיון⁵³ שהיה משקה כל המדינה והיו הכל⁵⁴ משבחין אותו אמר להם אחד שבחו למעין שמספיק לזה "It may be likened to a sanctuary of the Nymphs⁵⁵ which provided water to the whole city, and everybody used to offer praise to it. Somebody remarked to them: Offer praise to the source which supplies it (i. e. the Νυμφαῖον) [with water]."⁵⁶

---

⁴⁶ As εἰς is used instead of ἐν in Hellenistic Greek.

⁴⁷ Comp. the passage of *TP Shabbath* cited below. The verb זלף in the sense of sprinkling water (washing) in the bathhouse occurs there half a dozen times.

⁴⁸ I. e. is it not forbidden to use the waters of this Bathhouse? The waters probably belonged to this deity.

⁴⁹ This explanation is in harmony with the parallel passage in *TB 'Abodah Zar.* 58b–59a.

⁵⁰ *Shabbath* III. 3. 6a.

⁵¹ In the Genizah fragments: כריטה. J. N. Epstein (*Tarbiz* I, fasc. II, p. 126) accordingly emended our text: בטריס כריטס. There can be no doubt about the correctness of this emendation.

⁵² *Shemoth Rabba* XXXI. 3.

⁵³ This is the reading of Cod. Oxford, Hebr. 147, f. 220b. *Tanḥuma Mishpatim* 8, ed. prin. and ed. Venice read: לנימפיון. Comp. also *Arukh* s. v. נמפיון. The readings quoted by Krauss (*LW* 364) from the modern editions of the *Tanḥuma* are worthless. He further misunderstood the whole passage. The asterisk on Νυμφαῖον should be dropped there.

⁵⁴ So Cod. Oxford.

⁵⁵ Νυμφαῖον. See Liddell and Scott s. v. Νυμφαῖον II. The *Nymphaeum* was sometimes like a regular *castellum*. See Daremberg et Saglio IV, p. 313 ff.

⁵⁶ Comp. *Tosefta 'Abodah Zar.* VI. 5 (and parallels): מעין היוצא מבית עבודה זרה "A source which issues from a heathen sanctuary".

Again we read in *TP*:[57] ר' חייה בר ווא הווה לי קווקין והווה טיכי
דרומי ציירה בנווה אתא שאל לרבנין אמרין מכיון שהמים צפין על נבה דבר
של בזיון הוא "R. Hiyya b. Abba had a cup[58] in which the Fortuna
(τύχη) of Rome[59] was painted. He came and consulted the
Rabbis.[60] They said: 'Since the water is flowing over it (i. e.
the Fortuna)[61] the vessel is considered a common object'."[62]

We have seen that the Greco-Roman deities are mentioned
only incidentally in rabbinic literature, yet it is clear that the
Rabbis had a fair knowledge of these divinities,[63] their worship
and their festivals.[64]

In order to eliminate any possible imitation of the heathen
art of sacrificing the Rabbis imposed special restrictions on the
Jewish way of slaughtering. We read, for instance, in the
Mishnah:[65] אין שוחטין לא לתוך ימים ולא לתוך נהרות ולא לתוך כלים
אבל שוחט הוא לתוך א נ א [66] של מים. ובספינה על גבי כלים. אין שוחטין
לגומא כל עיקר. אבל עושה גומא בתוך ביתו בשביל שיכנס הדם לתוכה ובשוק
לא יעשה כן שלא יחקה את המינין "None may slaughter into the seas
or into rivers or into vessels. But they may slaughter into a
basin filled with water. And [when a man is] on a ship he may
slaughter on the outside of vessels. One may by no means
slaughter into a hole (or pit), but a man can make a hole within
his house for the blood to flow into it.[67] He may not however

[57] Ibid. III. 3, 42d. I quote from the *Genizah* fragment published in *Tarbiz*
III, p. 19.

[58] καυκίον. So correctly Krauss in *LW* II, p. 502. Comp. Liddell and
Scott, s. v. καῦκος.

[59] See Wissowa, *Religion und Kultus der Römer²*, p. 264.

[60] He feared that the Fortuna was worshipped by the previous owners.
It is not stated where the Rabbi acquired the cup. From *TP* (*Ma'aser Sheni*
IV. 1, 54a) we know that he once visited Rome.

[61] When the cup is filled with water.

[62] I. e. the heathen do not worship figures painted on common objects.
The images on such objects are considered only as ornaments. See *Mishnah*
'Abodah Zar. III. 3.

[63] See ibid. III. 1–3 passim.

[64] Saturnalia, Kalendae and others, see ibid. I. 3, passim.

[65] *Ḥullin* II. 9.

[66] This is the correct reading, see *Tosefeth Rishonim* II, p. 227, top.

[67] I. e. if the man slaughters the animal in the courtyard and does not want
the ground to be soiled with the blood, he is allowed to let it flow from the

do so in the market place lest it appear that he is following the laws[68] of the Gentiles."[69]

TB[70] explains that it is forbidden to slaughter into the sea because it may look as if the man is sacrificing to the Prince of the sea.[71] It further states[72] that one is not allowed to slaughter on board ship only if the blood flows directly into the sea, but it is permissible to let it fall into the sea after running over the sides of the ship. If a victim is slaughtered to Poseidon on board ship, its blood has to flow directly into the sea.[73] The rabbinic stipulation that an animal may be slaughtered into a basin[74] only if it contains dirty[75] water is also designed to counter a pagan practice.

It is further obvious from the language of the *Mishnah* that the heathen practice was to have only the head of the animal over the sea, or river, or hole[76] into which the blood gushed. Hence לשחוט לתוך הנהר, לתוך הגומא, which is the exact equivalent of σφάγειν εἰς τὸν ποταμόν, εἰς τὸν βόθρον, frequently

place of slaughter into a pit. But he must not slaughter over the pit. See *TB* ibid. 41b.

[68] My translation of the word יחקה is based on *Tosefta* ibid. (II. 19, 503₈) where the formulation is: מפני שעושה את חוקי מינין.

[69] On מינין, gentiles, see Lieberman *GJP*, p. 141, n. 196. The subsequent conclusion in the *Tosefta* ibid. (503₉) does not contradict this translation. A man who follows the practices of the heathen incurs the suspicion of being a heretic and is to be investigated.

[70] Ibid. 41b.

[71] *TP* (*Sanhedrin* VII. 19, 25d) relates that the Prince of the sea twice obeyed R. Joshua's orders; once in Tiberias and once in Rome. In the latter instance this prince of the sea, of course, was Neptune-Poseidon. For the Semitic name of the Prince of the sea as mentioned in later *Midrashim* see Ginzberg, *Legends of the Jews* VI, p. 8, n. 42. Princes of waters, rivers, mountains, hills, abysses, wildernesses, astral bodies are mentioned in *Seder Rabba Dibereshith, Batei Midrashoth,* ed. Wertheimer I, pp. 7–8.

[72] On the authority of a *Baraitha*. Comp. however *Tosefta* ibid. II. 19, and my remarks in *Tosefeth Rishonim* II, p. 227.

[73] Comp. Eur. *Hel.* 1088: αἵματος δ'ἀπορροαὶ ἐς οἶδμ' ἐσηκόντιζον. "The blood-gush spurted to the surge".

[74] I. e. σφαγεῖον.

[75] See *TB* ibid.

[76] The *Mishnaic* גומא means a small hole (or pit) into which the whole animal would hardly fit.

mentioned in connection with heathen sacrifices,[77] means to have
the blood gush directly into the river or the pit.[78] In the market-
place a Jew was forbidden to let the blood flow into a pit
because he may be considered to be following the laws of the
gentiles. Perhaps the Rabbis had the Romans in mind who
sometimes sacrificed in such a way that the blood was not
gushing directly into the pit.[79]

The Rabbis also refer frequently to the Egyptian deities.
Animal worship is not only mentioned in the tractate dealing
with idolatry,[80] but the term נעבד (a deified animal) occurs
throughout rabbinic literature.[81] Furthermore, Isis and Sarapis
are specifically mentioned. The *Tosefta*[82] numbers among the
idols "an image of a woman nursing [her child] and Sarapis."[83]
This is quoted in *TB*[84] which comments on it: מניקה על שם חוה
שמניקה כל העולם כולו. סר אפיס על שם יוסף שסר והפיס[85] את כל העולם
מניקה וקא בן דנקיטה והיא .כייל וכא גריוה דנקיט והוא .כולו "A
woman nursing [a child] represents Eve[86] who suckled the whole

---

[77] See Pausan. II. 12. 1; Strabo XV. 14; Herodot. VII. 113; Dittenberger
Syl³. 1024. 37. All these sources are referred to by Stengel, *Opferbräuche der
Griechen*, p. 120.

[78] This definitely solves the doubts of Stengel ibid.

[79] See S. Eitrem, *Opferritus und Voropfer der Griechen und Römer*, Kristiania 1915, p. 430.

[80] I. e. *'Abodah Zarah*. See *Tosefta* ibid. II. 1; V. 10; *TP* ibid. III. 6, 43a;
TB ibid. 22b, 54a passim.

[81] See, for instance, *Mishnah Zebaḥim* VIII. 1; IX. 3; XIV. 2; *Temurah*
VI. 1.

[82] *'Abodah Zar*. V. 1.

[83] דמות מניקה וסרפיס.   [84] Ibid. 43a.

[85] So Cod. New York, a Spanish manuscript of 1290.

[86] The Rabbis not only identified Eve with Isis (see below), but apparently
also compared the Biblical Eve to the Greek one. R. Simeon b. Yoḥai likened
Adam to a man who stored various kinds of fruits in a jar (חבית), and after
having placed a scorpion on them he sealed the jar hermetically. He warned
his wife not to open the jar under any circumstance. However, the latter was
overcome by her curiosity and opened the jar, whereupon she was stung by
the scorpion (I *Aboth deR. Nathan* I, ed. Schechter, p. 6 and parallels). This
parable was certainly appreciated by the people who were familiar with the
myth of the Greek Eve-Pandora who out of curiosity "took off with her hands
the great lid of the jar" (Hes., *opera et dies* 94: ἀλλὰ γυνὴ χείρεσσι πίθου μέγα
πῶμ᾽ ἀφελοῦσα) and let loose all the evils contained therein.

world. Sarapis stands for Joseph[87] who saw[88] and quieted [the

[87] M. Sachs (*Beitraege zur Sprach- und Alterthumsforschung* II, p. 99) was the first to understand the whole passage properly. He quoted Suidas s. v. Σάραπις, who mentions the identity of Sarapis with Joseph. (For other scholars who followed in his footsteps, see the references in Krauss' *LW* II, p. 412). Drexler in Roscher's *Mythologisches Lexicon* (II. 433) made reference to a number of articles dealing with the "Sarapis = Joseph" thesis. Most of them are not accessible to me. We shall refer to the sources found in the collection of Th. Hopfner's *FHRA*. The following Christian authors connect Sarapis with Joseph: Melito Sardianus, *Apol.* (ed. de Otto) 5 (*FHRA* p. 343); Tertullianus, *ad nat.* II, 8 (ibid. 380); Firmicus Maternus, *de errore prof. rel.* 13. 2 (ibid. 520); Paulinus Nolanus, *carm.* XIX 100 ff. (ibid. 647). According to the rabbinic tradition the body of Joseph was put in a metal coffin and thrown into the Nile etc. (*Tosefta Sotah* IV. 7 and parallels). It is similar to what according to an Egyptian tale (See Plut. *de Is. et Osir.* 13 passim) Typho did to Osiris (= Sarapis). This connection between the two legends was first pointed out by Jellinek (*apud* Weiss in his edition of the *Mekhilta*, Introduction, p. XXI). Comp. also J. H. Bondi, *Dem Hebraeisch-Phoenizischen Sprachzweige angehoerige Lehnwoerter*, p. 120 ff.

In the light of the preceding we may perhaps understand a very strange anonymous *Midrash* (?), quoted by Rabbi David Hanagid in his Arabic commentary on *Aboth* II. 7. According to it Hillel the Elder saw Pharaoh's skull floating on the water and he said to it: "Because thou drownedst they drowned thee etc." This sounds like sacrilege, for the continuation in the *Mishnah* ibid. is: "And at the last they that drowned thee shall be drowned" (The explanation of Rabbi David is along mystical lines). However, we know that the Rabbis sometimes interpreted the Mishnah by the same methods as they interpreted Scripture (See *TP Rosh Hashanah* I. 10, 57c. Comp. also I. Heinemann, *The Methods of the Aggadah* [Hebrew], p. 198, n. 28). It is therefore possible that the wording of the *Mishnah* (ibid. על דאטפת אטפוך וסוף מטיפיך יטופון) which repeatedly stresses the root טוף (*tuph*) conveyed to some later Rabbi the association with Typho who drowned Osiris, the ancient Pharaoh of Egypt. This association may have been suggested to the Rabbi by the legend that "A human head comes every year from Egypt to Byblos (Phoenicia) floating on its seven days' journey thence, and the winds drive it by some divine guidance and it does not turn aside but comes only to Byblos". (Luc., *de Syria dea* 7: κεφαλὴ ἑκάστου ἔτεος ἐξ Αἰγύπτου ἐς τὴν Βύβλον ἀπικνέεται πλώουσα τὸν μεταξὺ πλόον ἑπτὰ ἡμερέων, καὶ μιν οἱ ἄνεμοι φέρουσι θείῃ ναυτιλίῃ· τρέπεται δὲ οὐδαμά, ἀλλ' ἐς μούνην τὴν Βύβλον ἀπικνέεται). This head of Osiris which according to the legend floated from Egypt to Byblus had to pass on its way through the sea facing Palestine, and some Rabbi having heard of the legend made Hillel apply his famous saying to it: "Because thou drownedst they drowned thee, and at the last they that drowned thee shall be drowned".

[88] I. e. in advance. See '*Arukh* s. v. סר II.

fear]⁸⁹ of the whole world. [A genuine Sarapis is] only one who holds a measure (i. e. a *modius*) and is measuring,⁹⁰ and [a genuine Isis is] only one who is holding a child and nursing it" (i. e. Horus).

Again, it is likely that the *Mishnah*⁹¹ had the Egyptian cult in mind. We read there: המגפף והמנשק והמכבד והמרביץ והמרחיץ והסך והמלביש והמנעיל עובר בלא תעשה "He who embraces, or kisses [the idol], sweeps, or besprinkles [the floor before the idol], washes,⁹² anoints, clothes or shoes⁹³ [the idol] transgresses only a negative commandment."⁹⁴ Although every single act mentioned in the *Mishnah* is well known from the Greek and Oriental ritual, the *ensemble* of these acts suits the daily cult of the Egyptians in particular.⁹⁵

We see from the preceding material that the Rabbis were acquainted with the various rites of idolatry prevalent in the Middle East in their day.⁹⁶ It is therefore sometimes impossible to define precisely the heathen cult they had in mind in their allusions to certain rites of idolatry.

⁸⁹ I. e. by storing up grain for the seven years of hunger. The Rabbis interpreted Sarapis to consist of *sar* which means "he saw" in Aramaic and *appis* which means "he quieted" in this language. According to Firmicus Maternus (see above n. 87) Sarapis meant Σάρρας παῖς, for Joseph was Sarah's great grand-son (*Sarrae pronepos fuerat*).

⁹⁰ Comp. Tertullian, *ad. nat.* II. 8.   ⁹¹ *Sanhedrin* VII. 6.

⁹² In *TP* ('*Abod. Zar.* III. 6, 42d) it is stated that they used to wash the idol with water and rub it with salt. Comp. the Epistle of Jeremiah 23 and Arnobius, *adv. gent.* VII. 32 (*aliqua frictione cinderis*).

⁹³ *Tosefta Sanhedrin* X. 3, adds: והמעטף, "And he who covers" (with a garment). Perhaps this is a variant for והמנעיל (shoes), the latter coming by attraction (*ashgarah*, see above, p. 125, n. 54), since it is frequently associated with המלביש, see *TP Kiddushin* I, 7, 61a; *TB* ibid. 22b (and parallel) passim.

⁹⁴ But is not subject to the death penalty.

⁹⁵ See A. Moret, *Le rituel du cult divin journalier en Égypte* (Paris 1902), p. 87, n. 1 (on embracing and kissing); p. 200 ff. (on spreading sand before the idol, which required previous sweeping and subsequent sprinkling; see *Aruch Completum* VII, 249, s. v. רבץ); pp. 172, 175 (about besprinkling and washing); p. 190 ff. (about anointing) and p. 178 ff. (about clothing).

⁹⁶ The Rabbis expressly referred (*TB 'Ab. Zar.* 11b) to the temple of Heliopolis (Baalbek) and other temples. See N. Brüll in his *Jahrbücher* etc. I (1874), p. 138 ff.; Krauss, *Semitic Studies in Memory of A. Kohut*, p. 343; Isidor Lévy, *REJ* XLIII (1901), p. 192 ff.; Lieberman, *JQR* XXXVII (1946), p. 43.

THE THREE ABROGATIONS
OF JOHANAN THE HIGH PRIEST

It is stated in the *Mishnah* that Johanan the High Priest did away with three acts which were performed in the Temple. Rabbinic tradition explains this action of the High Priest. In order the better to understand the material which will be discussed, it is in place to say a few words about the method to be followed in the investigation of the sources. We must discriminate between the reasons openly given by the Rabbis in justification of a new enactment of theirs and the real motives which prompted it. *TB*[1] records: " 'Ulla[2] said: When an ordinance is issued in the West (i. e. Palestine) its reason is not disclosed for the first twelve months, lest there be some who may not agree with the reason and will slight the ordinance." This offers explicit testimony that the Rabbis were sometimes reluctant to reveal the reasons which moved them to enact a new law. Moreover, in order to make the people accept a new ordinance the Rabbis occasionally substituted some formal legalistic grounds for the real motive.

Good evidence to this effect is available in *TP*. The *Mishnah*[3] states: "A man may not go out [on the Sabbath] shoed with a nailstudded sandal." According to the sources[4] this prohibition resulted from the recollection of a disaster caused by the sight or the noise of the nailstudded sandals worn by the soldiers;[5] according to another version[6] Jews wearing

---

[1] *'Abodah Zarah* 35a.

[2] Flourished in the third century.

[3] *Shabbath* VI.2.

[4] *TP* a. l. 8a; *TB* ibid. 60a; *Debarim Rabba* ed. Lieberman, p. 81.

[5] פולחין in *Debarim Rabba* ibid. means soldiers, as in Palestinian Syriac; see F. Schulthess, *Lexicon Syropalaestinum*, p. 157 s. v. פלח and פלוח. In a Palmyrene bilingual inscription of the year 251 (ed. Vog, 22, G. A. Cooke, *North-Semitic Inscriptions*, p. 284) פלחא corresponds to the Greek στρατιώτης. Comp. also A. Büchler in *REJ* XL, 1900, p. 155 ff.; B. Jacob ibid. XLI, p. 216; W. Bacher ibid., p. 221.

[6] See *TP* and *TB* ibid.

this kind of sandals once stampeded in a panic[7] and many casualties were caused by the sandals.

The question was raised: If these are the reasons, why were the nailstudded sandals forbidden only on Saturdays and not on weekdays? *TP* (ibid.) gives the curious reply: לאו אורחיה דבר נשא מיהוי ליה תרין סנדלין חד לחולא וחד לשובתא "People do not usually own two [pairs of] sandals, one for the weekdays and one for the Sabbath."[8] In other words, if the Rabbis forbade the use of certain kind of objects on the Sabbath its use was *eo ipso* eliminated on weekdays as well; people would not buy shoes which they could not wear on the Sabbath. It is clear that the earlier Rabbis did not make public their reason for the injunction on the nailstudded sandals which, for social or sentimental reasons, they sought to ban altogether. Instead they linked the law to the Sabbath, a domain in which their competence could not be questioned, and thus achieved their actual purpose circuitously. Evidently a distinction must sometimes be drawn between the public reasons (for a decree) given by the authorities and the actual motives impelling the action.[9]

In the light of the preceding we shall be able properly to understand the material bearing on the abrogations of Johanan the High Priest.

We read in the *Mishnah*:[10] יוחנן כהן גדול העביר הודיית מעשר. אף הוא בטל את המעוררים ואת הנוקפים "Johanan the High Priest did away with the *Declaration*[11] concerning the Tithe. He also

---

[7] See H. Ehrentreu, *Magazin* etc., ed. Berliner and Hoffmann XX, 1893, p. 213.

[8] See the reason given in *TB* ibid. 60a, bot.

[9] Comp. also *TB* ibid. 14a passim.

[10] *Ma'aser Sheni* V. 15.

[11] הודייה is rendered "Confession" or "Avowal" by all the commentaries, translations and dictionaries. The *Mishnah* (ibid. 10) and the Talmuds repeatedly call it וידוי מעשר. However, וידוי originally is not "confession" but "declaration". The Septuagint (Lev. 5:5; 16:21; 26:40; Num. 5:7 passim) often translates the Hebrew התוודה ἐξαγορεύειν, which means "to declare". The same term was also used by the pagans. Plutarch (*de superst.* 7, 168d) expresses himself: ἐξαγορεύει τινὰς ἁμαρτίας αὐτοῦ, "He confesses (announces) various sins of his". Comp. also Dittenberg *Syl.*³ 1179 and 1180. The literal rendering of confession is ὁμολογία, see Liddell and Scott, s. v.

abolished the Awakeners and Knockers."[12] Let us first consider the "Knockers."[13] The *Tosefta*[14] explains it: את שמכין[15] אילו נוקפין העגל בין קרניו כדרך שעושין לעבודה זרה. אמר להן יוחנן כהן גדול[16] עד מתי אתם מאכילים את המזבח טריפות "The Knockers are those who strike the calf between its horns as they do in [the practice of] idol worship. Said Johanan the High Priest to them: 'How long will you feed the altar with *Terephoth*' "[17] We are told explicitly that the real reason for the removal of the "Knockers" was that they followed the practices of the heathen *victimarii*. This habit of stunning the ox before slaughtering was very widely used in pagan worship,[18] and the desire not to imitate the heathen rites motivated Johanan's abolition of the custom.[19]

ὁμολογέω II. 2; R. Petazzoni, *Harvard Theological Review* XXX, 1937, p. 8, n. 22 and p. 9 ibid.

The standard Hebrew confession began with the words (*Vayyikra Rabba* III. 3, according to codd. Vatic. and London): מודע כל מה שעשיתי וכו': "Let it be declared: Whatever I did etc." (The reading of the editions and of *TP* Yoma end, 45c, are to be corrected accordingly). On the identity of הודאה with וידוי see *Bereshith Rabba* LXXI. 5, 8282; *TP Shebu'oth* V. 1, 36a; ibid. VIII. 9, 38d; comp. also ibid. I. 8, end, 33b.

[12] The other reforms of Johanan the High Priest mentioned in the *Mishnah* ibid. are not related to these three abrogations.

[13] Most of modern scholars discount entirely the early rabbinic explanations of the *Mishnah*, and advance their own conjectures. See, for instance, Rapaport *apud* Geiger, *Lehrbuch zur Sprache der Mishnah* II, p. 11; Jacob Brüll, *Einleitung in die Mischnah* (Hebrew) I, pp. 17–18; comp. also *Jewish Studies in Memory of G. A. Kohut*, Hebrew part, p. 56 ff.

[14] *Sotah* XIII. 10.

[15] So ed. princ. and cod. Vienna.

[16] So ed. princ. and cod. Vienna.

[17] I. e. animals which are mortally wounded and may not be used for either food or sacrifice. *TP* (ibid. IX. 24a) reads נבילות, carcasses, instead of טריפות (comp. also *TB* ibid. 48a). This may be correct, for the struck animal sometimes looks only stunned, whereas it is actually dead; see P. Stengel, *Opferbräuche* etc., p. 114, n. 2.

[18] See *Odys*. XIV. 425; Apoll. Rhod. I. 425 ff.; P. Stengel ibid. pp. 110, 114. For archaeological evidence see J. Carcopino, *Mélanges d'arch. et d'hist.* XXVII, 1907, p. 233, n. 2 and plates V–VI ibid.

[19] He instituted instead special metal bands to hold the animal while it was being slaughtered. See *Mishnah Sukkah* end, Rashi ibid. 56a s. v. וטבעתה, *TP* ibid. 55d; *Sotah* IX. 11, 24a and parallel; *Mishnah Tamid* IV. 1; *Middoth* III. 5. Comp. ערוגת הבושם ed. Urbach, I, p. 61.

However he justified his abrogation of the practice on the ground that the animal became unfit for sacrifice after it was stunned.[20] Certainly, the High Priest's authority in all matters pertaining to the altar could not be challenged. Thus the public understood the High Priest's action in one way while its real purpose was something other.

Let us now proceed to the third abrogation, the abolition of the "Awakeners". All the rabbinic sources[21] agree that the "Awakeners" were those in the Temple who used to recite the verse (Ps. 44:24): "*Awake, why sleepest Thou, O Lord?*"[22] The fact that an objection was raised to the recitation of a verse from Scripture in the Temple because it was unseemly speaks for itself. Johanan had no intention to eliminate the verse from the Bible, for he probably understood it as a literary figure. Why then was he shocked by its recitation in the Temple?

Here again the chanting of this Psalm (in the morning) closely resembled a heathen ceremony. The Egyptian temples were, as was the Jewish Temple, closed at nights.[23] At the opening of the former the god was invoked in a hymn with the recurrent refrain: "Awake in peace."[24] The commencement of the daily service in the temple of Sarapis is portrayed by Porphyrius Tyrius[25] as following: "For even now, in the opening of the sanctuary of Sarapis the worship is performed through *fire* and water; *the singer of the hymns* making libation with the

---

[20] Comp. I. H. Weiss, דור דור ודורשיו II, pp. 28–29. He, however, completely misunderstood the purpose of the knocking.

[21] *Tosefta Sotah* XIII. 9; *TP* ibid. IX. 11, 24a; *TB* ibid. 48a.

[22] According to the *Tosefta* and *TB* ibid. it referred to the Levites who used to recite this verse daily. It has nothing to do with the daily singing of the Levites (*Mishnah Tamid* VI. 4), for it is stated here that they used to recite *the same* verse every day. *TP* does not mention the Levites but merely says: "Those who used to say: *Awake etc.*" This version seems to be more original, and the "Awakeners" may have been priests.

[23] See, A Moret, *Le rituel du cult divin journalier en Egypt*, p. 9 passim.

[24] Ibid., p. 122 ff.

[25] *De abstin.* IV. 9 (T. Hopfner, *FHRA* p. 467): ὥς που ἔτι καὶ νῦν ἐν τῇ ἀνοίξει τοῦ ἁγίου Σαράπιδος ἡ θεραπεία διὰ πυρὸς καὶ ὕδατος γίνεται, λείβοντος τοῦ ὑμνῳδοῦ τὸ ὕδωρ καὶ τὸ πῦρ φαίνοντος, ὁπηνίκα ἑστὼς ἐπὶ τοῦ οὐδοῦ τῇ πατρίῳ τῶν Αἰγυπτίων φωνῇ ἐγείρει τὸν θεόν.

water (i. e. of the Nile) *and exhibiting the fire;*[26] then standing
upon the threshold, he *awakens the god in the native Egyptian
language.*"[27] Johanan apparently abolished the whole ceremomy
of the singers who sang (in the morning) the Psalm: *"Awake
why sleepest Thou O Lord* [. . . *arise for our help and redeem us
for Thy mercy's sake]"*, for it sounded like a repetition of the
service in a heathen temple.[28] The above discussion makes it
very probable that the object of some of the abrogations of
Johanan was to purify the Temple service and to keep out of
it all traces of pagan worship. For reasons of tact he did not
divulge his purpose to the public. But the desired effect was
achieved, and the Rabbis gave him the deserved praise for it.

---

[26] See *Mishnah Tamid* I. 3.

[27] Comp. also Apuleius, *Metam.* XI. 20 (T. Hopfner ibid. 324 ff.); Arnobius,
Adv. gent. VII. 32. Comp. F. Cumont, *The Oriental Religions in Roman
Paganism*, Chicago 1911, pp. 95, 236.

[28] Rabbinic sources advance various reasons for the first abolition, i. e.
the elimination of the Declaration. (See *Tosefta Sotah* XIII, 3204, according
to the reading of cod. Erfurt. Comp. *TP* ibid. IX, 24a and parallel; *TB* ibid.
48a). The generally accepted opinion is that during the priesthood of Johanan,
the tithes were given to (or forcibly taken by) the priests instead of the
Levites. The statement of Deut. 26:13 (*And I gave it to the Levite etc.*) in the
Declaration would therefore be untrue. Accordingly, the High Priest, who
most probably supported the priesthood, was opposed to the Declaration
because it would remind the worshipper that he broke the law by letting the
tithes go to the priests, and therefore abolished it altogether. However, it is
very unlikely that Johanan revealed his motive publicly. He probably found
some other excuse. Perhaps his pretext is preserved in a different tradition
(see *Tosefta, TP* and *TB* ibid.): he claimed that the people in general did not
strictly observe the laws of tithes (i. e. gave them neither to the Levites nor
to the priests), and he therefore canceled the Declaration in order not to cause
some people to utter a lie in the Temple. Comp. now my conjecture in
Tarbiz XXVII (1958), p. 186, n. 34. In other words, as in the case of the
Knockers, he was guided by one reason while he formally motivated his action
by another.

HEATHEN PRE-SACRIFICIAL RITES
IN THE LIGHT OF RABBINIC SOURCES

It was shown that the authorities of the Jerusalem Temple
tried to eliminate the practices and rites which resembled those
of the heathen too closely. However, outside of the Temple
certain customs connected with the prospective victim, which
were sanctified by age, continued in force despite their identity
with heathen behavior.

An old *Mishnah*[1] describes the ancient ceremony of the
bringing of the Fist-fruits to Jerusalem:[2] "How do they take
up the First-fruits [to Jerusalem]? The men of all the smaller
towns that belonged to the *Ma'amad*[3] gather together in the
town of the *Ma'amad*; they spend the night in the open place
of the town and come not into the houses[4]. . . Before them goes
the bull (intended as a sacrifice), *its horns overlaid with gold
and a wreath of olive-leaves on its head.*[5] The flute is played before
them until they draw nigh to Jerusalem etc."

The Bible does not make the slightest suggestion about
adorning the sacrifice with a wreath and gilding its horns. Nor
does the *Mishnah* mention it anywhere save here. The entire

---

[1] Undoubtedly older than the destruction of the Temple.

[2] *Bikkurim* III. 2–3.

[3] See Schurer, *Geschichte* etc. II⁴, p. 338 and nn. 5, 6 ibid.

[4] The *Tosefta* (ibid. II. 8 and *TP* ibid. III, 2, 65c) explains that they did
not enter any house for fear of defilement (by possibly being under one roof
with a human corpse, or parts of it). A similar practice was adopted by the
pilgrim to Hierapolis, according to Lucian (*de Syria dea* 55) who depicted it
as follows: Starting from his house he passes into the road . . . He always
sleeps on the ground; for he may not go up to his bed before his pilgrimage is
completed and he comes back to his own country (ἄρας δὲ ἀπὸ τῆς ἑωυτοῦ
ὁδοιπορέει . . . καὶ ἐς πάμπαν χαμοκοιτέων· οὐ γὰρ οἱ εὐνῆς ἐπιβῆναι
ὅσιον πρὶν τήν τε ὁδὸν ἐκτελέσαι καὶ ἐς τὴν ἑωυτοῦ αὖτις ἀπικέσθαι).
Comp. *TP 'Abodah Zarah* II. 2 (end), 41b. The *Tosefta* (*Bikkurim* ibid.)
stresses that the First-fruit carriers were treated like every one else upon
their return to their homes.

[5] According to *Aggadath Shir Hashirim* II, ed. Schechter, p. 28 (= *Midrasch
Suta*, ed. Buber, p. 24) the participants in the procession wore golden crowns
on their heads (ועטרה של זהב בראשן), but it is apparently a scribal error. The
text is to be corrected in accordance with our *Mishnah* and *Yalkut* a. l.; see
Schechter ibid. p. 108.

ceremony described above is not even hinted in the Bible. The text of Scripture (Deut. 26:1–11) does not imply that First-fruits are to be brought by a group of people; it appears to be a private duty incumbent on the individual. The entire procedure is recorded in the *Mishnah* not in the form of a law but as an account of a custom. It was only natural that an occasion like the *Bikkurim* should assume the character of a πανήγυρις, a popular festival. Philo also describes it as such,[6] although he does not speak of the details portrayed in our *Mishnah*.[7] It is not surprising that the πανήγυρις shared all the features of a religious public festival customary among all the Mediterranean nations of the time.

The bull was adorned with a wreath[8] and his horns were overlaid with gold. This is a regular heathen rite. Diomedes promises Athene to sacrifice a heifer whose horns he will overlay with gold;[9] it was agreeable to the deity. Theophrastus[10] maintains: οὐ γὰρ ἄν ποτε τοῦ Θετταλοῦ ἐκείνου <τοῦ> τοὺς χρυσόκερως βοῦς καὶ τὰς ἑκατόμβας τῷ πυθίῳ προσάγοντος

---

[6] *De spec. leg* II, XXXIV–XXXV, 215–216. See Grätz in *MGWJ* XXVI, 1877, p. 433 ff.

[7] Philo states that there were no sacrifices on this occasion. It is clear from the context that he means to say that there were no sacrifices prescribed as on the other holidays. But it is likewise obvious that he did not know of the rabbinic law which requires a sacrifice on this occasion. See *Mishnah Bikkurim* II. 4; *Tosefta* ibid. II, 10130, *TP* ibid. a. l.

[8] στέμμα. See Aristoph. *Pax* 948; Lucian, *de sacr.* 12; P. Stengel, *Die griechischen Kultusaltertümer*[3], p. 108, n. 7; G. Wissowa, *Religion und Kultus der Römer*[2], pp. 416–417 and n. 1. ibid. On the pictures of the Synagogue in Dura-Europos, the bull (intended as a sacrifice) seems to be adorned with a wreath; see E. L. Sukenik, בית הכנסת של דורא אברופוס, pp. 139, 141. It is, of course, taken from heathen life as mirrored in pagan literature and works of art. Our *Mishnah* is older by some two hundred years than the Dura-Europos Synagogue; see D. Hoffmann, *Die erste Mischnah*, p. 15.

In *Aboth deR. Nathan* (XXXIV) XXXV we find כבשים המצוייירים, "painted sheep," as prospective victims. This is undoubtedly the correct reading (See the variants recorded by Prof. Finkelstein, *A. Marx Jubilee Volume*, Hebrew part, p. 355, n. 89), as we hope to prove elsewhere.

[9] *Il.* X. 294 (=*Odys*. III. 384): χρυσὸν κέρασιν περιχεύας. See also *Odys*. ibid. 437. Virgil, *Aen.* IX. 627: et statuam ante aras aurata fronte iuvencum. "I shall place a young bullock with gilded horns before your altars". Comp. also Prudentius, *Perist.* X. 1024.

[10] As quoted by Porphyrius, *de abst.* II. 15.

μᾶλλον ἔφησεν ἡ πυϑία τὸν Ἑρμιονέα κεχαρίσϑαι ϑύσαντα τῶν ψαιστῶν ἐκ τοῦ πηριδίου τοῖς τρισὶ δακτύλοις. "Otherwise the Delphic priestess would not have said once, when that Thessalian sacrificed a hundred oxen with *gilt horns* to Apollo, that the man of Hermione who had offered a pinch of barley-meal taken with three fingers out of his bag had made the more gratifying sacrifice."[11] In certain solemn public sacrifices it was the accepted rule in the Roman Empire[12] to cover the horns of bulls and heifers with gold.[13]

The behavior of the people agreed with the conventional character of public religious festivals, and the proper authorities did not protest. But it does not seem likely that the prescribed public sacrifices of the Temple service were garlanded and gilded; there is not a single allusion to it in the vast rabbinic literature which deals with the Temple sacrifices. The decoration of the bull who came with the *Bikkurim* was exceptional; it was a concession to the people who considered it a הידור מצוה, "an adorning of a pious deed."

[11] An interesting parallel is found in *Vayyikra Rabba* III. 5, where it is related that King Agrippa once decided to sacrifice a thousand burnt-offerings in one day. He bade the priest not to accept offerings from anybody else. A poor man, however, prevailed upon the priest to sacrifice two doves of his on that day. It was shown to King Agrippa in a dream that the offering of the poor man was more gratifying to the Lord than his sacrifices. It is further related (ibid.) that a priest, who regarded disdainfully *a handful* (קומץ) of *flour* offered by a poor woman, was told in a dream that her gift was equivalent to a sacrifice of her life.

We are not told the nature of the thousand holocausts offered by Agrippa. It was perhaps a χιλιόμβη brought in behalf of the Roman emperor (see below n. 12). Our text is probably of the fourth century, and it mirrors the customs of its time.

[12] See Henzen, *Acta fr. Arv.*, p. 144; P. *Stengel* ibid. p. 108, n. 9. S. Eitrem, *Opferritus and Voropfer* etc., p. 195, n. 3. Macrobius (*Sat.* III. 5. 8) quotes *Aen.* IX. 627 (see above n. 9) as an example of Virgil's exactness in his description of sacrifices.

[13] TP (*Bikkurim* III. 3, 65c) adds an interesting detail: יחיד שנתעצל ולא בא מביא גדי וקרניו מצופות כסף, "An individual who procrastinated and did not join the procession [of First-fruit carriers] has to bring a kid whose horns are overlaid with silver". Some commentators who were not aware of the popular custom reflected in this passage misinterpreted it; see Ratner in אהבת ציון וירושלים on *Bikkurim*, p. 151. Its meaning however cannot be doubted.

THE CONSECRATION OF A VICTIM
IN HEATHEN RITES

According to Jewish law any object becomes sacred as soon as the owner dedicates it to God even by word of mouth. The *Mishnah*[1] formulates it: אמירתי לגבוה כמסירתי להדיוט "Dedication to God by word of mouth is equal to the act of delivery to a common person." On the other hand, regarding consecration to idols the Rabbis ruled:[2] אמר שור זה לעבודה זרה בית זה לעבודה זרה לא אמר כלום שאין הקדש לעבודה זרה "If one says: This ox is [dedicated] to an idol, or this house is [dedicated] to an idol, he has said nothing, because there is no dedication to an idol."[3] If however some act was performed on the animal for the purpose of offering it to an idol it could not be used on the Jewish altar; it became מוקצה, *Muktzeh* (set aside for a sacrifice to an idol). The *Tosefta*[4] rules: מאמתי נקרא מוקצה משנעשה בו מעשה "When does an animal become *Muktzeh*?[5] From the time that an act (of consecration) was done to it." The *Tosefta* does not specify the deed which will make it *res sacra* and thereby disqualify it from the Jewish altar.[6]

But TB[7] has preserved a number of opinions on this point.[8] According to one the consecration becomes effective from the time the animal was "put under guard" (שעושין לו שימור), i. e. after it was examined for fitness to be sacrificed.[9]

Another Rabbi explains that the consecration becomes effec-

---

[1] *Kiddushin* I. 6.

[2] *Tosefta 'Ab. Zar.* V. 10, 469₆; ibid. *Temurah* IV. 3, 552₂₉; *TB 'Ab. Zar.* 44b.

[3] See G. Wissowa, *Religion und Kultus der Römer*², p. 385, n. 5.

[4] *'Ab. Zar.* V. 9, 469₅ and parallel.

[5] I. e. consecrated to an idol.

[6] In case the heathen was prevented from slaughtering the victim and it was seized by the Jews.

[7] *Temurah* 29a.

[8] On the ruling of Resh Lakish which is recorded ibid. 28b, see below n. 22.

[9] This is the accepted interpretation of שימור in rabbinic literature; see *Sifre* I, 142 (to Num. 28:2), ed. Horovitz, p. 188 and the sources referred to in n. 14 ibid.

tive when the animal is delivered to the attendants[10] of the idol and is fed *Karshinim*[11] which is the property of the latter.[12]

The concluding opinion is that of R. Johanan[13] that the consecration takes effect when the animal is shorn and an act of worship is performed with it[14] (עד שיגזז ויעבדו בו).

But Hezekiah, a contemporary of R. Johanan, taught that the *consecratio* is performed by "Pouring wine to an idol between the horns of the animal."[15] The four preceding opinions of the Rabbis about the consecration of the victim indicate that they were not unfamiliar with the several rites of the various cults. Let us analyze these opinions in the order in which they are recorded.

1. THE *PROBATION* MAKES THE *CONSECRATIO* EFFECTIVE. According to rabbinic law the public Daily Whole-offering as well as the Paschal Lamb had to be examined by specialists (to find whether they are perfect) four (or three) days before they were laid on the altar.[16] A special college existed in Jerusalem of inspectors of intended sacrifices, who drew their fees

---

[10] משרתים, ὑπηρέται.

[11] A kind of vetch, ὄροβος, see E. Löw, *Die Flora der Juden* II, p. 484 ff.

[12] עולא אמר ר' יוחנן עד שימסרוהו לטשרתי ע'ז ... עולא נמי כי קאמר הוא ד ס פ י
.ליה כרשיני ע'ז (So cod. Mun.)

[13] Flourished in the third century.

[14] I have translated the passages of the Talmud almost verbatim. As we shall presently see they are perfectly understandable in the light of heathen practices. Some commentators who were not familiar with the heathen rites tried to give the passages a forced interpretation. Maimonides, however, guided by the simple meaning of the words interpreted them correctly (ה איסורי מזבח IV. 4), although he too was unaware of the true significance of these rites.

[15] *TB 'Ab. Zar.* 54a (according to cod. Mun.): שניסך לע'ז יין בין קרניה. The Talmud cites it as an example of נעבד, "worshipped animal," but argues that according to Hezekia's formulation not the animal is worshipped but the idol. It is obvious that the definition of Hezekiah deals with the *consecratio* of the victim which the Rabbis wanted to extend to the regulation regarding animals worshipped.

[16] See *Mekhilta Bo* V, ed. Horovitz, p. 16; *Sifre* I, 142, ed. Horovitz, p. 188 and parallels referred to in n. 14 ibid. On the inspection of private sacrifices see *TP Bezah* II. 4, 61c and parallel.

from the Temple treasury.[17] Philo[18] relates that "the most highly esteemed of the priests, selected as the most qualified for the inspection in regard to blemishes, examine them (i. e. the sacrifices) from the head to the extremities of the feet." He states further that this examination is conducted most minutely and exactly.[19] This inspection was also applied by the heathens carefully and conscientiously.[20] The author of the first opinion in *TB* saw in this *probatio* by the heathens the actual *consecratio* of the victim.[21]

2. CONSECRATION BY WAY OF FEEDING THE ANIMAL BY THE ATTENDANTS OF THE HEATHEN TEMPLE. We have found no evidence in classical literature that the feeding of the victim was important as a special pre-sacrificial act.[22] However, Plutarch in describing the practices at Delphi[23] states that in addition to the examination of the body of the sacrifice the soul of the

---

[17] *TP Shekalim* IV. 3, 48a; *TB Kethuboth* 106a.

[18] *De spec. leg.* I. XXXIV (166 ff.): οἱ δοκιμώτατοι τῶν ἱερέων ἀριστίνδην ἐπικριθέντες εἰς τὴν τῶν μώμων ἐπίσκεψιν ἀπὸ κεφαλῆς ἄχρι ποδῶν ἄκρων ἐρευνῶσιν.

[19] However, it is possible that he was influenced by the Egyptian practice; see Herodot. II. 38.

[20] See Herodot. ibid.; Aristoph. *Lysistr.* 84; Tertullian, *ad. nat.* I. 10; Lucian, *de sacr.* 12; B. Brissonius, *de formulis et solemnibus populi Romani verbis* I, XXI, p. 12; Stengel, *Die griechischen Kultusaltertümer*[3], p. 121, nn. 13, 14; G. Wissowa, *Religion und Kultus der Römer*[2], p. 416 and n. 2 ibid.

[21] Of course, the Rabbi did not discriminate between public and private heathen sacrifices.

[22] From the style of the Talmud it appears that the Rabbi does not refer to the general fattening of the heathen sacrifices (see on it Plut., *Cleomed.* XXXVI; G. Wissowa ibid., p. 416, n. 4; Stengel ibid., p. 121, n. 15), but to a single act. This fattening was termed פטום לעיג by the Rabbis (see *Bereshith Rabba* LXXXVI, 1054₆. Comp. also *TB Sotah* 43a and parallels).

According to the view of Resh Lakish (*TB Temurah* 28b) the consecration becomes valid only after [the animal was fattened for] seven years. See *Targum* to Jud. 6:25 and *Redak* ibid. We omitted the opinion of Resh Lakish in our analysis because he deals with an animal set apart for eventual worship, not for sacrifice (see *TB* ibid.). Hence this kind of *Muktzeh* has nothing to do with the animals consecrated to be sacrificed.

[23] *De defectu orac.* 49.

victim was also tested. He says (ibid.): "They test the soul[24] by setting barley-groats[25] before the bulls and peas before the boars; the animal that does not taste them is not considered healthy."[26] What purpose the sacrifices were meant to serve[27] does not concern our inquiry. The important fact is that in some heathen sanctuaries the prospective victim was fed by the priests as a final test. The Rabbis considered this act a consecration.

A highly interesting detail regarding the treatment of the victim immediately before it was slaughtered is preserved in the *Mishnah*. We read there:[28] השקו את התמיד בכוס של זהב. אף על פי שהוא מבוקר מבערב מבקרין אותו לאור האבוקות "They gave [the lamb that was to be] the Daily Whole-offering to drink from a golden bowl. Although it had been inspected the evening of the day before, they inspect it again by the light of torches." Neither the *Mishnah* nor the Talmud supplies the reason for the practice of watering the victim before it was slaughtered.[29] It seems to have been an ancient rite related to the inspection with which it is associated in the *Mishnah*.[30]

This custom of which there is no hint in Scripture was probably prevalent among other nations as well. On a Greek painting[31] Nike is represented as pouring water from a pitcher

---

[24] According to Jewish law the prospective victim has to be healthy (*Mishnah* Bekhoroth VI. 7). One Rabbi rules (ibid. VII. 6) that an animal which is not of sound mind (שוטה. See also *Mishnah Baba Kamma* V. 6) is not "of the choicest", as the law requires it (see Deut. 12:11).

[25] In Palestine vetches (see above n. 11) was a staple animal fodder.

[26] τὴν δὲ ψυχὴν δοκιμάζουσι, τοῖς μὲν ταύροις ἄλφιτα τοῖς δὲ κάπροις ἐρεβίνθους παρατιθέντες. τὸ γὰρ μὴ γευσάμενον ὑγιαίνειν οὐκ οἴονται.

[27] See Legrand in *Revue des études grecques*, 1901, p. 55, n. 1.

[28] *Tamid* III. 4.

[29] The mediaeval commentators (see Rashi, Ḥullin 90b; *Aruch Completum*, ed. Kohut IV, p. 267, s. v. כס IV) explain that it is easier to skin an animal which drank before it was slaughtered (see *TB Bezah* 40a).

[30] It is possible that the lamb was given water to drink as a final test of its good health; perhaps they simply wanted the thirsty animal (see Arist., *hist. anim.* VIII. 12. 1, about the thirst of the sheep which were fed for the purpose of fattening them) not to look miserable. But whatever its original explanation, the act became an integral part of the sacrificial ritual.

[31] Of the middle of the fifth century B. C. E.

(ὑδρία) into a bowl for a decorated bull about to be sacrificed.[32] A. Furtwängler[33] remarks that Nike's performance is an entirely incidental action[34] in the sacrificial rite. But in the light of the preceding we may perhaps surmise that the painting portrays the customary final ritual act before the slaughtering of the victim.

3. CONSECRATION BY WAY OF CUTTING SOME OF THE VICTIM'S HAIR AND OFFERING IT TO THE GODS. R. Johanan's opinion, which is conclusive, is that "the consecration takes effect when the animal is shorn and an act of worship is performed with it." It was the regular practice of the Greeks to cut some hair of the victim immediately before slaughtering and offer it to the gods.[35] The Rabbi correctly took the offering of the hair as the actual *consecratio* of the victim.[36] R. Johanan defined the *consecratio* according to the *graecus ritus* which was followed by many heathens in Palestine, Syria and Egypt.

4. CONSECRATION BY WAY OF POURING WINE BETWEEN THE HORNS OF THE VICTIM. R. Johanan's older contemporary, Hezekiah, ruled that the consecration becomes effective "When he poured wine between the horns of the victim."[37] The phrase ניסך יין בין קרניה is verbatim *vinum fundit inter cornua*, an expression of frequent occurrence in Latin literature.[38] It is of no import whether this is part of *probatio*, a test of the sensi-

---

[32] A. Furtwängler and K. Reichhold, *Griechische Vasenmalerei* I, plate 19; P. Stengel, *Die griechischen Kultusaltertümer³*, plate V, fig. 22.

[33] In his comment on this picture, p. 83.

[34] Eine ganz nebensächliche episodische Handlung.

[35] *Il.* XIX. 254; *Odys.* III. 445. Comp. *Il.* III. 273. For many other references to this practice in Greek classic literature see P. Stengel, *Opferbräuche der Griechen*, pp. 40–47.

[36] Comp. Liddell and Scott, s. v. καταρχεσθαι II. 2; Stengel, ibid., p. 41 seq.; idem, *Die griechischen Kultusaltertümer³*, pp. 111, 260.

[37] See above n. 15.

[38] Comp. Ov. *met.* VII. 594: et fundit purum inter cornua vinum; Virg. *Aen.* IV. 61: inter cornua fundit; Silius ital., *Punica* XIV. 461: et large sacra inter cornua fundit. See A. S. Pease in his edition of Virgil, *Aen.* IV, p. 138, n. 61.

tivity of the animal,[39] or part of *immolatio* according to the
Romanus ritus.[40] The Rabbi regarded the sprinkling of the wine
on the head of the victim[41] as the final act of consecration. He
issued his ruling on the basis of the practice of the Roman
troops in Palestine and the neighboring countries.[42]

All these rabbinic passages[43] regarding the *Muktzeh*, which
hitherto were almost meaningless, become pertinent in the light
of the actual heathen practices of the time.

[39] See Serv. *ad Aen.* IV. 61 and VI 244; Plut. *quaest. conv.* VIII. 8. 3, 729f;
idem, *de defectu orac.* 49. Comp. Legrand, referred to above, n. 27.

[40] In which cutting of the victim's hair apparently did not take place.
See G. Wissowa's remark (*Religion und Kultus der Römer*[2], p. 417, n. 7) on
Virg., *Aen.* VI. 245.

[41] See Wissowa ibid., p. 417, n. 6; Latte in PW *RE*, IX. 1, s. v. *immolatio*,
p. 1128.

[42] As soon as the *immolatio* was performed, all the decorations were apparently removed from the victim (see Latte ibid.). This is confirmed by the
Mishnah (*Temurah* VI. 1) which ruled that only the consecrated animal
becomes forbidden, not its decorations (for they constituted a temporary
dressing only and were to be removed when the animal was sacrificed).

[43] Some of the above-mentioned passages were discussed by me in *Mélanges
Grégoire, Annuaire de l'Institut de Philologie et d'Histoire Orientales et Slaves*
IX, 1949, p. 414 ff.

BLEMISHES IN SACRIFICES

It is self evident and natural that animals for sacrifice be of the choicest.[1] The Rabbis style[2] such offerings מובחר, "the choicest."[3] According to the Palestinian Talmud[4] the lambs for the Daily Whole-offering were so large that their legs reached the ground even when they were carried on camels. Private offerings also were sometimes chosen from the flocks of Kedar[5] which were already famous in Biblical times.[6] The Talmud perhaps did not exaggerate in the above-mentioned description of the large size of the lambs. Herodotus relates[7] that the Arabians have marvelous varieties of sheep. Their tails are sometimes so long that "they would get wounds by rubbing them on the ground.[8] But as it is, every shepherd there knows enough of carpentry to make little carts (ἀμαξίδας) which they fix under the tails, binding the tail of each several sheep on its own cart." We find the same in the *Mishnah*:[9] "Rams may not go out [on Saturday] with their cart (בעגלה) under their tail." *TB*[10] explains the purpose of the carts: כי היכי דלא ליחמטן אליתייהו "So that they might not hurt (literally: knock) their tails."[11] It appears from the *Mishnah* that this kind of sheep was also extant in Palestine.

---

[1] See Deut. 12:11; Gen. 4:4 and *TP Megillah* I. 12, 72b.

[2] See Kosowsky, *Concordance to the Mishnah*, p. 353; idem, *Concordance to the Tosefta* II, p. 67 passim.

[3] For the localities from which the choicest animals came, see *Tosefta Menaḥoth* IX. 13, 52622 and *TB* ibid. 87a.

[4] *Pe'ah* VII. 4, 20a, bot. Comp. *Bereshith Rabba*, LXV. 17, p. 729. Comp. the opinion of R. Judah in the *Tosefta* and *TB* ibid.

[5] See *Tosefta Ḥagigah* II. 11, 2367 and parallels in *TP* and *TB*. The reading of the *Tosefta* was perhaps influenced by Isa. 60:7.

[6] Isa. ibid.   [7] III. 113.

[8] ἕλκεα ἂν ἔχοιεν ἀνατριβομενέων πρὸς τῇ γῇ τῶν οὐρέων.

[9] *Shabbath* V. 4.

[10] Ibid. 54b.

[11] The account of Herodotus confirms fully the explanation of Rashi that חמט means to "hurt". Rabbenu Hananel a. l. and *'Arukh* s. v. חמט explain it differently.

The *Mishnah*[12] devotes a whole chapter to the description
of the choicest produce[13] to be used for Meal-offerings[14] and to
the specification of the best oils and wines for sacrificial purposes. It states:[15] לא היו כונסים אותו בחצבים גדולים אלא בחביות
קטנות. ואין ממלא את החבית עד פיה כדי שיהיה ריחו נודף. אינו מביא לא
מפיה מפני הקמחון ולא משוליה מפני השמרים אלא מביא משלישה ומאמצעה
"They did not put [the wine] in large store-vessels, but in small
jars, and they did not fill the jars up to the brim, so that its
vapors might escape. They did not take the wine that was in
the mouth of the jar because of the scum nor that of the bottom
because of the lees, but from the third part that was in the
midst thereof."[16]

This corresponds to the description of the quality of the
wine accepted in ancient times. We read in the *Geoponica*:
"When transferring wine from the storage jars to small vessels
one must observe the seasons of the stars."[17] "The wine which
is transferred into the pitchers should not fill them up to the
brim but until a little below the neck, so that it may not suffo-
cate but be able to breathe."[18] "The sages,[19] particularly

---

[12] *Menaḥoth* VIII.

[13] Comp. also M. Olitzki, *Flavius Josephus und die Halacha*, Berlin 1885,
p. 41.

[14] According to the *Tosefta* ibid. IX. 3, 52535 (comp. *TB* ibid. 85a) special
fields were set aside (מיוחדות) for the purpose of producing the best grain.
Comp. the exegesis of *eximius* by Veranius as quoted by Macrobius, *Sat.*
III. 5. 6.

[15] Ibid. 7.

[16] Comp. *Tosefta* ibid. IX. 10, 52615 ff. for different details.

[17] VII. 6. 6: χρὴ δέ, ἡνίκα ἀπὸ τῶν πίθων εἰς μικρὰ ἀγγεῖα μεταβάλ-
λομεν τὸν οἶνον φυλάττεσθαι τὰς ἐπιτολὰς τῶν ἀστέρων.

[18] Ibid. 10: Δεῖ δὲ τὸν μεταγγιζόμενον εἰς τὰ κεράμια οἶνον, οὐ μέχρι
τοῦ χείλους τῶν κεράμων ἐμβάλλεσθαι, ἀλλ' ἕως ὑποκάτω μικρὸν τοῦ
τραχήλου, ὥστε μὴ πνίγεσθαι, ἀλλὰ διάπνοιαν ἔχειν.

[19] Ibid. 7–8: Συμβουλεύουσι δὲ οἱ σοφοί, μάλιστα δὲ Ἡσίοδος,
ἀνοιγομένου πίθου, τὸν ἐν τῇ ἀρχῇ τοῦ πίθου οἶνον, καὶ τὸν περὶ τὸν
πυθμένα δαπανᾶν, τὸν δὲ μέσον τοῦ πίθου οἶνον φυλάττειν, ὡς ἰσχυρότερον
καὶ μονιμώτερον, καὶ πρὸς παλαίωσιν ἐπιτήδειον. ὁ μὲν γὰρ πρὸς τῷ
στόματι τοῦ πίθου οἶνος, ὡς προσομιλῶν τῷ ἀέρι, ἀσθενέστερός ἐστι
διαπνεόμενος· ὁ δὲ πρὸς τῷ πυθμένι ταχέως τρέπεται, ὡς πλησιάζων τῇ
τρυγί·

Hesiod,[20] advise that when a jar is opened the wine at the top be consumed and the wine in the middle be conserved as being more potent and more lasting and suitable for aging. For the wine at the mouth of the jar being in contact with the air is weaker as a result of exhalation; that near the bottom quickly turns because of its proximity to the lees."[21]

But what provoked the greatest care was that the victim be without defect. Scripture enjoins that all sacrifices be perfect, but it lists (Lev. 22:21–24; Deut. 15:21) only a comparatively small number of defects which renders the animal unacceptable for the altar. However, the Rabbis record[22] a detailed series of such blemishes many of which are not mentioned in the Bible.

The oral law to this effect certainly followed an ancient tradition. There were certain rules regarding defects that make the animal unfit for sacrifice, which were common to Jews and non-Jews alike. The mere consideration by the gentiles of a certain flaw in an animal as disqualifying it from sacrifice affected the Jewish law. What is improper for the table of the idol can certainly not be brought on the Jewish altar.[23] We can therefore expect striking similarities between the Jewish and non-Jewish rules regarding defects and blemishes. We shall cite an interesting example:

Huic tantum animali omnium quibus procerior cauda non statim nato consummatae ut ceteris mensurae; crescit uni donec ad restigia ima preveniat. quamobrem victimarum probatio in vitulo ut articulum suffraginis contigat: breviore non litant.[25]	זנב העגל שאינו מגיע לערקוב. אמרו חכמים כל מרבית העגלים כן כל זמן שהן מגדילין הן נמתחות. לאיזה ערקוב אמרו ר' חנינא בן אנטיגנוס אומר לערקוב שבאמצע הירך.[24]
"Of all the animals that have a comparatively long tail this (i. e. the bull) is the only one whose	"If a calf's tail does not reach the knee-joint? The

---

[20] *Opera et dies* 368 ff.

[21] The *Tosefta* (*Baba Mezi'a* VI. 14, 384₂₁) states that in Jerusalem they sold wine from the top of the jar, from its middle and from the bottom at different prices (see also ibid. 13, 384₁₈).

[22] *Mishnah Bekhoroth* VI. 1–12; *Tosefta* ibid. IV. 1–16 passim.

[23] See Mal. 1:8.

[24] *Mishnah* Ibid. VII. 11.

[25] Plinius, *nat. hist.* VIII. 70, 182–183.

tail is not of the proper size from birth; and in this animal alone it continues to grow until it reaches right down to the feet. *Consequently the test of victims in case of a calf is that the tail must reach the joint of the hock; if it is shorter the sacrifice is not acceptable".*

sages said: The majority of calves have this characteristic;[26] while they grow their tails grow longer. Of which knee-joint did they speak? R. Ḥaninah b. Antigonos says: The knee-joint in the middle of the thigh".[27]

Both these texts are striking in their similarity. A comparison of both makes it obvious that although the tail of a calf is small at birth and it continues to grow, it must be at least long enough to reach the joint of the hock. If it is shorter than this it is considered a defect. When the Sages of our *Mishnah* said: "The majority of calves have this characteristic," they meant that the tails of most calves reach at least to the knee-joint. If they are no longer than these it does not matter, for they continue to grow with the growth of the animal. There is no divergence of opinion in our *Mishnah* between the Sages and R. Ḥaninah b. Antigonos. Both explain the first clause which ruled: "If the calf's tail does not reach the knee-joint [it is a blemish]." The Sages explain why the short tail of a calf is not considered a defect if it reaches the knee-joint; R. Ḥaninah b. Antigonos defines the exact location of that joint.[28]

However, if the Rabbis may have taken notice of the heathen judgment of bodily defects which disqualified animals from the altar, they certainly ignored other prerequisites of prospective victims required by the pagans. For instance, the Rabbis ruled[29] that only the Red Heifer becomes disqualified for the ritual purpose if a "yoke came upon her"[30] even by chance, not

[26] See below.

[27] *Tosefta* ibid. IV. 14, 53921 and *TB* ibid. 41a explain that it means the upper of the two joints in the hind legs.

[28] The comparison with Plinius seems to prove the correctness of Rashi's interpretation of the *Mishnah* against the opinion of Maimonides. Comp. also Rav Hai המקח והממכר, gate XLV, 83b.

[29] *Sifre* I, 123, ed. Horovitz, p. 153. Comp. the sources referred to in n. 1 ibid.

[30] See Num. 19:2.

with the intention of work (בעול שלא לעבודה); but no yoke renders any other animal unfit for sacrifice. Similarly, a Red Heifer which was broken is disqualified, but no other victim is affected by it.[31]

This ruling meant to emphasize that the Jews do not follow the heathen practice in this respect. Diomedes said in his vow to Athene: "I shall sacrifice a heifer . . . *unbroken which no man has yet led beneath the yoke.*"[32] The Romans also sometimes adopted this practice. They had a class of victims called *iniuges*, i. e. that were never broken nor came under the yoke.[33] The Rabbis did not recognize such laws for victims that were to be offered on the Jewish altar.

Likewise, they decided[34] that an animal which was shorn did not thereby become unfit for sacrifice.[35] In this too the Jews did not follow the custom of the heathen who stipulated of certain sacrifices that they should be *intonsa*, i. e. that they should have never been shorn.[36] At first blush the rabbinic declaration that the shearing of an animal does not at all affect its fitness for the altars seems to be superfluous; there is no reason to suppose that this should have any influence. But the Rabbis were aware of the heathen sacred law, and they taught the Jews to ignore this practice. In the last two instances the exegesis of the Rabbis was aimed at the heathen *leges sacrae*, although they did not specifically mention them.

However, the Talmudic sources are sometimes more explicit. We read in the *Mishnah*:[37] לא היו כופתים את הטלה אלא

---

[31] See *TB Sotah* 46a; *Tosefta Parah* II. 5, 631₁₉ and *Tosefeth Rishonim* III, p. 214.

[32] *Il.* X. 292 (=*Odys.* III. 382): ῥέξω βοῦν . . . ἀδμήτην, ἣν οὔ πω ὑπὸ ζυγὸν ἤγαγεν ἀνήρ.

[33] Macrobius, *Sat.* III. 5. 5: iniuges vocatur, id est quae nunquam domitae aut iugo subitae sunt. See Wissowa, *Religion und Kultus der Römer*², p. 416, n. 4.

[34] *TP Pesaḥim* IX. 4, 37a.

[35] From *Pirkei R. Eliezer* XXI and *Midrash Aggada* (Gen. IV. 5, ed. Buber, p. 11) it would appear that unshorn sheep were preferred for sacrificing.

[36] See Virg. *Aen.* XII. 170 and Servius a. l.

[37] *Tamid* IV. 1.

מעקידים אותו "The lamb[38] was not [wholly] bound but only tied."[39] According to one Babylonian Rabbi,[40] the Jews did not [wholly] bind the lamb so as not to imitate the gentiles [who use to bind the sacrifice]. As far as we know, the Greeks and the Romans did not bind their sacrifices, as is obvious from all the existing paintings.[41] But the Babylonian Rabbi undoubtedly referred to an Oriental cult. The Egyptians, apparently, used to bind the legs of the victim very tightly.[42]

A general question is in order at this point. Did the Jews stress the apparent voluntary submission of the victim to its fate? The heathen attached the greatest importance to the external behavior of the sacrifice. Whenever the victim showed signs of resistance it was a bad omen; by artificial means they contrived to produce the impression that the animal agreed to be sacrificed.[43] They used not to drag the victim by force, for the very resistance of the animal demonstrated that it was not acceptable to the divinity.[44] The practice of the Jews in ancient times to stun the victim before it was slaughtered[45] indicates that they too attached importance to the non-resistance of the sacrifice.

We have traces of such popular beliefs in many places in our literature. It is related in the *Midrash*[46] that they tried to

[38] I. e. the Daily Whole-offering.

[39] The LXX render both כפת and עקד συμποδίζειν. But the Rabbis discriminated between the two verbs. עקד according to them (see *TB Shabbath* 54a. Comp. *Tosefta* ibid. IV. 3, 11510 and variants ibid.) meant "the tying together of the forefoot and the hindfoot, or the two forefeet or the two hindfeet". The animal was prevented by this kind of tying from running away, but not from walking; see *Mishnah Shabbath* V. 3. According to Maimonides the lamb was not tied at all, but simply held by its forefeet and hindfeet; see above, p. 141, n. 19.

[40] *TB Tamid* 31b.

[41] See Latte in PW *RE* IX. 1, s. v. *immolatio*, p. 1228.

[42] See the upper figure in *Annales de philosophie chrétienne*, March 1870, p. 20.

[43] See P. Stengel, *Die griechischen Kultusaltertümer*³, p. 63, nn. 8–10.

[44] See B. Brissonius, *de formulis et solemnibus populi Romani verbis* I, XXII, p. 13; Wissowa, *Religion und Kultus der Römer*², p. 416, n. 6.

[45] See above, p. 141 ff.

[46] *Tehilim* XXII, ed. Buber, p. 196.

draw a bull towards the altar but it refused to go. A poor man
came and stretched out a bundle of endives to it; the bull ate
it[47] and followed the poor man to the altar. In a dream the
owner of the bull heard the act of the poor man commended.
Similarly it is told in the *Midrash*[48] that the bull destined to be
Elijah's sacrifice[49] followed the prophet willingly, whereas the
one intended as the victim of the Ba'al's prophets resisted so
violently that all the false prophets were not able to make
it budge.[50]

In the light of this we shall perhaps better understand a
certain procedure adopted in the cases of the Red Heifer and
the Scape-goat. The *Mishnah*[51] relates: וכבש היו עושים מהר הבית
להר המשחה . . . שבו כהן השורף את הפרה ופרה וכל מסעדיה יוצאין להר
המשחה "They made a causeway from the Temple Mount to the
Mount of Olives . . . by it the priest that was to burn the Heifer
and the Heifer and all her attendants went forth to the Mount
of Olives." The *Mishnah* (ibid.) explains that this procedure
was adopted so as to avoid possible defilement by an unknown
grave in the depth of the earth. The causeway was built in a
way which would prevent any such defilement. The commentaries realized the difficulty of the explanation. According to
Jewish law the Heifer could never be defiled as long as it was
alive; why then go to the expense[52] and trouble of leading the
Heifer through the embankment?

The true reason for the causeway is probably implied in the
immediately following *Mishnah*: לא היתה פרה רוצה לצאת אין
מוציאין עמה שחורה . . . ולא אדומה וכו' "If the Heifer refuses to go
forth they may not send out with her a black heifer . . . nor

---

[47] Comp. *Vayyikra Rabba* III. 5. The version in the later source (i. e.
Midrash Tehilim) seems to be more original.

[48] *Tanḥuma* מסעי 6, ed. Buber, p. 165.

[49] See I Kings 18:25 ff.

[50] Comp. also *Mishnah Sukkah* II, end.

[51] *Parah* III. 6. See *Tosefta* ibid. III. 9, 632₂₄ ff. and *Tosefeth Rishonim*
III, p. 219.

[52] According to the *Tosefta* (*Shekalim* II, p. 176₃) and *TP* (ibid. IV. 3,
48a) such a causeway used to cost the high priests more than sixty talents of
gold.

another Red Heifer etc."[53] Here it is clearly stated that the Red Heifer was not dragged by force.[54] The causeway *supplied with a rampart*[55] made it easier to lead the Heifer, for it could be easily lured to go forward.

A causeway was also provided for the Scape-goat and its leader "Because the Babylonians[56] used to pull its hair,[57] crying to him: 'Bear [our sins] and be gone! Bear [our sins] and be gone!' "[58] Here the *Mishnah* openly admits that the causeway was built on account of the popular desire to get rid of the Scape-goat as soon as possible. The popular impatience may also have stemmed from the fear that the goat might escape. A high and narrow embankment made the flight of the goat much more difficult. From *TP*[59] it is obvious that the flight of the goat was considered a bad omen.[60] The escape of an animal about to be sacrificed was regarded by the heathen as a sign of disaster.[61]

Certain definite fears were common to the ancient world. The reasons given by the Rabbis for the causeway are based on good tradition. They belong to the many motives which tended to legalize old practices which the authorities were not able to uproot;[62] the Rabbis gave the ancient customs a good Jewish dressing.

[53] Comp. the similar stratagem recorded in *Bereshith Rabba* LXXXVI. 2, p. 1052.

[54] Comp. משנה אחרונה a. l. The explanation given by the author is unacceptable to me; see *TP Pesaḥim* VI. 1, 33a.

[55] See *TP Shekalim* IV. 3, 48a.

[56] According to the *Tosefta Yoma* IV.13, 188₁₁ (and parallels): Alexandrians.

[57] Comp. the Epistle of Barnabas, VII. 8 and S. Lieberman, in *A. Marx Jubilee Volume* (Hebrew part), p. רצ״י, n. 52.

[58] *Mishnah* ibid. VI. 4.

[59] *Yoma* VI. 3, 43c.

[60] Comp. also the questions addressed to R. Eliezer, regarding a case where the goat or its leader would get sick (*Tosefta* ibid. IV. 14, 188₁₅ ff.). See the view of R. Eliezer, regarding the causeway for the Red Heifer, in *Tosefta Parah* III. 7, 632₁₆.

[61] See G. Wissowa, *Religion und Kultus der Römer*², p. 416, n. 6 ff.

[62] See Lieberman *GJP*, p. 103 ff. A similar method was followed by the Christian church fathers; see J. Toutain, *Nouvelles études de mythologie et d'histoire des religions antiques*, Paris 1935, p. 193.

The inquiry into the heathen sacrificial rites and practices may help us to understand some rabbinic figures and symbols. For instance, the Rabbis state:[63] כל הקבור בארץ ישראל כאלו קבור תחת המזבח . . . וכל הקבור תחת המזבח כאלו קבור תחת כסא הכבוד "He who is buried in the Land of Israel is as if he were buried under the altar.[64]. . . And he who is buried under the altar is as if he were buried under the throne of the Divine Majesty."[65] This statement of the Rabbis is quite surprising. To bury under the altar means to commit sacrilege,[66] for it would defile the sacrifices offered on it. The prophet Haggai reproaching the priests charged (2:14): *"And that which they offer there is unclean."* The Palestinian Talmud[67] explains that the Prophet had in mind the victims which became unclean because they found the skull of Ornan the Jebusite[68] under the altar. The skull, the Rabbis say,[69] was discovered by the exiles on their return from Babylonia[70] when they were engaged in enlarging the altar.[71] The discovery of a skull under the altar would certainly upset the Jews,[72] although, said the Rabbis, by grace of the

---

[63] *Aboth deR. Nathan* XXVI, ed. Schechter, 41b and parallels, see below.

[64] See also *Tosefta 'Abodah Zarah* IV, 466[3]; *TB Kethuboth* 111b.

[65] See Lieberman, *Tosefeth Rishonim* II, p. 192.

[66] The Rabbis maintain (I *Aboth deR. Nathan* XII, 25b; *TB Shab.* 152b) that the souls of the righteous are treasured under the throne of the Divine Majesty (נגנזות תחת כסא הכבוד). But there is, of course, a great difference between the expression of the "soul being treasured under the throne" and "the body being buried under the altar".

[67] *Sotah* V. 3, 20b.

[68] See I Chr. 21:18 ff. II Sam. 24:18 ff.

[69] *Aggadath Shir Hashirim* III. 4, ed. Schechter, p. 33; Rabbi Abigedor Cohen Zedek (in his commentary to Songs, ed. Bamberger, p. 21) quotes it in the name of the *Pesikta*.

[70] On the seemingly contradictory view of *TP* (*Pesaḥim* IX. 1, 36c) see Lieberman, הירושלמי כפשוטו, p. 508.

[71] See *Mishnah Middoth* III. 1, *TB Zebaḥim* 61b, Rashi ibid. s. v. שיתין, and דקדוקי סופרים, p. 116, n. 1.

[72] Titus Livius (I. 55. 5) records the legend that when they were digging the foundations of the temple of Jupiter the Capitoline, they found a human head with its features intact (caput humanum integra facie). The Romans considered it a good omen, interpreting it to signify that the place would be the head of the world.

Lord the sacrifices offered on the altar before the skull was removed were not disqualified.

The question therefore may be raised again: What did the Rabbis mean by exalting him who was buried under the altar and comparing such burial to that under the throne of the Divine Majesty? Perhaps we shall find the answer in the rabbinic conception concerning the attempted offering of Isaac. The Rabbis looked upon the ram sacrificed by Abraham as though it were Isaac.[73] In the view of the Rabbis the ashes of the burnt ram formed the foundations of the inner altar.[74] They further relate that when the Jews returned from the Babylonian exile they looked for the exact place of the outer altar. They established the correct spot because they found the ashes of Isaac heaped and deposited in that place.[75] According to this version the ashes of Isaac formed the foundations of the outer altar.[76]

Altars built of ashes of victims were quite common among the heathens. Pausanias states:[77] "[The altar of the Olympian Zeus] is made of the ashes of the thighs of the victims sacrificed to Zeus, just like the altar at Pergamus. The altar of the Samian Hera is also made of ashes etc."[78] In view of this we suggest that the parable of the Rabbis, in which they liken

[73] See *BR* LVI, 9, p. 606 and parallels referred to by Theodor a. l.; J. Mann, *The Bible as Read and Preached in the Old Synagogue* I, Hebrew part, p. 67 and the parallels referred to in n. 135 ibid.; Ginzberg, *Legends of the Jews*, V, p. 252, n. 245. See now the excellent article of S. Spiegel in *A. Marx Jubilee Volume*, Hebrew part, p. רע״א ff. Comp. *Tosafoth* in *TB Ta'anith* 16a, s. v. אפר.

[74] *Pirkei R. Eliezer* XXXI, end; *Midrash Haggadol* Gen., ed. Schechter, p. 325, ed. Margulies, p. 358; *JQR*, N. S. VII, 1916, p. 132.

[75] *TB Zebaḥim* 62a, according to the correct reading and explanation by Rabbi Judah b. Barsilai of Barcelona in his commentary to ספר יצירה, p. 109.

[76] As correctly observed by Rabbi David Luria in his commentary to *Pirkei R. Eliezer* XXXI, 72a, n. 71. Comp. also *Targum* to I Chr. 21:15.

[77] V. 13. 8: πεποίηται δὲ ἱερείων τῶν θυομένων τῷ Διὶ ἀπὸ τῆς τέφρας τῶν μηρῶν, καθάπερ γε καὶ ἐν Περγάμῳ. Τέφρας γὰρ δή ἐστι καὶ τῇ Ἥρᾳ τῇ Σαμίᾳ βωμός κτλ.

[78] See also ibid. 14.8 and 10; 15. 9 and IX. 11. 7. Comp. Frazer a. l. III, p. 557; P. Stengel, *Die griechischen Kultusaltertümer*³, p. 13, n. 18.

burial in the Land of Israel to burial under the altar, was an ancient phrase adapted to the ashes of Isaac.[79] The latter formed the foundation of the altar, directly under the throne of the Divine Majesty.[80] This will still be better understood in the light of a Semitic heathen custom. Porphyrius reports[81] that the Dumatii,[82] a people of Arabia, annually *sacrificed a boy whom they buried under the altar* which was used by them as a god.

The Rabbis converted a pagan rite[83] into material for a Jewish legend, and they transformed a reality of heathen cult[84] into a Jewish symbol. The ashes of Isaac are deposited under the altar directly beneath the throne of the Divine Majesty; "He who is buried in the Land of Israel is as if he were buried under the altar . . . And he who is buried under the altar is as if he were buried under the throne of the Divine Majesty."

We repeat again: In these chapters only some of the pre-sacrificial rites were discussed. But they are sufficient to demonstrate the common patterns of worship which prevailed in the Mediterranean world during the first century B. C. E. and C. E.

---

[79] There may have been a view among the Jews that Adam was buried under the altar; see L. Ginzberg, *Legends of the Jews* V, p. 125 ff., n. 137. However, the Rabbis could hardly hold such views. See the opinion of R. Yanai in *TP Nazir* VII. 2, 56b and comp. *TB* ibid. 54a.

[80] *Tanḥuma* וירא 41, ed. Buber 55a (*Aggadath Bereshith* XXXI. 1): שעשה את המזבח מכוון כנגד כסא הכבוד "[Abraham] has built the altar directly beneath the throne of the Divine Majesty". Comp. *Mekhilta, Shirah* X, ed. Horovitz, p. 150 and parallels referred to in the notes ibid. See also P. Stengel, ibid., p. 12, n. 1.

[81] *De abst.* II. 56: Καὶ Δουματηνοὶ δὲ τῆς 'Αραβίας κατ' ἔτος ἕκαστον ἔθυον παῖδα, ὃν ὑπὸ βωμὸν ἔθαπτον, ᾧ χρῶνται ὡς ξοάνῳ.

[82] See Gen. 25:14; Is. 21:11.

[83] I. e. the building of altars of victims' ashes.

[84] The burying of the sacrificed boy under the altar.

THE TEMPLE: ITS LAY-OUT AND PROCEDURE

The attitude of the ancients towards their sanctuaries was expressed in certain laws which marked their respect for the holy places. There was, of course, a rule common to Jew and gentile that ritually unclean persons or people improperly dressed were barred from the temple premises.[1] To these the Orientals, the Greeks[2] and the Romans[3] added certain moral transgressions as well as the state of mourning over relations.[4] According to Jewish law, a man who touched a dead body is allowed to enter the Temple Mount[5] whereas a mourner is barred from it during the first two (or three) days of mourning.[6] Although the strict *Halakhah* does not exclude morally

---

[1] See A. Bickerman, *Syria* XXV, 1946–48, pp. 70–71; Lieberman *JQR* XXXVII, 1946, p. 45 nn. 32, 33. Comp., however, Herodot. II. 64.

[2] See W. M. Ramsay, *The Cities and Bishoprics of Phrygia* I, Oxford 1895, p. 149, No. 41; Th. Wächter, *Reinheitsvorschriften im griechischen Kult*, Giesen 1910, p. 8 ff.; E. Fehrle, *Die kultische Keuschheit im Altertum*, p. 231 ff.; P. Stengel, *Die griechischen Kultusaltertümer*[3], p. 155 ff.; A. D. Nock, *Harvard Theological Review* XXVII, 1934, p. 73, n. 61; S. Spiegel, ibid., p. 121 ff.

[3] See B. Brissonius, *de formulis et solemnibus populi Romani verbis*, I, IV, p. 4; Th. Wächter ibid., p. 10, n. 2; Wissowa, *Religion und Kultus der Römer*[2], p. 416, n. 3.

[4] κῆδος. See Dittenberger, *Syl.*[3], 982 and 983; Wächter ibid. pp. 49, n. 1, 56 ff. and 62; Frazer, *The Golden Bough, Adonis, Attis, Osiris* II, New York 1935, p. 228, n. 1. Death *per se* seems to impart a kind of contamination to the relations of the deceased. When Xenophon in the course of sacrificing heard that his son fell in battle he stopped and removed the garland from his head. He resumed the act only when he decided that the glorious death of his son was not to be lamented (Plut. *cons. ad Apoll.* 119a, passim). Similarly in Jewish law mourning, legally, is not related to contact with the dead or attendance at the funeral. The relative of the dead becomes a mourner even when the corpse has not been recovered (as in case of drowning).

[5] *Mishnah Kelim* I. 8.

[6] See below. Contact with a dead body makes the person unclean whether he is related to the deceased or not. Sight of a corpse in the open or presence at a funeral four cubits away from the corpse does not impart uncleanliness.

unclean persons[7] or people in mourning[8] from the Temple, there is good ground to assume that in practice they were barred from the sanctuary at some time during the second commonwealth. The minor tract *Semaḥoth*[9] states that a mourner is not to enter the Temple Mount during the first two (or three) days of his mourning.[10] From *TB*[11] it appears that his exclusion from the Temple proper lasted all the seven days of mourning.[12]

A restriction is imposed only on the High Priest who is not allowed to attend a funeral or to see the coffin (*Mishnah Sanhedrin* II. 1). Comp. Lucian, *de Syria dea* 53.

[7] See *Mishnah Bekhoroth* VII. 7 and *Tosafoth Yom Tob* ibid. Comp. *Tosafoth Yebamoth* 7a s. v. שנאמר, referred to by Rabbi 'Akiba Eiger a. l.

[8] According to Biblical law the period of mourning (אנינה) associated with the partaking of some sacred food (see Lev. 10:19; Deut. 26:14) may have consisted of one day only. Distress caused only by death (of a near relative) imparted some kind of contamination. (*TP Pesaḥim* VIII. 8, 36b and parallels: אין אנינה טמאה אלא למת בלבד). Of course, it had nothing to do with contact with the dead body, see above, n. 6.

[9] VI. 11, ed. Higger, p. 134. Comp. the reading of Naḥmanides, תורת האדם ed. Venice, 71a.

[10] Comp. *Mishnah Mo'ed Katan* III. 5 and *TP* ibid. 82b; *Bereshith Rabba* C. 8, p. 1290 and notes ibid.; *Semaḥoth* ibid. 2–7. From all these sources it is obvious that in post-Biblical times the first stages of mourning lasted two or three days. Comp. העמק שאלה on שאילתות, Jerusalem 1948, p. 196 and note ibid.

[11] *Mo'ed Katan* 15b; *Tosefta Zebaḥim* XI. 1, 495 27 and my note in *Tosefeth Rishonim* II, p. 214.

[12] The only exception was made for the High Priest. He remained in the Temple even during the time of his mourning (Lev. 10:7; 21:12. See *Mishnah Sanhedrin* II. 1; *Tosefta Zebaḥim* XI. 3, 495 31 and parallels). *TB* (*Mo'ed Katan* 14b) formulates it: כהן גדול דכל השנה כרגל לכולי עלמא דמי, "A High Priest all through the year is like any other person on a holiday". Gellius (X. 15. 16) defines the status of the Flamen Dialis in identical terms: Dialis cotidie feriatus est. "Every day is a holiday for the Dialis". The same applied to the Rex sacrorum. See Macrob. *Sat.* I. 16. 9; G. Wissowa, *Religion und Kultus der Römer*[2], p. 507, n. 1.

In ancient times the Flamen Dialis was not allowed to pass a single night outside of Rome (Liv. V. 52. 13. See Wissowa ibid., p. 505, n. 5). The Jewish High Priest was not allowed to leave Jerusalem (Maimonides in כלי המקדש V. 7, from an unknown source. Comp. *Mishnah Sanhedrin* II. 1). The Dialis never enters a place of burial and never touches a dead body (Gellius ibid.). The same is true of the Jewish High Priest (Lev. 21:11). The death of the Dialis' wife deprives him of his sacrificial office for ever (see Wissowa ibid.,

The *Targum*[13] expressly states that sinful persons (חטאיא
וחייביא) do not enter the [Holy] House.[14] It likewise appears from
the *Mishnah*[15] that an excommunicated person was barred from
entering the Temple.[16]

For our purpose the ruling of an old *Mishnah* is even more
instructive. We read there:[17] כל הנכנסים להר הבית נכנסין דרך ימין
ומקיפין ויוצאין דרך שמאל חוץ ממי שאירעו דבר שהוא מקיף לשמאל. מה
'לך מקיף לשמאל. שאני אבל . . . שאני מנודה וכו "Whoever enters the
Temple Mount enters on the right, goes round, and leaves from
the left,[18] save any whom aught befell, for he goes round to the
left. 'What aileth thee that thou goest to the left?' 'Because
I am a mourner . . . Because I am under a ban' etc." As said
before, the mourner and the person under a ban were not allowed
to enter the Temple itself, but in the Temple Mount[19] they
turned to the left because the left was a token of misfor-
tune. Here again we come across the general attitude of the
time.

The proper behavior in entering a temple, according to the
Pythagorean symbol, was to enter from the right and leave
from the left,[20] exactly like the statement of our *Mishnah*. The

p. 506, n. 4, end). The death of the wife of the Jewish High Priest prevents
him from officiating in the Temple on the Day of Atonement. See *Mishnah
Yoma* I. 1. The other particulars of the Dialis enumerated by Gellius (X. 15)
were not shared by the Jewish High Priest.

[13] II Sam. 5:8. Comp. Ps. 24:3–4 and Spiegel, *op. c.* (above, n. 2, end), 126.

[14] Comp. also *Targum* to Cant. 6:6. The cleanliness from the defilement
of robbery mentioned there refers to the priests and Levites and not to the
sacrifices and tithes.

[15] *'Eduyoth* V. 8 (according to the correct explanation of G. Allon, *Tarbiz*
IX, 1938, p. 278 ff.).

[16] Comp. also Joseph. *Ant.* XIX. VII. 4, 332; ibid. VIII. III. 9, 96 and
G. Allon ibid., p. 279, n. 10, and p. 283, n. 20. See also the interpolation in
contra Ap. II. XXVI, 205.

[17] *Middoth* II. 2. Comp. *TP Sukkah*, V. 8, 55d.

[18] Comp. also *Mishnah Zebaḥim* VI. 3; *TB* ibid. 64b.

[19] The mourner was admitted to it after the second (or the third) day of
his mourning, but was barred from the Temple itself for five (or four) days
more; see above.

[20] Jambl. *de vit. 'Pyth.* 156: εἰσιέναι δὲ εἰς τὰ ἱερὰ κατὰ τοὺς δεξιοὺς
τόπους παραγγέλει, ἐξιέναι κατὰ τοὺς ἀριστερούς. Comp. Ezek. 46:8–9.

use of the left was standard in chthonian rites,[21] which is in keeping with the behavior of the mourner and the excommunicated person. The Jews paid no heed to the original meaning of the custom. In the course of time it became merely a pattern of behavior, and the Jews did not hesitate to follow it.[22]

A *Baraitha*[23] reads: נעשית[24] ריבות ושתים ובשמונים "[The veil of the Temple] was made by eighty-two young girls." A mediaeval author[25] explains that "the girls did not reach the age of puberty (*menses muliebres*), and were consequently ritually pure." A. Büchler called attention[26] to the Syriac Apocalypse of Baruch (X.19) and to *Pesikta Rabbathi*[27] where it is clearly stated that the girls who were weaving the veil of the Temple were virgins. S. Krauss[28] correctly associated the reading of our *Mishnah* with the story in *Protevangelium Iacobi* (X.1). It is related there that the council of the priests (συμβούλιον τῶν ἱερέων) decided to make a veil for the Temple. And the priest said: καλέσατέ μοι ὀκτὼ[29] παρϑένους ἀμιάντους ἀπὸ τῆς φυλῆς Δαυίδ κτλ. "Call unto me eight undefiled virgins[30]

[21] See S. Eitrem, *Opferritus und Voropfer d. Griechen und Römer*, Kristiania 1915, p. 41 ff. R. 'Akiba alluded to this chthonian rite in his reference to the *Minim* (*Tosefta Yoma* III. 2, 18511 *TB* ibid. 40a; see סופרים דקדוקי a. l.). It is obvious (see *TB* ibid.) that the question necessarily involved the moving of the Scape-goat to the left. Comp. also *Mishnah Parah* III. 3 and *Tosefta* ibid. 63137 and see below n. 33.

[22] See the excellent review article by A. D. Nock, "Sarcophagi and Symbolism" in the *American Journal of Archaeology* vol. L, 1946, p. 150, n. 4.

[23] Interpolated in the *Mishnah, Shekalim* VIII. 5. See J. N. Epstein המשנה לנוסח מבוא, p. 952.

[24] This is the correct reading, see Epstein ibid.

[25] The commentary on *Tamid* (29b) ascribed to *RABAD*.

[26] *JQR* XVI, 1904, p. 20, n. 1.

[27] XXVI, ed. Friedmann, 131a.

[28] *Festschrift in honor of A. Harkavy*, German part, p. 177 (addenda and corrigenda to p. 62, n. 5). Comp. *Tarbiz* XI, 25, n. 3; ibid., p. 223.

[29] Some mss. read ἑπτά, seven; some omit the number, but from the continuation of the story it is clear that there were eight virgins.

[30] Here παρϑένοι ἀμίαντοι most probably mean לדמים בתולות, virgins who never menstruated (comp. *Mishnah Niddah* I. 4). See *Protev.* ibid. VI.1: τὰς ϑυγατέρας τῶν 'Εβραίων τὰς ἀμιάντους, where it means small girls who did not yet reach the age of puberty. This sense is particularly obvious in VIII. 2, where it is stated that when Mary became twelve years old (i. e. the age of

of the tribe of David etc." The author who maintained that when called to participate in the work of the veil Mary was twelve years old probably wished to emphasize that she was morally undefiled.[31] But in the light of the rabbinic sources it is obvious that the information about the παρθένοι ἀμίαντοι (in its technical sense) was probably taken from a well informed Jewish source. As suggested above, παρθένοι ἀμίαντοι in the strict sense of the word means "virgins who have not yet menstruated" regardless of their age. But in our case it means virgins who have not reached the age of puberty, a very natural precaution when working on an object of the sanctuary.[32] The virgins were below the age of twelve,[33] the normal age of puberty.

To sum up. A college of eighty-two[34] noble virgins below the age of puberty participated in the weaving of the veil of the Temple;[35] they drew their salaries from the treasury of the Temple.[36] The veils on which there were embroidered lions and eagles[37] were exhibited to the public before they were used in the Temple.[38]

This, of course, reminds us of the girls who wove the Peplos

---

puberty), the priests decided to remove her from the Temple, because "she may pollute the sanctuary of the Lord". (μήπως μιάνῃ τὸ ἁγίασμα κυρίου. Cod. C: μήπως ἐπέλθῃ αὐτῇ τὰ γυναικῶν καὶ μιάνῃ κτλ.).

[31] X. 1: ἀμίαντος ἦν τῷ θεῷ.

[32] See *Tosefta Kelim, Baba Bathra* I. 2, 590₂₁ (and parallels).

[33] A similar procedure was adopted in the preparation of the water of purification. Small boys of seven or eight acted as the water carriers (*Tosefta Parah* III. 2, 631₃₂, according to the correct reading of the mediaeval authorities; see Lieberman, *Tosefeth Rishonim* III, p. 215). Comp. Th. Hopfner, *Griechisch-Aegyptischer Offenbarungszauber* I, p. 236 No. 846. See above, n. 21.

[34] It is a round number; comp. *TP Berakhoth* II. 5, 4d, bot. The remark of Samuel (*TP Shekalim* VIII. 4, 51b; *TB Tamid* 29a) about the exaggerated numbers refers to the end of our *Mishnah*, and not to the number of the girls, which is an interpolation in our *Mishnah*; see above n. 23 and comp. the commentary of Rabbi Judah b. Barsilai of Barcelona on ספר יצירה, p. 27 ff.

[35] Two veils were prepared every year; see *Mishnah* ibid. Comp. *Tosefta* ibid. III. 15, p. 178₂₇.

[36] *Tosefta* ibid. II. 6 and parallels.

[37] *TP* ibid. 51b. Comp. Joseph. *bel. iud.* V. 5. 4, 212.

[38] *Mishnah* ibid. 4.

of Athene. They all were of noble birth, and some of them were between seven and eleven years old.[39] The number of the workers (ἐργαστῖναι) on the robe sometimes grew to one hundred or one hundred and twenty.[40] When finished, the robe of Athene was carried in procession at the Panathenaic festival.[41]

The similarity between the Jewish way of weaving the veil of the Temple and the Athenian manner of preparing the Peplos is quite striking. However, we have no sound grounds to establish any connection between the two. It is quite natural that weaving and embroidery are done by women, and it is altogether normal for sacred objects to be guarded from possible contamination. Since girls are subject to periodic uncleanliness it is certainly in the nature of things that young virgins who did not reach the age of puberty be chosen for handling the sacred objects. It is again a pattern naturally common to human sanctuaries.

It is well known that much of the external architecture of the Temple of Herod was in Greek style.[42] It is obvious from the Hellenistic sources that the Temple served as a depository for private citizens.[43] The *Mishnah*[44] states: "Hillel the Elder ordained that he[45] could deposit[46] his money in the [Temple] chamber." It is safe to assume that this money was deposited in the Treasury Chamber of the Temple.[47]

---

[39] *Etym. magn.* 149.19: τέσσαρες δὲ παῖδες ἐχειροτονοῦντο κατ᾽ εὐγένειαν ἀρρηφόροι, ἀπὸ ἐτῶν ἐπτὰ μέχρις ἔνδεκα. See A. Mommsen, *Heortologie*, p. 184 ff.; Frazer, Pausanias II, 574 ff.; ibid. III, 592 ff.; L. Deubner, *Attische Feste*, Berlin 1932, p. 11 ff. and Plate I. 1 ibid.

[40] See Frazer ibid. II, p. 575, n. 6.

[41] See Deubner ibid., p. 29 ff.

[42] See Schürer, *Geschichte* etc. II⁴, p. 64 ff.

[43] II Macc. III. 10; Jos. *bell. iud.* VI. 5. 2, 282; See Schürer *Geschichte* etc. II⁴, p. 325 ff.; E. Bickerman, *Annuaire de l'Institut de Philol. et d'Hist. Orientales et Slaves* VII (1939–44), p. 14 ff.

[44] *'Arakhin* IX. 4.

[45] I. e. the seller of a house who wishes to protect his right to redeem it.

[46] חולש, literally: to cast in.

[47] The money was probably put in a vessel together with a note containing the name of the man to whose credit the money was deposited. See Bickerman, *ibid.*, p. 18.

In addition to the regular yearly payment to the Temple there were, of course, special contributions in gold made by Jews.[48] These often included *ex voto* offerings in gold. A rich woman, for instance, once made a vow that if her daughter recovered from her illness she would give the equivalent of her weight in gold [to the Temple].[49] A special chest in the Temple was designated for those who wanted to contribute gold[50] לכפרת which perhaps means "For redemption."[51] This gold was used to make golden plates for the Holy of Holies only,[52] and apparently could not be spent on Temple repairs (בדק הבית) in general.

Gold was also contributed in the form of leaves, berries and clusters which were hung on the golden vine standing over the entrance to the Sanctuary.[53] The golden chain dedicated by king Agrippa to the Temple[54] was probably also a votive offering as an expression of gratitude.[55] All this gold was not stored in one chamber.[56] There is also no evidence of the existence of a special chamber exclusively for the *Shekalim*.[57]

It appears that the same rooms contained not only coins but gold-dust as well. If we are right in our assumption we shall the better understand the precautions taken against the man who entered the Treasury Chamber for the purpose of taking part of the *Terumah*.[58] He was not allowed to wear a tunic with

---

[48] For contributions of gentiles, see Schürer ibid. p. 360 ff.

[49] *Tosefta 'Arakhin* III. 1, 54526. Comp. *Mishnah* ibid. V. 1.

[50] *Mishnah Shekalim* VI. 5–6 and *TP* ibid.

[51] I. e. *ex voto* offerings; see commentaries and מלאכת שלמה a. l.; *Aruch Completum* s. v. כפר, p. 305a.

[52] See *Tosefta* ibid. III. 6, 1787 and variants ibid.

[53] *Mishnah Middoth* III. 8. On the golden vine see Jos., *antiq.* XV. 11. 3, 395; *bel. iud.* V. 5. 4, 210. Comp. the numerous parallels quoted by A. B. Cook, *Zeus* II, p. 281, n. 4.

[54] Joseph. *antiq.* XIX. 6. 1, 294.

[55] Herodot. relates (I. 90) that Croesus sent his shackles to Delphi as a reproach to the gods.

[56] See *Mishnah Shekalim* V. 6.

[57] See Exod. 30:13.

[58] On the access to the Treasury Chamber, see *Tosefta* ibid. II. 15, 1776 and *TP* ibid. V. 3, 49a. Comp. *Tosefeth Rishonim* I, p. 182.

folds[59] or to wear shoes or sandals.[60] He was compelled to talk all during his stay in the Chamber,[61] in order not to be suspected of putting money in his mouth. In addition, his body, *including his hair*, was inspected upon his leaving the Chamber.[62] A man with long curly hair[63] was altogether barred from taking of the *Terumah*,[64] lest he be suspected of hiding gold in his hair.[65]

All these precautions remind us of the anecdote told by Herodotus[66] about Alcmeon whom Croesus permitted to take out of his treasury as much gold as he could carry on his person. The former put on a wide tunic leaving a deep fold in it[67] and shod himself with the most spacious buskins that he could find. He then packed the fold of his tunic and his buskins with gold-dust; in addition, he strewed dust in the hair of his head and

---

[59] פרגוד חפות, παραγώδης. The spelling παραγώδης is found several times in one ms. of Ioannes Lydus' *de magist. pop. rom.* (see the variants in ed. Wuensch, pp. 21, n. 20; 58, n. 22; 69, n. 7). The word חפות is explained by 'Arukh (s. v. חפ) to mean "with sleeves". According to Lydus (ibid. I. 17): παραγαῦδαι (or: παραγώδαι), χιτῶνες ... περιχερίδας ἔχοντες. "The *paragaudae* ... are tunics with sleeves". However ps.-Rashi to *Bereshith Rabba* LXXV. 5 and a marginal note in cod. Oxf. a. l. (see Theodor-Albeck ibid., p. 883, n. 5) explain חפה as synonymous with חיק, κόλπος, *sinus*, bosom. Comp. also *Aruch Completum* III, p. 468. I therefore prefer to render פרגוד חפות — like παραγώδης κολπωτός — a "bosomed" tunic, a tunic with folds. Comp. the χιτὼν κολπωτός (usually worn by women) mentioned by Plut., *reg. et imp. apophth.* 173c.

[60] *Mishnah Shekalim* III. 2. Comp. *TB Yebamoth* 102b.

[61] *Tosefta Shekalim* II. 1, 175₉; *TP* ibid. III. 2, 47c.

[62] *TP* ibid.

[63] קווץ. Maimonides trying to rationalize the tradition explained the word to mean a poor man who is sick and tired of life, and who might be suspected of stealing in a fit of despair. All the other commentaries rejected this interpretation of the word and took קווץ in its usual meaning. See, for instance, Me'iri a. l., p. 74.

[64] *TP* ibid.

[65] This injunction may have been only purely theoretical, but it is reported in the name of R. Ishmael who in his youth must have attended the Herodian Temple. As the son of a high priest (see *Tosefta Halla* I. 10, 98₁₀) he most probably knew the nature of the gold deposited in the Treasury Chamber.

[66] VI. 125.

[67] ἐνδὺς κιθῶνα μέγαν καὶ κόλπον βαθὺν καταλιπόμενος τοῦ κιθῶνος.

took more of it in his mouth.[68] The injunction on a man with
long curly hair not to enter the Treasury Chamber (despite the
usual search) could make sense only if the Chamber contained
gold-dust.

We do not know the exact location of the Treasury Chambers,[69] but we have good reason to assume that they were
behind the innermost recesses of the Temple.[70] We read in the
Sifre:[71] מקום היה אחורי בית הפרוכת[72] ששם בודקים יוחסי כהונה "There
was a place behind the Holy of Holies where the priestly gene-
alogy was investigated." However, according to the Mishnah[73]
and the Tosefta[74] they investigated the priestly pedigree in the
Lishkath Haggazith which was situated in the North end (or the
South end) of the Temple.[75] Nevertheless there is no divergence
of opinion between the sources. It is obvious from the Mishnah
and the Tosefta (ibid.) that the final investigation of the priestly
lineage took place in the Lishkath Haggazith, and there the decision of the High Court[76] was rendered. The chamber behind
the Holy of Holies was used for the preliminary examination of
the pertinent documents which were deposited in this chamber.
This is the regular ὀπισϑόδομος, the back chamber, common
to the gentile temples.[77]

Thus the Treasury Chambers were ὀπισϑόδομοι which, like
in all other temples of the time, contained among other items —
such as the votive offerings and the private deposits — the
priestly archives as well.

Let us now turn our attention to the summit of the Temple

[68] ἐς τὰς τρίχας τῆς κεφαλῆς διαπάσας τοῦ ψήγματος καὶ ἄλλο λαβὼν
ἐς τὸ στόμα.

[69] See A. Schwarz, MGWJ LXIII, 1919, p. 246 ff.

[70] See Joseph. bel. iud. V. 5. 2, 200.

[71] I, 116, ed. Horovitz, p. 133₁₂.

[72] So Yalkut and cod. Vat. Comp. Tosefta Temurah IV. 8, 556₂; ibid.
Zebaḥim VII. 1, 489₁₈; TB Yoma 21a; Zebaḥim 55b; Temurah 30b passim.

[73] Middoth, end.

[74] Ḥagigah II. 9, 235₁₇ and parallels.

[75] Middoth V. 4 and variants ibid. Comp. Schürer, Geschichte etc. II⁴,
p. 264.

[76] For in this place its regular sessions were held.

[77] See Van Buren in PW RE XVIII, p. 686 ff. s. v. Opisthodomos.

building in Jerusalem. The *Mishnah*[78] states that on its roof the Temple had a "raven-scarer" (כלה עורב) one cubit high. The form of the scarecrow is not described in the early rabbinic sources.[79] Rabbenu Shemaiah a. l. explains that it was spikes fixed in the roof. This opinion agrees with the description of Josephus who stated:[80] "From its top protruded sharp golden[81] spikes to prevent birds from setting upon and polluting the roof." Eupolemus,[82] in his portrayal of Solomon's Temple, related:[83] "He made also two brazen rings of chain work, and set them upon machinery rising twenty cubits in height above the Temple, and they cast a shadow over the whole Temple; and to each net-work he hung four hundred brass bells of a talent in weight, and the net-works he made solid that the bells might sound and frighten away the birds,[84] that they might not settle upon the Temple nor nest upon the panels of the gates and porches, and defile the Temple with their dung."[85] This description by Eupolemus has no historic value, for it is based on the translation of the Septuagint.[86] The translators probably ascribed

---

[78] *Middoth* IV. 6.

[79] See the various commentaries quoted and referred to by Kohut, *Aruch Completum* IV, p. 226, s. v. כל.

[80] *Bel. iud.* V. 5. 6, 224: κατὰ κορυφὴν δὲ χρυσέους ὀβελοὺς ἀνεῖχεν τεθηγμένους, ὡς μή τινι προσκαθεζομένῳ μολύνοιτο τῶν ὀρνέων.

[81] According to *TB Shabbath* 90a and *Menahoth* 107a the "raven scarer" was of iron.

[82] According to Euseb., *praep. ev.* 451, ed. Gifford I, p. 562; Freudenthal, *Hellenistische Studien* II, p. 298. Prof. E. Bickerman kindly referred me to the description of Eupolemus.

[83] ποιῆσαι δὲ καὶ δακτυλίους δύο χαλκοῦς ἀλυσιδωτούς, καὶ στῆσαι αὐτοὺς ἐπὶ μηχανημάτων ὑπερεχόντων τῷ ὕψει τὸν ναὸν πήχεις κ', καὶ σκιάζειν ἐπάνω παντὸς τοῦ ἱεροῦ· καὶ προσκρεμάσαι ἑκάστῃ δικτύϊ κώδωνας χαλκοῦς ταλαντιαίους τετρακοσίους· καὶ ποῆσαι ὅλας τὰς δικτύας πρὸς τὸ ψοφεῖν τοὺς κώδωνας καὶ ἀποσοβεῖν τὰ ὄρνεα, ὅπως μὴ καθίζῃ ἐπὶ τοῦ ἱεροῦ, μηδὲ νοσσεύῃ ἐπὶ τοῖς φατνώμασι τῶν πυλῶν καὶ στοῶν, καὶ μολύνῃ τοῖς ἀποπατήμασι τὸ ἱερόν.

[84] Heracles in one of his labors chased away the birds of the Stymphalian lake by a bronze rattle which made a terrible noise. See Diod. Sic. IV. 13. 2.

[85] The translation is of Gifford ibid. III, p. 479.

[86] II Chr. 4:12–13. See Gifford ibid. IV, p. 371.

to the Temple of Solomon the existence of a mechanism used in the Egyptian temples of their time.[87]

The very opposite is maintained by Rabbenu Hananel[88] who contended that the Temple of Solomon had no raven-scarer at all.[89] He drew his conclusion from II *Aboth deR. Nathan*[90] which, among the miracles wrought in the Temple, counts: ולא נמצא זבוב בבית המטבחים ... ולא עבר העוף(ר) על גביו "And no fly was found in the slaughterhouse [of the Temple],[91] . . . and no bird passed over the Sanctuary." From this statement the Rabbi inferred that there was no need for a raven-scarer in the Temple of Solomon.[92] However nobody will doubt the evidence given by the *Mishnah* and Josephus that the Herodian Temple did have a raven-scarer on its top.

Furthermore, it is recorded in the *Baraitha di-Mlekheth ha-Mishkan*[93] that the *altar* of the Tabernacle was provided with a raven-scarer.[94] All this will be properly understood in the light of sanctuary buildings of the time.

It is a well established fact that the ancient statues very often had discs[95] or spikes[96] on top to protect them from pollution by birds. In particular similar measures had to be taken in temples.[97] Pausanias counts among the wonders of the altar at Olympia that "the kites molest none of the people who sacrifice at Olympia."[98] Plinius likewise tells that the kites never

---

[87] See below.   [88] *TB Shabbath* 57b.

[89] See *Tosafoth 'Arakhin* 6a, s. v. כגון.

[90] XXXIX, ed. Schechter, p. 105.

[91] See *Mishnah Aboth* V. 5.

[92] According to the opinion of R. Jose b. Bun (in *TP Yoma* I. 4, 39a) the miracles took place in Solomon's Temple only. But see below.

[93] XI, ed. M. Friedmann, p. 71. It is a *Tannaitic* source; see Friedmann ibid. p. 7. The date of the final compilation is unknown.

[94] The reading is attested by the mss. and quotations from mediaeval authors; see ibid., p. 73; its authenticity is beyond question.

[95] Schol. to Aristoph. *aves* 1114. See H. Lechat, Μηνίσκος, in *Bulletin de Correspondance Hellénique* XIV, 1890, p. 337 ff.

[96] See the figures reproduced in Daremberg et Saglio *Dictionnaire* etc. III, pp. 1718–19.

[97] See E. Petersen, *Athen. Mittheil.* XIV, 1889, p. 233 ff.

[98] V. 14. 1: οἱ γὰρ ἰκτῖνες . . . ἀδικοῦσιν οὐδὲν ἐν Ὀλυμπίᾳ τοὺς θύοντας.

snatch any edible from the altar at Olympia.[99] Lucretius[100] maintains that crows (*cornices*) never approached the temple of Pallas Tritonia on the Acropolis of Athens even "when the altars were smoking with offerings."[101] Petersen[102] cleverly remarked that these miracles were based on facts. Effective precautions were taken to make it impossible for big birds of prey to nest or even to rest in the temples and their vicinity. Sharp spikes were planted on the flat surfaces which prevented the big birds from resting on them. And then the miracle happened; those feathered creatures got out of the habit of dwelling near the temples and consequently did not annoy the sacrificers too much.

The same situation existed in Jerusalem.[103] The flesh of the sacrifices was salted on the Ramps (כבש) of the altar.[104] Many victims were burnt on the altar which stood in an open place,[105] and the odor certainly attracted the big birds of prey. Kites[106] and ravens abound in Palestine. The audacity of the kites is well known. Aristotle relates:[107] "They say that [in Elis] there are kites which snatch the meat from persons carrying it through the market-place, but do not touch the flesh offered in sacrifice." Similarly it is told in *TP*:[108] "A man was carrying meat

---

[99] *Nat. hist.* X. 12. 28 (referred to by Frazer, III, p. 558): Milvi . . . nihil esculenti rapere numquam . . . Olympiae ex ara.

[100] *De rerum nat.* VI, 750.

[101] Non cum fumant altaria donis. Comp. also below, n. 107.

[102] Ibid. (see above n. 97), p. 235.

[103] The stone which was in the Holy of Holies in the Jerusalem Sanctuary (the *Eben Shetiyyah*) was considered by the Jews as the navel of the world. It was the Jewish μεσόμφαλος, γῆς ὄμφαλος, like the Navel-stone of the Greeks. See Frazer, Pausanias, vol. V, pp. 318–319; Eisler, *Philologus* LXVIII, p. 117 ff.; Feuchtwang *MGWJ* LIV, 1910, p. 719 ff.; ibid. LV, 1911, p. 43 ff.; Ginzberg, *Legends of the Jews*, V, p. 15 ff.

[104] *Tosefta Menaḥoth* VI. 3, 519₂₆; *TB* ibid., 21b.

[105] See the commentary of Rabbi Simeon Duran on *Aboth* V. 5, s. v. ולא כבו.

[106] The LXX translates the Hebrew דיה (Deut. 14:13) ἰκτῖνος.

[107] *Mirab.* 123, 842a: εἶναι δέ φασι, παρ' αὐτοῖς καὶ ἰκτίνους, οἳ παρὰ μὲν τῶν διὰ τῆς ἀγορᾶς τὰ κρέα φερόντων ἁρπάζουσι, τῶν δὲ ἱεροθύτων οὐχ ἅπτονται.

[108] *Shekalim* VII. 5, 50c; '*Abod. Zar.* II. 9, 41d. Comp. *TB Baba Mezi'a* 24b.

in the market place;[109] a kite appeared and snatched it from him."[110]

In order to keep the birds away from the Temple area, "raven-scarers" were probably planted not only on the roof of the Temple but also near the altar (see above), on the stoas and columns.[111] All these precautions helped the miracle, and indeed no bird flew over the Temple.

Pausanias, after recounting the wonderful behavior of the kites in regard to the altar of Olympia, adds[112] that the Eleans are said to sacrifice to Zeus the Averter of Flies (Ἀπόμυιος) when they are about to drive the flies out of Olympia.[113] We have seen[114] that the rabbinic source also connects the same two miracles, that no fly was found in the slaughterhouse of the Temple and that no bird flew over the Sanctuary.

The birds were averted with the aid of "raven-scarers," but the Jews had neither an Ἀπόμυιος (Fly-averter) nor a Μυίαγρος (Fly-catcher).[115] They had no need of them. The dry Jerusalem climate and the draughty air on the Temple Mount offered sufficient help to the miracle, and no flies were seen in the slaughterhouse. Some of the ancient Rabbis explicitly expressed their opinion to this effect. Very strict measures were taken[116] to prevent the High Priest from a *pollutio nocturna* on the Day of Atonement, although according to the miracles of the Temple[117] such a thing would never happen to

---

[109] Somewhere in Babylonia.

[110] חד בר נש הוה מהלך בשוקא טעין קופד אתא דייתא וחטפתיה מיניה.

[111] I have not been able to find a parallel to Eupolemus' "raven-scarer" in the form of bells. This was probably one of the many inventions of the Alexandrian mechanics who by some device placed the bells high above the temple. The bells perhaps operated by force of the wind.

[112] V. 14. 2.

[113] Frazer a. l. III, p. 558, adduces a series of parallels from Greek and Latin authors who assert that the flies disappear (or perish) immediately after the sacrifice is offered.

[114] Above, p. 174.

[115] Some special ingredients were probably included in the sacrifices to these gods, the smell of which either exterminated or drove away the flies.

[116] See *Mishnah Yoma* I. 4; *TP* ibid. 39a; *TB* ibid. 18a

[117] *Mishnah Aboth* V. 5 and parallels.

the High Priest on that day. R. Abun remarked[118] that those precautions had to be taken because it is written (Deut. 6:16): *"Ye shall not try the Lord your God."*[119] A miracle is well deserved only when all the proper natural actions have been performed to create the miracle.[120]

Usually the ancients did not deny the miraculous "facts" which happened in the temples. Although the Jews tried to rationalize some wonders performed in heathen temples[121] they did not deny the stories themselves. Measures were taken all over the ancient world to make miracles possible in the temples, and the resulting wonders were accepted everywhere in the same spirit.

We shall now conclude with the later mechanical improvements introduced into the Temple of Jerusalem. The *Mishnah*[122] relates: "Ben Katin[123] made twelve stop-cocks for the laver (כיור, LXX: λουτήρ) which before had but two. He also made a device (μηχανή[124]) for the laver that its water should not be rendered unfit by remaining overnight." The nature of this μηχανή is not clear. We know from the *Mishnah*[125] that it was made of wood, and that, according to a Rabbi of the fourth century,[126] it had a wheel by which the huge mass of the laver

---

[118] *TP* ibid.

[119] A more forceful remark about another miracle in the Temple is available in *TP* Shekalim VI. 4, 50a. Comp. also *TB Pesaḥim* 64b.

[120] As a matter of fact Josephus relates (*Ant.* XVII. 6. 4, 166) that a *pollutio nocturna* once did happen to the High Priest, a fact also corroborated by I *Aboth deR. Nathan* (XXXV, ed. Schechter, p. 105) and by *TP* (*Yoma* I. 1, 38d top and parallels; see Ratner אהבת ציון וירושלים a. l. p. 8). See Schürer, *Geschichte* etc. II⁴, p. 270, n. 7. But exceptions do not invalidate a miracle (comp. also the *Baraitha* quoted in *TB Pesaḥim* 64b); it is simply a bad portent. See Pausanias V. XIV. 1.

[121] See *Debarim Rabba* ed. Lieberman, p. 75 and n. 7 ibid.

[122] *Yoma* III. 10.

[123] See Ratner (אהבת ציון וירושלים) on *TP Yoma*, p. 60) who tries to identify him with Ben Gamala mentioned in the preceding *Mishnah*. On the latter see Schürer, *Geschichte* etc. II⁴, p. 273 and n. 21 ibid.

[124] מוכני or מיכני; see *Der Mišna-Traktat Tamid*, ed. A. Brody, p. 48, n. 44; ibid. 62, n. 22; H. L. Ginsberg, *MGWJ* LXXVII, 1933, p. 423, n. 3.

[125] *Tamid* I. 4; III. 8.

[126] *TB Yoma* 37a.

full of water was moved.[127] According to some tradition, a μηχανή was also employed to lift the Red Heifer on the pile of wood, where it was to be slaughtered.[128]

The sources do not state whether the μηχαναί were prepared in Palestine or imported from the outside. From the Tosefta[129] we know that the bronze gates of Nicanor were imported from Alexandria.[130] When some vessels of the Jerusalem Sanctuary got out of order, the authorities resorted to artisans from Alexandria.[131] Specialists from that city were brought to Jerusalem for the purpose of baking the Show-bread and preparing the incense,[132] but they failed in their mission. Thus we see that the Temple authorities frequently utilized the skill of the Alexandrian professionals.

Now Hero Alexandrinus relates[133] that at the entrance of the Egyptian temples the vessel containing lustral water (περιρραντήριον[134]) was supplied with a bronze wheel, and when the wheel was turned the water for sprinkling flowed from the vessel.[135] The wheel in the laver at the Herodian Temple seems to have had a different function (see above). The devices of the Egyptian priests went so far as to introduce an automaton for selling holy water; after dropping one coin of five drachmae the lustral water automatically flowed out.[136] The mechanism of this automaton was very simple,[137] and its production would be

---

[127] Comp. however, Maimonides' commentary a. l.

[128] Tosefta Parah III. 9, 623₂₄. Comp. Tosefeth Rishonim III, p. 218.

[129] Yoma II. 4, 183₂₂; TB ibid. 18a.

[130] See Schürer Geschichte etc. II⁴, p. 64, n. 165.

[131] Tosefta 'Arakhin II. 3–4, 544₂₀ ff. and parallels.

[132] Tosefta Yoma II. 5–6, 183 ff. and parallels.

[133] Pneumatica XXXII, ed. Schmidt, p. 148.

[134] See P. Stengel, Die griechischen Kultusaltertümer³, p. 22, n. 6; E. Bickerman, Syria XXV, 1946–48, p. 71, n. 1.

[135] ἐπιστραφέντος τοῦ τροχοῦ ὕδωρ ἐξ αὐτοῦ ἐπιρρέειν εἰς τὸ περριρραίνεσθαι.

[136] Hero ibid. XXI: εἰς ἔνια σπονδεῖα πενταδράχμου νομίσματος ἐμβληθέντος, ὕδωρ ἀπορρέει εἰς τὸ περριρραίνεσθαι. Comp. the editor's note on p. 111, n. 1. See also H. Diels, Antike Technik, Leipzig und Berlin 1924, p. 68 and n. 3 ibid.

[137] See the description of Hero and fig. 22 ibid. Comp. also Diels ibid., p. 69.

very inexpensive. The μηχανή of the laver in the Jerusalem Temple was probably not automatic,[138] but it was a new device which was possibly constructed by the Alexandrian mechanics who invented the various contrivances for the περιρραντήρια of the Egyptian temples.

Again we see that the many ways of behavior in the Temple of Jerusalem, many features in its structure and furniture were common to all the sanctuaries of the time. This, of course, detracts nothing of the exclusive holiness of the place; it only increases its many attractions by appealing to human nature and feeling.

[138] An automatic device which was counted among the wonders of the world existed in Jerusalem, according to Pausanias VIII. 16. 4. Comp. Th. Reinach, *Textes d'Auteurs Grecs et Romains Relatives au Judaïsme*, p. 172.

THE NATURAL SCIENCE OF THE RABBIS

The problem of how well the Rabbis of the first four centuries were informed regarding the natural sciences can certainly
not be solved in one chapter. Even a superficial perusal of the
four volumes of I. Löw,[1] or the work of Lewysohn,[2] J. Preuss[3]
and others[4] will convince the reader that many parallels exist
between the rabbinic natural science and that of the Greeks
and the Romans of that time. For our purpose it will be sufficient to discuss in this chapter some details which will tend to
demonstrate the necessity of a thorough and methodical examination of the rabbinic material bearing on this field. For no
definite opinion can be pronounced until all that the Rabbis
said about it is collected. Correct texts and exact information
as far as possible regarding time and place of the particular
scholar mentioned there must be established.

It would be of special interest to investigate the scientific
definitions of the Rabbis, their general principles and their
classification of natural facts and phenomena. For instance, the
Rabbis offer the following definition:[5] זה הכלל כל המוציא עליו
מעיקרו הרי זה מין ירק וכל שאינו מוציא עליו מעיקרו הרי זה אילן "This is
the general rule: Any plant that sheds forth its leaves from its
roots is a species of herb, and any plant that does not shed forth
its leaves from its roots is a species of tree." TP[6] elaborates:
"That which grows [branches] from its stem is a species of tree,
from its roots is a species of herb. An objection was raised

[1] Die Flora der Juden, Wien, 1926–1934.
[2] Die Zoologie des Talmuds, Frankf. a. M., 1858.
[3] Biblisch-talmudische Medizin; see below, n. 62.
[4] See Strack, Introduction to the Talmud and Midrash, p. 193 ff.
[5] Tosefta Kil'aim III. 15, 785 and parallels; see Lieberman, Tosefeth Rishonim I, p. 91 ff.
[6] Ibid. V, end, 30a: את שהוא עולה מגזעו מין אילן משרשיו מין ירק. התיבון הרי
הכרוב הרי הוא עולה מגזעו. כאן בודאי כאן בספק.

[against this definition]: Why, the cabbage branches from its stem [yet it is considered an herb]? [The reply]: The latter is a sure case,[7] and the former [applies to the] uncertain."[8] The Rabbis sought to give an exact definition of tree and herb. But by the example of the cabbage plant they demonstrated that their delimitation holds true only in doubtful cases; there are exceptions to the general rule.

Theophrastus[9] classifies all plants in four groups: trees, shrubs, under-shrubs and herbs.[10] "A tree," he says, "is a thing which grows from the root with one stem having many branches[11] and knots, and it cannot be easily uprooted ... An herb is a thing which sends forth its leaves from the root, has no [main] stem, and the seed is borne in the stalk."[12] However, immediately after this definition Theophrastus points out that the latter can be applied only generally and on the whole, for in some instances this definition overlaps. He further develops the idea[13] that an exact classification of plants is impossible, and in some cases he suggests classification by other principles, such as size, comparative robustness or length of life. The cabbage, he says, has the character of a tree since it grows only one stem (and consequently branches from it), although it is certainly not a tree.[14] For this reason, he asserts, some call the cabbage a tree-herb (δενδρολάχανον).

The Greeks and the Rabbis describe and reason in a similar way, with the difference that for the Rabbis it was not a matter

---

[7] I. e. there is a tradition that cabbage is considered an herb, and therefore we disregard the definition.

[8] I. e. the definition is applied only to uncertain cases where there is no clear tradition whether the given plant is a tree or an herb.

[9] Hist. pl. I. 3. 1.

[10] The Rabbis do not single out shrubs and under-shrubs as special classes; see Otzar Hageonim, Berakhoth I, p. 91.

[11] I. e. the branches grow from the stem and not from the roots, like the definition in TP.

[12] δένδρον μὲν οὖν ἐστι τὸ ἀπὸ ῥίζης μονοστέλεχες πολύκλαδον ὀζωτὸν οὐκ εὐαπόλυτον ... πόα δὲ τὸ ἀπὸ ῥίζης φυλλοφόρον προϊὸν ἀστέλεχες, οὗ ὁ καυλὸς σπερμοφόρος.

[13] Ibid. 4.

[14] See ibid. VI. 1. 2.

of logical classification, but an issue of practical value. For the purpose of certain rituals[15] the Jew had to know whether the particular plant is an herb or a tree. The Rabbis did not have to consult special treatises on botany for their needs. The Jewish peasant was fully acquainted with the products of the earth in his vicinity. Even abstract generalizations about plant species may have been based on observation dictated by the duty of fulfilling the laws of the Torah. It was practical life itself which gave birth to the different classifications of herbs into groups such as,[16] תבואה קיטנית ירק, cereals,[17] pulse (literally: "small vegetable")[18] and greens. In order to avoid the sowing of Kil'aim, the Rabbis arranged[19] many plants into families and species.[20]

The same religious motives prompted them to give a series of general rules regarding animals and their nature.[21] At least part of their information was based on personal observation;

---

[15] Such as 'Orlah, Kil'aim and benedictions to be pronounced before partaking of the food.

[16] Sifra Kedoshim I. 7, ed. Weiss 87b and parallels.

[17] Theophrastus (ibid. VII. 1. 1) divides the herbs into pot-herbs and cereals.

[18] It seems to be the same vegetable which in Egypt and Palestine was called λεπτολάχανον. See vita Porphyrii by Marcus the Deacon 102, and the long note in the edition of H. Grégoire and M. A. Kugener, p. 144. It was usually eaten raw (see ibid. and comp. Sifre II, 105 ed. Finkelstein, p. 1653. See the editor's note ibid., p. 16412). The Egyptian sources (Apophthegmata Patrum, PG LXV, 152c and pap. Oxyrh. 1656) mention both beans and λεπτολάχανα together. The reason is that the Egyptian beans were considered a species of greens (and not kitnith) when they were fresh (Mishnah Nedarim VII. 1) and a kind of cereal when they were dry (Tosefta ibid. IV. 3, 27917; TP ibid. 55b).

[19] Mishnah, Tosefta and TP Kil'aim.

[20] Comp. also Tosefta Nedarim III. 6–IV. 3, p. 2794–17.

[21] See Lewysohn, Zoologie des Talmuds, p. 6 ff. He seems to have overlooked the fact (p. 14) that the rule laid down by the Mishnah (Niddah VI. 9: כל שיש לו קרנים יש לו טלפים): "All animals that have horns have cloven hoofs" is recorded by Aristotle, de anim. hist. II. 2. 9, 499b16. Similarly the rule given by the Baraitha (TB Ḥullin 59a, see Lewysohn ibid.): Any animal that has no teeth in the upper jaw is certain to be ruminating and cloven footed (except the camel) is also reported by Aristotle, de part. anim. III. 14, 674a23 ff.; de anim. hist. II. 17. 5, 507a34 ff.

there were Rabbis who themselves examined the anatomy of the human body;[22] some performed experiments on animals[23] and others deduced their conclusions by simply watching the phenomena of life. For example, we read in *TB*:[24] "It was inquired:[25] Does the hair grow from its roots or at its tips . . . [Judge from the fact that] when old men dye their beards, these grow white again at the roots. From this we can infer that hair grows from the roots. This proves it." Aristotle[26] simply remarks: "If a hair be cut, it does not grow at the point of section; but it gets longer by growing upward from below."

However, some passages in rabbinic literature concerning natural science suggest that they are not the result of observation, but are borrowed from literary sources or oral information.[27] The Rabbis wished to be guided by the *Halakha* even in regard of legendary beings. They discuss whether or not the dead "Field-men"[28] and the dead sirens[29] impart impurity like human beings.

The *Mishnah*[30] rules: "If a man touches the flesh of a mouse which is half flesh and half earth he becomes unclean; but if he touches the earth he remains clean." The existence of such a mouse was taken for granted by many ancient authors.[31]

---

[22] *TB Bekhoroth* 45a.

[23] *TB Ḥullin* 57b and *Vayyikra Rabba* XX. 4; ibid. XIX. 1.

[24] *Nazir* 39a: אִיבַּעֵי לְהוּ הָאי מֵזִיא מַלְתַּחַת רַבִּי אוֹ מִלְעֵיל . . . כַּד צִבְעִין סָבֵי דִיקְנְהוֹן חוֹרִין עִיקְבֵי נִימְהוֹן שׂ׳ט מַלְתַּחַת רַבִּי שׂ׳ט.

[25] It corresponds to the Greek technical term ζητεῖται, it is asked; see above, p. 48, n. 12.

[26] *De anim. hist.* III. 11. 10, 518b: οὐκ αὐξάνεται δὲ θρὶξ ἀποτμηθεῖσα, ἀλλὰ κάτωθεν ἀναφυομένη γίνεται μείζων.

[27] Comp. *Tosefta Bekhoroth* I. 10–11, 534 37 ff.; *TB ibid.* 7b bot. and see Lewysohn, ibid., p. 9.

[28] אַדְנֵי הַשָּׂדֶה. *Mishnah Kil'aim* VIII. 5; *Sifra*, ed. Weiss, 51d. See Lewysohn ibid., pp. 64 and 356; Ginzberg, *Legends of the Jews*, vol. V, p. 50, n. 148; Lieberman, *Tarbiz*, VIII, p. 367.

[29] *Sifra*, ed. Weiss, 49d.

[30] *Ḥullin* IX. 6: עַכְבָּר שֶׁחֶצְיוֹ בָּשָׂר וְחֶצְיוֹ אֲדָמָה הַנּוֹגֵעַ בַּבָּשָׂר טָמֵא בָּאֲדָמָה טָהוֹר. Comp. *TB ibid.* 127a and *Sifra* 52b.

[31] See Ovid. *met.* I. 423 seq.; Pomponius Mela, *Chorogr.* I, 9. 3, 52.

Plinius cites it[32] as a "fact" which could confirm the credibility of other wonderful creatures. He reports: "But the inundation of the Nile gives credit to all these things by a marvel that surpasses them all. For when it subsides little mice are found with the work of generative water and earth uncompleted: in one part of their body they are already alive, while the most recently formed part of their structure is still of earth."[33] It is exactly the mouse described by the Rabbis. It appears from the account of Plinius that the parts of earth in the mouse subsequently turn into flesh; this is also the belief of the Rabbis.[34] Maimonides in his commentary[35] maintains that many people have claimed to have seen such a mouse.[36] The information about that kind of mouse the Rabbis probably got from Egyptian sources. When the alledged existence of the miraculous creature was brought to their attention they commented on its would-be *Halakhic* status.[37]

It is therefore evident that the rabbinic sources can sometimes be understood only in the light of the natural "science" of the time. We shall quote a few examples. The *Tosefta*[38] rules: אין משרבטין ומסרטין[39] את הבהמה ואין נופחים בקרביים ואין מטילין בשר בתוך המים "It is forbidden to whip or to scratch cattle [for the purpose of giving it an appearance of fatness][40] or to inflate the

---

[32] *Nat. hist.* IX. 84, 179.

[33] Verum omnibus his fidem Nili inundatio adfert omnia excedente miraculo; quippe detegente eo musculi reperiuntur inchoato opere genitalis aquae terraemque, iam parte corporis viventes novissima effigie etiamnum terrena.

[34] See *TB Sanhedrin* 91a.

[35] *Ḥullin* IX. 6.

[36] Comp. also בועז in *Mishnah* ed. Romm. The book referred to by the author is inaccessible to me.

[37] See Lieberman, *Studies in Memory of Moses Schorr* (Hebrew), New York 1944, p. 184 ff.

[38] *Baba Mezi'a* III, end, 379₂.

[39] So ed. prin. Cod. Vienna: אין מסרטין את הבהמה. Zuckermandel does not record the variant מסרטין from the editions and cod. Vienna.

[40] And thereby deceive the purchaser. *TB* (ibid. 60b) explains the word משרבטין in a different way. But from *TP Shabbath* VII. 2, 10c, it is evident that משרבטין in regard to בהמה means to whip the animal with a rod. It will be demonstrated below that this was the Palestinian explanation of the *Tosefta*. Comp. the second explanation of the latter in *TB* ibid.

entrails, or to soak meat in water."[41] The commentaries explain
the prohibition of inflating the entrails to refer to entrails displayed in a shop. One is not allowed to inflate them and to
give them an appearance of a larger size for the purpose of deceit.

However TP[42] discusses the question of whipping (למיחבוט)
cattle,[43] or inflating it (למינפוח) during the mid-festival days.
It is therefore obvious that the inflation of the entrails has to
do with living cattle and not with those displayed in the butcher
shop. It is likewise evident that the practice of whipping and
inflating the cattle was performed by the husbandmen for some
other reason and not only with the intention of cheating; for the
question is only whether one is allowed to do these things during
the mid-festivals, but it is taken for granted that one may do
it in the week days.

It appears that the whipping of the cattle was practiced in
order to affect the color of the skins.[44] The reason for inflating
the cattle is disclosed by Aristotle.[45] He maintains that the
older cattle will fatten if they be fed after an incision has been
made into their hide and air blown thereinto.[46] Similarly,
Plinius asserts[47] that the oxen and cows fatten by making an
incision in the hide and blowing air into the entrails with a
reed.[48] Now the meaning of the operation is quite clear. The
peasants believed that by blowing air into the entrails of the
animal it would absorb more water and actually fatten.[49] But

[41] To make it look fat, for the purpose of deceiving the purchaser.

[42] *Betza* III. 7, 62b.

[43] See Rabbenu Hananel on *TB* ibid. 28a and Ratner אהבת ציון וירושלים
a. l., p. 30. Z. W. Rabinovitz (שערי תורת ארץ ישראל, p. 285) correctly associated
the text in *TP* with our *Tosefta*.

[44] See *TP Shabbath* referred to above n. 40.

[45] *De anim. hist.* VIII. 7 (9). 1, 595b.

[46] ἐάν τις τὸ δέρμα ἐντεμὼν φυσήσῃ.

[47] *Nat. hist.* VIII. 70, 178: si quis incisa cute spiritum harundine in viscera
adigat.

[48] Perhaps we should read in the *Tosefta* ibid. (see above n. 39): אין משרבטין
את הבהמה ואין מסרטין ונופחין בקרבים, "One is not allowed to whip cattle, nor to
make an incision and blow air into the entrails".

[49] Just as they used to fatten sheep by mixing salt with their food. See
Aristotle ibid. VIII. 10 (12). 1, 596a.

fattening by the inflation of the entrails was only an illusion; it
had to be subsequently fed in order actually to increase its fat
content. The prohibition against inflating the cattle was directed
against the process of making it look fat without feeding it in
order to cheat the purchaser.

Again we read in the *Mishnah*:[50] מקבלין עגלין וסייחין למחצה
ומגדלין אותן עד שיהיו מ ש ו ל ש י ן וחמור עד שתהא טוענת "A man
may undertake the care of calves and foals in return for half
the profits and rear them until they have reached the third of
their growth;[51] and of a she-ass until it can bear a burden."
It is evident from the rule pertaining to asses that the rearing
is to be continued until the animal becomes fully able to work.
In case of oxen the custom was to break them when they were
three years old. Plinius states:[52] "Oxen should be broken when
three years old; after that is too late and before that too early."

This supports the reading ש ל ש י ן [53] which can mean only
three years old.[54] The calves are to be reared until they reach
the age of three years. They are not yoked before that age and
consequently are useless to the husbandman.

In *TP*[55] we read: רב חייה בר אשי הוה יתיב קומי דרב חמיתיה מבעת.
אמר ליה מהו כן. אמ' ליה חמרתי מעברה והיא בעיה מילד ואנא בעי מרבעתה
עד דלא תצנן "R. Hiyya b. Ashi was sitting before Rab who
noticed that the former was worried. When he asked him:
What is the matter? he replied: My ass is gestating and she is
about to cast, and I want to copulate her before she cools off."[56]

[50] *Baba Mezi'a* V. 4.

[51] This is the explanation of משולשין by Rashi and his followers. Comp.
also his commentary on Genesis 15:9 and Ibn Ezra ibid.

[52] *Nat. hist.* VIII. 70, 180: domitura boum in trimatu, postea sera, ante
praematura.

[53] Ed. Naples, W. H. Lowe, Kauffman (the latter reads שלושין and is corrected by a later hand to משולשים) and *TP*. Comp. also מלאכת שלמה a. l. See
דקדוקי סופרים on *TB* ibid. 68a, p. 192, n. א and *Tosafoth Yom Tob* a. l.

[54] As correctly explained by Alfasi in an Arabic responsum (cited in
שטה מקובצת a. l.) and by Maimonides ibid. מלאכת שלמה refers to *Mishnah
Parah* I. 1 where it is explicitly stated that שלשית means three years old.

[55] *Yebamoth* IV. 11, 6a and *Niddah* I. 4, 49b.

[56] This is the meaning of צנן in our context. See *Tosefta Mo'ed Katan*
II. 11, 231[7]; *TP Pesaḥim* IV. 8, 31b. *Bereshith Rabba* (XX. 6, 189[6]) reads:
שמא תיצן ו ת מ ו ת, "Lest she catch cold and *die*". This is an obvious scribal

It is evident from the anecdote that the Rabbi was eager to mate his ass immediately after her delivery lest she cool off afterwards. His anxiety may be understood only in the light of the beliefs of his time.

Aristotle maintains:[57] Seven days after parturition the she-ass submits to the male, and it is best impregnated if put to the male on this particular day, but she will also receive it afterwards. Plinius[58] merely asserts: It has been observed that she-asses are best coupled on the seventh day after parturition. He further declares:[59] equas autem post tertium *diem*[60] aut post unum ab enixu utiliter admitti putant; coguntque invitas. "It is thought advisable to have the mare covered after three days, and even after *one day* of her foaling. When they are unwilling compulsion is used." Apparently it was the custom to mate the mare immediately after her parturition. The passage in *TP* indicates that it was customary in Babylonia and Palestine[61] to cover the asses on the same day that they cast their foals.

The field of medicine is widely represented in rabbinic literature. Dr. Julius Preuss in his voluminous book[62] treats

error (or a lapsus from p. 1337 ibid.). The commentaries on *TP* misunderstood the passage completely. Jastrow, *Dictionary*, p. 1445, s. v. רבץ II, translated ואנא בעי מרבעה "And I want to assist at her *lying down* (for delivery) before she cools off".

[57] *De anim. hist.* VI. 23. 2, 577a: Τεκοῦσα δὲ βιβάζεται ἑβδόμῃ ἡμέρᾳ, καὶ μάλιστα δέχεται τὸ πλῆσμα ταύτῃ βιβασθεῖσα τῇ ἡμέρᾳ. λαμβάνει δὲ καὶ ὕστερον.

[58] *Nat. hist.* VIII. 69, 172: feminas a partu optime septimo die impleri observatum.

[59] Ibid. X. 83. 179.

[60] This is the reading of all the mss. in ed. Sillig. Only β (see *praefatio* ibid., p. V) has: *annum*.

[61] The story itself took place in Babylonia, but since it is reported in Palestinian sources with no comments it seems to have been taken for granted in that country. This suggests that both countries followed the same practices in our case.

[62] *Biblisch-Talmudische Medizin*, Berlin 1911, and reproduced ibid. 1921. It is still the standard book on the subject. It is a matter of regret that Jewish scholars do not make more frequent use of this valuable book. Prof. H. Torczyner published (*Louis Ginzberg Jubilee Volume*, Hebrew part, p. 217 ff.) a learned article on the story of R. Meir who pretended that he felt pain in his eye and asked a woman to spit in it. (The woman's tyrannical husband

this subject with great erudition. The field of popular medicine
is also not devoid of interest. Notwithstanding their knowledge
of the actual effectiveness of cures in certain diseases, the
Rabbis did not entirely discourage the popular remedies. For
instance, they stated categorically:[63] "Let nobody tell you that
he was bitten by a mad dog and survived," but this did not
prevent them from recording remedies against rabies which were
accepted by the ancient physicians.[64] We shall discuss some
instances which escaped the notice of Preuss.

In *Shir Hashirim Zuta*[65] it is stated: והרשעים נמשלו לכלבים
שאין מהם הנייה שנאמר כלם כלבים אלמים לא יוכלו לנבוח. מה הכלב הזה
שהוא [נושך] את האדם בקש ממנו נימה (למדונו) [למכתו][66] אינו יכול

had ordered her to spit in the face of the famous Rabbi). Emending the text,
Torczyner claimed that the woman did not actually spit in the eye of the
Rabbi but used an incantation accompanied by the customary expectoration
in front of the latter. But both rabbinic and non-Jewish sources inform us
explicitly that saliva is a proved remedy against various eye diseases, as
correctly recorded by Preuss ibid., p. 321 ff. As a matter of fact Plinius
(*nat. hist.* XXVIII. 22, 76) says expressly that a *woman's* fasting spittle
(Mulieris quoque salivam ieiunam. Saliva ieiuna = rabbinic רוק תפל) is considered a powerful remedy against bloodshot eyes. The assertion that the
woman actually spat in the eye of the Rabbi is also confirmed by an otherwise
unknown rabbinic source quoted by Rabbi David Hanagid in his commentary
on *Aboth* I. 12, 8a. A similar rabbinic anecdote is preserved in the commentary to the same *Mishnah*, published in *Machzor Vitry*, p. 473 (Comp. ps.-Rashi
ibid.) which states: ורוק שלך רפואתי ורוקקת לו בעיניו, "And thy spittle is my
remedy, and she spits in his eyes".

Incidentally, the whole thesis of Dr. Torczyner is based on the misprint
of a single letter in our editions of *Debarim Rabba* V. 15. מתפסק is to be read
מתעסק, fidgeting (see אות אמת a. l.). A *Genizah* fragment of this *Midrash*
published in הצופה לחכמת ישראל XIII, p. 113, reads: עשה ר' מאיר עצמו כאלו הוא
חושש בעינו, "R. Meir pretended that he felt pain in his eye". The source quoted
by Rabbi David Hanagid (see above) read: "R. Meir began to tie his eyes".
All this corresponds to the reading in *TP* (*Sotah* I. 4, 16d), which Torczyner
discredited.

[63] *TP Berakhoth* VIII. 6, 12b; *Yoma* VIII. 5, 45b.

[64] See Preuss ibid., pp. 224, n. 7 and 225, n. 1.

[65] VI. 6, ed. Buber, p. 36; *Aggadath Shir Hashirim*, ed. Schechter, p. 40,
l. 1192. I copy from the quotation in *Yalkut Hamakhiri* on Is. 56:10, p. 216.

[66] The ח was split into וו and hence was read למכונו, and subsequently
corrected to למדונו. Ed. Schechter reads למרוט; in his manuscript the וו was
combined into a ט.

לכך נמשלו ככלבים שאין בידם לא מעשה טוב ולא מצוה. The passage
makes no sense. We must therefore preface some remarks before
translating it. The *Midrash* comments on the verse (Is. 56:10):
"*They are all dumb dogs, they cannot bark.*" TP[67] gives the symp-
toms of a mad dog. "These are the signs ($\sigma\eta\mu\epsilon\hat{\iota}\alpha$) of a mad
dog: His mouth is open, the saliva is dripping, his ears flap,
his tail is hanging between his thighs, he walks along the edges
[of the road] and dogs bark at him; some say: He also barks
but his voice is not heard."[68] Philostratus, telling the miraculous cure of a mad dog, adds:[69] "He began to bark, a thing
which mad dogs rarely do, and folding back his ears he wagged
his tail."

It is therefore most plausible to assume that the Rabbis
refer here to a mad dog which cannot bark; they want to
demonstrate that no benefit can be drawn from the body of
such a dog.[70] Among the remedies against the bite of a mad
dog Plinius counts[71] the insertion into the wound of some burnt
hairs from the tail of the dog which inflicted the bite. Now
our passage becomes comprehensible. It says: "And the wicked
ones are likened to dogs from [whose body] no benefit can be
derived, as it is said (Is. 56:10): '*They are all dumb dogs, they
cannot bark*'. [They are] like this [kind of] dog which [bites]
the man, yet will allow no one to procure a hair from him for
the wound. Therefore they[72] are compared to dogs, because
they have neither good deed nor charity[73] [to their credit]."

[67] *Yoma* VIII. 5, 45b; *TB* ibid. 83b.

[68] All these signs are, of course, correct, and they are based on sound
observation. Their formulation and arrangement give the impression of a
passage from a standard medical treatise. Comp. the signs of a mad dog
($\kappa\nu\nu\dot{o}s$ $\lambda\nu\sigma\sigma\hat{\omega}\nu\tau os$ $\sigma\eta\mu\epsilon\hat{\iota}\alpha$) enumerated by Philumenus (*de venenatis anima-
libus* I. 1. 1 ff.), Paulus Aegineta (V. 3, ed. Heiberg in *CMG* IX, p. 8) and
Theophanes Nonnus (*epitome de curatione morborum* 271, ed. Bernard, 1795,
p. 324, see notes ibid.).

[69] *Vita Apoll.* VI. 43: $\varphi\omega\nu\dot{\eta}\nu$ $\tau\epsilon$ $\dot{\alpha}\varphi\hat{\eta}\kappa\epsilon\nu$, $\ddot{o}\pi\epsilon\rho$ $\ddot{\eta}\kappa\iota\sigma\tau\alpha$ $\pi\epsilon\rho\dot{\iota}$ $\tauο\dot{\upsilon}s$ $\lambda\upsilon\tau$-
$\tau\hat{\omega}\nu\tau\alpha s$ $\tau\hat{\omega}\nu$ $\kappa\upsilon\nu\hat{\omega}\nu$ $\xi\upsilon\mu\beta\alpha\acute{\iota}\nu\epsilon\iota$, $\kappa\alpha\dot{\iota}$ $\tau\dot{\alpha}$ $\hat{\omega}\tau\alpha$ $\dot{\alpha}\nu\alpha\kappa\lambda\dot{\alpha}\sigma\alpha s$ $\ddot{\epsilon}\sigma\epsilon\iota\sigma\epsilon$ $\tau\dot{\eta}\nu$ $ο\dot{\upsilon}\rho\dot{\alpha}\nu$ $\kappa\tau\lambda$.

[70] Contrary to sheep which supply us with wool etc., see the *Midrash* ibid.

[71] *Nat. hist.* XXIX. 32, 98: intus ipsius caudae pilos combustos inseruere
volneri.

[72] I. e. the wicked ones.

[73] For מצוה, $\dot{\epsilon}\nu\tauο\lambda\dot{\eta}$, charity, see Lieberman, *JBL* LXV, 1946, p. 69 ff.

Again we read in *TB*:[74] לא לישתי מיא אלא בגובתא דילמא מתחזי
ליה כלביה[75] ומסתכן "Let him[76] not drink water save out of a tube,
lest he see his dog,[77] and be endangered." The Rabbis attributed
hydrophobia to the horror evoked by the image of the mad dog
which the bitten man would supposedly see in the water.
Naḥmanides and Rabbenu Baḥya in their commentaries on
Num. 21:9 refer to our text in *TB* and remark that this is also
recorded in the "medical books." I was not able to find any
reference to it in the early Greek and Latin medical works.

The first physician who mentions it is Paulus Aegineta[78] who
informs us that "it is thought that the bitten man sees in the
water the image of the dog who inflicted the bite."[79] From
Paulus it was taken over in later medical literature.[80] However,
Paulus Silentiarius[81] already refers to this belief in an amatory
epigram: "They say that a man bitten by a mad dog sees the
brute's image in the water."[82] The rabbinic text which credits
Abaye[83] with the advice to a man bitten by a mad dog that he
drink water from a tube in order to avoid the image of the dog
seems to be the earliest instance on record of the previously
cited belief.

Many of the popular remedies mentioned in rabbinic literature (and especially in the Babylonian Talmud) probably have
their origin in the Orient where they were acquired by the
Rabbis through direct contact with the eastern peoples. However, the Greek and the Roman records are important for the

---

[74] *Yoma* 84a.

[75] This is the reading of the mss. and mediaeval authorities; see דקדוקי
סופרים a. l., p. 281 nn. מ and נ.

[76] I. e. the man bitten by a mad dog.

[77] I. e. the image of the mad dog reflected in the water.

[78] Flourished in the beginning of the seventh century.

[79] V. 3, ed. Heiberg, p. 820: οἴεσθαι τὸν δακόντα κύνα ἐν τοῖς ὕδασιν
εἰκονίζεσθαι.

[80] See Theophanes Nonnus ibid. (see above n. 68).

[81] Flourished in the sixth century; see I. Merian-Genast, *de Paulo Silen-
tiario Byzantino*, Lipsiae 1889, p. 2 ff.

[82] *Anthol. Palat.* V, epigr. amat. 266 (265): Ἀνέρα λυσσητῆρι κυνὸς
βεβολημένον ἰῷ ὕδασι θηρείην εἰκόνα φασὶ βλέπειν.

[83] Flourished in the first half of the fourth century C. E. in Babylonia.

understanding of the rabbinic sources dealing with popular medicine and similar subjects. They sometimes help us to establish definitively the correct reading in the rabbinic text. We find, for instance, in the *Tosefta*:[84] מי שנשכו נחש ... גוזזין לו כרישין[85] "If one was bitten by a snake . . . leek from the ground may be cut for him [on the Sabbath]." But one mediaeval authority[86] reads in the *Tosefta* כרשינין[87]. I. Loew[88] prefers the reading כרישין, leeks, because this reading is also quoted by Rabbenu Hananel. Of course, this evidence is not decisive. Only if we can establish the vegetable popularly used in the treatment of the bite of a serpent will we succeed in finally determining the correct reading. Indeed, Plinius[89] claims that leek (*porrum*) with vinegar is employed against the bites of wild beasts as well as of serpents and other venomous creatures.[90] The reading כרישין is therefore assured.

Furthermore, even Jewish figurative expressions can be properly understood in the light of the accepted popular notions regarding animal life. For example, the Jews[91] called לשון הרע (slander, calumny, denunciation) לשון] שלישי[92] or לישנא תליתאי, the third tongue.[93] Sirach[94] also uses the same expression: γλῶσσα τρίτη πολλοὺς ἐσάλευσεν . . . γλῶσσα τρίτη γυναῖκας ἀνδρείας ἐξέβαλεν. "The third tongue hath shaken many . . . the third tongue hath cast out brave women." The

[84] *Shabbath* XV. 14, 1347 and *TB Yoma* 83b.

[85] Allium Porrum, πράσιον, leek.

[86] See Lieberman, *Tosefeth Rishonim* I, p. 145. This reading is corroborated by cod. Oxford of *TB* ibid.

[87] Vicia, ὄροβος, vetch.

[88] *Flora der Juden* II, p. 134.

[89] *Nat. hist.* XX. 21. 45.

[90] Bestiarum morsus ex aceto, item serpentium aliorumque venenatorum. See Sillig's note in his edition vol. III, p. 301.

[91] *TP Pe'ah* I. 1, 16a; *Vayyikra Rabba* XXV. 2; *Pesikta deR. Kahana* IV, 32a; *Bemidbar Rabba* XIX. 2; *Debarim Rabba* V. 10; *Tanḥuma* IV, ed. Buber, 54a; *Midrash Tehilim* CXX. 4, ed. Buber, p. 504.

[92] *TB 'Arakhin* 15b; *Midrash Tehilim* XII, 2, ed. Buber, p. 106, and see n. 22 ibid.

[93] The Aramaic תליתאי may also be translated the threefold, the triple; see *TB Shabbath* 88a and see below, n. 100.

[94] XXVIII. 14–15.

Rabbis remarked:[95] "Why do they call it (i. e. calumny) 'the third tongue', because it kills three: the slanderer, him who accepts the slander and the slandered person." M. Friedmann understood[96] that the interpretation of the Rabbis is only homiletical, and he explained תליתאי, שלישי to mean strong, vehement, a rough tongue.

However, the only correct explanation of the expression is given by Bochart[97] who properly understood that לישנא תליתאי originally meant the three-forked, the triple tongue, viz. the snake. He quotes many classic authors who mentioned the three-forked tongue of the serpent both literally and figuratively.[98] The nearest parallel to the Jewish personification of the *delator* by the snake is presented by the remark of Seneca:[99] "Here a savage serpent drags its huge body along, darts out its forked tongue and seeks against whom it is to come death dealing." It is therefore clear that לישנא תליתאי originally meant the triple tongued,[100] the serpent whose quick vibrations of the tongue gives the observer the impression that it is three-forked.[101]

It is likely that the expression δίγλωσσος, double-tongued,[102] is nothing but another appellation for the snake. Bochart,[103] describing serpents, cites many instances of *lingua duplex* of the snake. Plautus expresses himself:[104] "He's like a snake with that two-forked villainous tongue of his." רכיל (Lev. 19:16) is rendered לישנא תליתאי (threefold tongue) by the Palestinian

---

95 See above n. 91.

96 *Beth Talmud*, ed. Weiss, V, p. 200, n. 12.

97 *Hierozoicon*, part I, I, ch. 4, p. 25 ff.

98 Although Bochart was referred to by Schleusner (*Lexicon in LXX* etc. s. vv. γλῶσσα and τρίτος. See also M. Grünbaum, *Neue Beiträge z. Semitischen Sagenkunde*, p. 288) none of the modern editors of Sirach paid attention to it. For a similar neglect by the editors of Ben Sira, see Lieberman *REJ* XCVII, 1934, p. 54.

99 *Medea* 686: Hic saeva serpens corpus immensum trahit trisidamque linguam exertat et quaerit quibus mortifera veniat.

100 See above, n. 93.

101 See Bochart ibid.

102 Septuagint Prov. 11:13; Sirach V, 9, 14; VI. 1; XXVIII. 13.

103 Ibid., p. 24.

104 *Persa* 299: tamquam proserpens bestiast bilinguis et scelestus.

Targumim a. l., and the same Hebrew word in Proverbs (11:13) is rendered δίγλωσσος by the Septuagint ibid. Hence, γλῶσσα τρίτη and δίγλωσσος refer to the same creature. Similarly ψίθυρον καὶ δίγλωσσον (the whisperer and double-tongued) mentioned by Sirach[105] are probably synonymous. The ψίθυρος, the whisperer, is the rabbinic designation[106] for the delator-serpent; he is identical with δίγλωσσος, the double-tongued.

It was stated above that the Rabbis interpreted the expression "the three-forked tongue" to signify that it kills three persons. The *Midrash*[107] preserved another exposition which corresponds to the expression double-tongued. It states: הלשון הזה הורג שנים האומרו והמקבלו "This [vicious] tongue kills two: the slanderer and him who accepts the slander." Both terms — the three-forked tongue and the double-tongued — can be correctly understood only in the light of the designation of the snake's tongue by the ancients.

We have sought to demonstrate in the several chapters of this book the great similarities between the methods, behavior, practices and notions prevalent among Jews and gentiles alike. Although some of them may have been the heritage left by a more distant and simpler age, many of the others were nevertheless probably the result of direct contact and close relations among the various peoples in the Hellenistic Mediterranean world.

---

[105] XXVIII. 13.

[106] See *Shemoth Rabba* IX. 3 and the parallel in *Tanḥuma* ibid. For לחש, whisper, as the hiss of a snake, see *Mishnah Aboth* II. 10 and comp. *Tosefta Menaḥoth* XIII. 21, 533₃₅, *TB Pesaḥim* 57a.

[107] *The Mishnah of R. Eliezer*, ed. Enelow, p. 176.

APPENDIX I (To p. 78, n. 249)

‏בת קול‏ Bath Kol

We read in the *Tosefta*:[1] ‏משמת חגי זכריה ומלאכי נביאים האחרונים‏
‏פסקה רוח הקודש מישראל ואף על פי כן היו משמיעין להן בבת קול‏ "When
the latter prophets, Haggai, Zechariah and Malachi died the
Holy Spirit departed from Israel; nevertheless they were informed [of the unknown] by means of a *Bath Kol*." Rabbi Meir
Abulafia[2] remarks that the Palestinian Talmud explains *Bath
Kol*, ‏בת קול‏, to mean ‏הברת קול‏, a reverberating sound, an echo.[3]
Rab Sa'adiah Gaon[4] compares it to an echo rebounding from
the mountains.[5]

From the earlier sources[6] it is obvious that *Bath Kol* very
often means simply *vox, verbum*,[7] a voice or a word heard
without seeing the person who uttered it, or a word heard from
a person who was not conscious of the import of his saying,
i. e. the *Bath Kol* is nothing but φήμη or κληδών.[8] *TP*[9] and
TB[10] read in the above-mentioned *Tosefta*: ‏היו משתמשי ן‏

[1] *Sotah* XIII. 2, 31822.

[2] In his ‏יד רמה‏ to *Sanhedrin* 11a.

[3] This explanation is not extant in our editions of *TP* but is found in
codd. Leiden and Rome of *TP Sotah*, See Lieberman ‏הירושלמי כפשוטו‏ (Jerusalem
1934), Introduction, p. ‏כ'ה‏. The quotation in *Tarbiz* XVIII, 1947, p. 24, n. 9,
is not exact. Comp. *Shir Rabba* I. 2, ed. Rom 6[d].

[4] Quoted in *Machzor Vitri*, p. 556; see Introduction ibid., p. 196.

[5] The Syriac translation of *Sap. Solom.* (‏חכמתא רבתא‏ XVII. 18) reads:
‏או קלא דברת קלא מן בינת טולא‏, "or a sound of an echo (*bath Kol*) from between
the mountains".

[6] *Mishnah Yebamoth* XVI. 6 and parallels; see E. A. Urbach in *Tarbiz*
XVIII, 1947, p. 23 ff.

[7] See Payne Smith *Thesaurus Syriacus*, p. 596, s. v. ‏ברת קלא‏.

[8] See P. Stengel, *Die griechischen Kultusaltertümer*[3], p. 55 and below
n. 17.

[9] *Sotah* IX. 14, 24b.

[10] Ibid. 48b.

בבת קול "They were wont to make use of the *Bath Kol*."[11] The expression להשתמש ברוח הקודש or להשתמש בבת קול is awkward in Hebrew. It looks like a literal translation of the Greek χρῆσϑαι (with the Dative) which means both to make use and to consult a god or an oracle.[12] The Hebrew phrases should accordingly be rendered: to consult a *Bath Kol*, to consult the Holy Spirit.

The manner of consulting the *Bath Kol* is reported many times in rabbinic literature. *TB*[13] relates: ואמר ר' שפטיה אמר ר' יוחנן מנין שמשתמשין בבת קול שנא' ואזניך תשמענה דבר מאחריך "R. Shefatiah said in the name of R. Johanan: Whence do we know that we may consult a *Bath Kol*? Because it is said (Isa. 30:21): '*And thine ears shall hear a word*[14] *behind thee saying*' etc."[15] R. Johanan himself followed it. We are told[16] that R. Johanan and Resh Lakish desired to see Samuel personally. Before undertaking the journey to Babylonia, they decided to follow the "hearing"[17] of a *Bath Kol* (נלך אחר שמיעת בת קול). They passed the synagogue where they heard a school-boy reciting the verse: "*And Samuel died*."[18] They concluded that Mar Samuel of Babylonia is no longer alive, and they consequently abandoned their project.[19]

This procedure of consulting the verses casually uttered by children in the synagogue was the most frequent among the Rabbis.[20] Such verses answered the questions of the consultants.

[11] This expression also occurs in *TB Megillah* 32a. In *Bereshith Rabba* (XXXVII. 7, 349₆) we read: שהיו משתמשין ברוח הקודש, "They were wont to make use of the Holy Spirit".

[12] See Liddell and Scott s. v. χράω A. III and C. II.

[13] *Megillah* 32a.   [14] *Verbum* = *Bath Kol*.

[15] Comp. the similar version in the name of R. Eleazar in *TP Shabbath* VI. 9, 8c.

[16] *TP* ibid.

[17] Perhaps שמיעה = שמועה, κληδών, which means tidings, repute (comp. סנאי שומעניה and שפירן שומעניה in *TB Megillah* 25b, which correspond to κληδών αἰσχρά and κληδών καλή) and an omen contained in a chance uttering. The latter is indeed the real substance of the *Bath Kol*, see below.

[18] I Sam. 28:3.   [19] Comp. *TB Ḥullin* 95b.

[20] *TB Ḥagigah* 15a ff. (*Koheleth Zuta* VII. 8, ed. Buber, pp. 110–111; *Midrash Mishle* VI. 20, 29a); ibid. *Gittin* 68a; *Esther Rabba* (to Esth. 3:9), ed. Romm 13a.

In *TB Gittin* 56a this means of divination is ascribed to Nero! It is further

The Egyptians had a similar way of divination.[21] According to Plutarch's explicit statement[22] the Egyptians think that small children possess the power of prophecy,[23] particularly "when they are playing in temples and happen to say things."[24] This is also confirmed by Pausanias who, in describing the oracle of Hermes in Pharae, reports:[25] "He who wants to inquire from the god whispers his question in the ear of the god. Then he stops his own ears and leaves the market place. When he is gone a little way outside, he takes his hands from his ears and whatever words he hears he regards as an oracle."[26] Pausanias

related there that the emperor shot an arrow towards the East, but it altered its course and fell [towards] Jerusalem. He then shot one towards the West and then towards the other directions of the wind and achieved the same result. It is hard to decide whether the Rabbis described a practice which was customary in their time or had in mind the mantic devices of the king of Babylonia (see Ezek. 21:26). The Palestinian *Midrashim* (*Ekha Rabba* Proem. 23, ed. Buber 10a; *Koheleth Rabba* and *Zuta* to Eccl. 12:7) which comment in detail on the performance of the king provide no particulars about the means of divination by arrows. Jerome (to Ezek. ibid., *PL* XXV, 206c) contents himself with the observation: hanc autem Graeci βελομαντίαν sive ῥαβδομαντίαν nominant. It seems that βελομαντεία was in use in the time of Jerome. In *Midrash Tehilim* (LXXIX. 2, ed, Buber 180a) the βελομαντεία of the king of Babylonia is described in the following way: He shot an arrow meant for (לשם) Antiochia, one meant for Tyre and one meant for Laodicea. These arrows broke. But when he shot an arrow meant for Jerusalem it did not break. This indicated to him that Jerusalem was to be destroyed by him. Here again we cannot be positively sure that the Rabbis described the heathen practices of their time. Their account may have been guesswork. Comp. Th. Nöldeke, *Archiv f. Religionswissenschaft* XVI, 1913, p. 308 ff.

[21] See Bouché-Leclercq, *Histoire de la divination* III, p. 387 and n. 3 ibid. He refers to Dio Chrys., *Orat.* XXXIII. 13, to Ael., *hist. anim.* XI. 10 and Pausanias VII. 22. 4.

[22] *Is. et Osir.* 14, 356e, overlooked by Bouché-Leclercq.

[23] Comp. *TB Baba Bathra* 12b.

[24] παιζόντων ἐν ἱεροῖς καὶ φθεγγομένων ὅ τι ἂν τίχωσι. From the description of Xenophon of Ephesus (*Ephesiaca* V. 4. 11) one does not gain the impression that the children playing in the temple area of Apis uttered their prophecies by chance. Comp. also Plinius, *nat. hist.* VIII, 71, 185.

[25] VII. 22. 3.

[26] καὶ ἥστινος ἂν ἐπακούσῃ φωνῆς, μάντευμα ἡγεῖται. In *TP Shabbath* (VI. 9, 8c) it is related (I translate according to the correct text of the *Yerushalmi Fragments from the Genizah*, ed. L. Ginzberg, p. 28, and in the quotation

adds: "The Egyptians have a similar way of divination at the temple of Apis." Thus it is evident that in Egypt the method of divination was to learn from what children who are in the temple or its premises happened to say. It is worthy of note that many of the Greek writers stress the special veracity of this omen. The Jews adopted the same course, substituting the school or the synagogue for the heathen temple. This was not considered forbidden divination but a σημεῖου (אות) from Heaven, a kind of prophecy.[27]

The Christians also believed in the efficacy of this mode of divination, and did not disapprove of it. Antony decided to become a monk[28] when he heard Matt. 19:21 read in the church as he entered it. It appeared to him that the passage was read for his sake.[29]

Augustine recounts:[30] audio vocem de *divina*[31] domo cum cantu dicentis et crebro repetentis quasi pueri an puellae, nescio: tolle lege, tolle lege.[32] "I heard the voice of a boy or a girl coming from the divine house[33] which repeatedly uttered in a sing-song manner: take up and read, take up and read."

---

of הכותב לעין יעקב to *TB Megillah* towards the end): "R. Jonah and R. Jose were going to visit R. Aḥa who happened to be sick. They said: Let us follow the 'hearing of a *Bath Kol*' (see above n. 17). They heard a woman asking her friend: Has the lamp gone out? It has not, she said. And [indeed] the lamp of Israel was not extinguished" (i. e. R. Aḥa was not dead). In this case we have an omen which is similar to that practiced in Greece.

[27] See *TP Shabbath* VI, 9, 8c and TB *Ḥullin* 95b. Comp. the interpretation of Rabbi Aaron of Lunel in his ארחות חיים II, p. 619; the stories told in the above sources argue against his interpretation.

[28] Athanasius, *vita S. Antonii* 2, *PG* XXVI, 841c.

[29] ὡς δι' αὐτὸν γενομένου τοῦ ἀναγνώσματος.

[30] *Confess.* VIII. 12. 29.

[31] This is the reading of cod. Sessorianus, the oldest (seventh or eighth century) and best manuscript. All other manuscripts read: *vicina*, which was adopted in all later editions. However, Knöll (*CSEL* 33, p. 194₁₃) correctly followed the best text (See praefatio ibid., p. V and p. VII).

[32] Comp. the vision of Porphyrius (Mark le Diacre, *vie de Porphyre* 45, ed. Grégoire et Kugener, p. 38) where the empress Eudoxia told him: λάβε ἀνάγνωθι. The editors (p. 119) surmise that the expression is taken from our passage in the Confessions.

[33] I. e. the church.

Following the example of Antony who became converted by such an oracle (*tali oraculo*), he took the book of the Apostle, opened it and read in silence from the first chapter that his eyes fell upon.[34] This represents a double divination. Augustine was directed to read the Epistle of Paul (Rom. XIII. 13 ff.) by the utterance of children. The passage on which his glance fell accidentally contained the portent.

The belief in an omen indicated by the chance reading of a passage from a sacred book was quite current among the Jews.[35] The Rabbis had also a tradition[36] that King Josiah hid the Holy Ark because he happened to read in the Torah (Deut. 28:36): "*The Lord shall carry thee, and thy king whom thou shalt set over thee, unto a nation that thou hast not known etc.*" Fearing that the Holy Ark would be removed to a foreign country he decided to conceal it. The mediaeval rabbinic authorities[37] knew a passage in the Palestinian Talmud (not extant in our editions) that when the Scroll was unfolded before the king it happened to open at the above mentioned verse. He consequently concluded that the verse contains a prophetic reference to himself.[38] This was a variant of a *Bath Kol*, and it was also considered to be a σημεῖον from Heaven, a true prophecy.

An examination of the *Bath Kol* prophecies reveals that almost all of them were explicitly expressed and needed no special interpretation. As a matter of fact, the Rabbis emphasized this characteristic; the prophecies of the Jews were phrased clearly and specifically. They remarked:[39] "[It is written]: *That they should be ready against that day* (Esth. 3:14).

[34] Et legi in silentio capitulum, quo primum coniecti sunt oculi mei.

[35] See *TB Ḥullin* 95b, *Tanḥuma*, ed. Buber Jetro 7. Comp. Maimonides Responsa, ed. Freimann 374, p. 344, and n. 2 ibid.; *Birkei Josef* on Yoreh De'ah 179, 6. Prof. Morton Smith calls my attention to I Macc. III. 48. Comp. also Lucas IV. 17 and the International Crit. Comment. *a. l.*

[36] *TP Shekalim* VI. 1, 49c; *TB Yoma* 52b.

[37] See Ratner in ירושלים ציון אהבת a. l. p. 36. Comp. also *Lekaḥ Tob* to Ex. 16:32, 57a, bot.

[38] Comp. also *TP Sukkah* V. 1, 55b.

[39] *Esther Rabba* to Esth. 3:14, ed. Romm 13c: א'ר לוי אומות העולם נבואתם סתומה ואינן יודעין אם ליהרג ואם להרוג . . . אבל ישראל נבואתן מפורשת להיות היהודים עתידים ליום הזה להנקם מאויביהם.

R. Levi said: The prophecy of the nations of the world is ambiguous, so that they do not know whether [they are to prepare]
to be killed or to kill . . . But the prophecy of Israel is clear:
*That the Jews should be ready against that day to avenge themselves
on their enemies"* (Esth. 8:13).   M. Sachs correctly surmised[40]
that the Rabbis were ridiculing the heathen ambiguous oracles
like those given to Croesus and Pyrrhus.[41]

The Rabbis stressed this fact again:[42] "Why is [the Jewish
oracle] called *Urim* and *Tumim*? *Urim*, because they make
their words clear.[43] *Tumim*, because they fulfill[44] their words.[45]
If you should ask why they did not fulfill their words in Gibeath
Benjamin,[46] [the answer is] that [the fault lay with the people]:
they did not ascertain whether they would triumph or be
defeated.[47] But later when they did ascertain, they[48] cooperated,
as it is said (Judg. 20:28) etc.   *And the Lord said: go up, for
tomorrow I will deliver him into thy hand."*[49]

Hence, the Rabbis made it a special point to stress that the
Jewish oracles were not equivocal and ambiguous. No special
devices were needed to interpret them.

---

[40] *Beitraege z. Sprach- und Alterthumsforschung* I, p. 42.

[41] See Cicero, *de divin.* II 56, 115–116. Comp. ibid. I, 24. 50.

[42] *Sifre Zuta*, ed. Horovitz, p. 321₂₃; *TB Yoma* 73b. Comp. also דקדוקי
סופרים on *Berakhoth*, p. 8, n. מ. I copy from the version in *TB*: למה נקרא שמן
אורים ותומים אורים שמאירין את דבריהם. תומים שמשלימין את דבריהם ואם תאמר בגבעת
בנימין מפני מה לא השלימו. הם שלא ביחנו אם לנצח אם להנגח ובאחרונה שביחנו הסכימו
שנא' וכו' ויאמר ה' עלו כי מחר אתננו בידך.

[43] *Urim* means lights in Hebrew.

[44] *Tameim*, to fulfil, see *TB Sanhedrin* 39b.

[45] The Septuagint likewise translates אורים ותומים δήλωσις καὶ ἀλήθεια.
Comp. however I. Heinemann, *The Methods of the Aggadah* (Hebrew), Jerusalem 1949, p. 170.

[46] See Jud. 20:23–25.

[47] Comp. *TB Shebu'oth* 35b.

[48] I. e. the *Urim* and *Tumim*.

[49] Comp. also *TP Yoma* VII. 3, 44c.

APPENDIX II (to p. 86)

The Publication of the Torah

To avoid possible forgery the Torah, according to the
Rabbis, was "published" by means of deposition in the ark.
The Jewish sages also discuss the publication of the Torah
from another point of view. We read in the *Midrash*:[1] א"ר אלעזר
אעפ"י שנתנה התורה מסיני לא נענשו ישראל עליה עד שנתפרשה להם באהל
מועד. לדיוטגמה שהיא כתובה ומחותמת ונכנסה למדינה ולא נתחייבו עליה בני
המדינה עד שנתפרשה להם ב[דימוסיה של][2] מדינה. כך אעפ"י שהתורה נתנה
בהר סיני לא נענשו עליה עד שנתפרשה להם באהל מועד "R. Eleazar[3]
said: Although the Torah was revealed on Mount Sinai Israel
was not punished for its transgression until it was promulgated[4]
to them in the Tent of Meeting. It was like a $\delta\iota\acute{\alpha}\tau\alpha\gamma\mu\alpha$ (edict)
which had been written and sealed and brought to the city, but
in respect whereof the inhabitants of the city are not bound
until it has been *promulgated*[5] to them in the public place[6] of

---

[1] *Shir Hashirim Rabba* to Cant. 2:3. Comp. *Vayyikra Rabba* I. 10.

[2] The bracketed words are extant in *Vayyikra Rabba* ibid.

[3] Flourished in the third quarter of the third century.

[4] See below, n. 5.

[5] The word פרש, פרס, to display, to stretch out, was a technical term for
the promulgation of an edict. See *Aruch Completum s. v.* דטגמא and פרוזדגמא;
Prof. Finkelstein's additional instances in *JQR* XXXII (1942) p. 387, n. 1
and add: *Midrash Tehilim* CXIX. 46, ed. Buber, p. 499. The Semitic פרש
(פרס) most likely translated the Latin [edictum] proponere, $\pi\rho o\tau\acute{\iota}\vartheta\epsilon\sigma\vartheta\alpha\iota$
(Eusebius, *Hist. eccl.* VIII. 5. Comp. also Sophocles, *Greek Lexicon*, p. 953).
Eusebius frequently uses the expression $\dot{\alpha}\pi\lambda o\tilde{\upsilon}\nu \beta\alpha\sigma\iota\lambda\iota\kappa\grave{\alpha} \gamma\rho\acute{\alpha}\mu\mu\alpha\tau\alpha, \beta\alpha\sigma\iota\lambda\iota\kappa\grave{\alpha}$
$\delta\iota\alpha\tau\acute{\alpha}\gamma\mu\alpha\tau\alpha$ etc. (Ibid. VIII. 2. 4; 17. 2; IX beginning; X. 9. 8; *De mart.
Pal.*, beginning) which is literally the equivalent of פרש דיוטגמא. Indeed, the
Syriac translation of Eusebius (published by Wright and Maclean from a
dated manuscript of 462, see Preface ibid., p. V) renders the verb $\dot{\alpha}\pi\lambda o\tilde{\upsilon}\nu$ פרס
(See ibid. pp. 324, 353–354 and 357. Brockelman, *Lexicon Syriacum*[2], 600b
quotes only one instance from the late Julian Romance of the use of this verb
in the sense of promulgation).

[6] The text has בדימוסיה, $\delta\eta\mu o\sigma\acute{\iota}\alpha$.

the city. In the same way, although the Torah was revealed on Mount Sinai Israel was not punishable for its transgression until it was promulgated to them in the Tent of Meeting." The Rabbi argued according to the legal practice of the Roman government. An edict had to be displayed δημοσίᾳ, in a public place;[7] until then the people were not punishable for its transgression.[8]

Similarly, some Rabbis maintained, the gentiles were not punishable for the transgression of the Torah until it was inscribed on the stones by Joshua.[9] It is by virtue of the publication of the Torah on those στῆλαι, that the Gentiles received their death sentence (ἀπόφασις של מיתה) for its transgression.[10] For, according to the Rabbis, the nations of the world sent their *notarii* to copy for them the Torah which was inscribed on the stones in seventy languages.[11] Apparently the Rabbis conceived that the *notarii* in their turn inscribed it on στῆλαι which they then deposited in their sanctuaries or archives.[12] They maintain that some of those nations whom the Torah had forbidden Israel to attack subsequently produced their στῆλαι as evidence against David when he planned to conquer them.[13]

It is noteworthy that according to a Rabbi of the second century neither the whole Torah nor Deuteronomy was in-

---

[7] See F. F. von Schwind, *Zur Frage der Publikation im römischen Recht*, München 1940, pp. 84, 86.

[8] See ibid., p. 92.

[9] See Deut. 27:4–8; Josh. 8:32.

[10] *TP Sotah* VII, 21d; comp. *Tosefta* ibid. VIII. 6, 3112 ff.

[11] *Tosefta* and *TP* ibid. and parallels.

[12] See von Schwind ibid., p. 47.

[13] *Bereshith Rabba* LXXIV. 15, 8724 ff. The editions and some mss. read there פיסטוליות (ἐπιστολαί, letters) instead of אסטליות (στῆλαι, blocks of stone). But the latter reading is attested by the majority of, and the best codd. The reading אפיסטולי in *Yelamdenu* to Deut. 4:7 recorded in 'Arukh (s. v. אסטולי) in the name of some books is likewise erroneous. The correct reading is the first one mentioned there: אסטולי, στῆλη. Comp. the parallel passage in *TP* 'Abodah Zarah I. 1, 39b, where it is stated: וכתב על ליבן והרנוך "And [Jeroboam] inscribed on their hearts (i. e. of the golden calves. It is more likely that ליבן is a scribal error for אבנין, stones, i. e. he inscribed on στῆλαι): 'And they will kill thee'" (Comp I Kings 12:27 והרגוני, *And they will kill me*).

scribed on the stones but only those portions in which the
nations of the world would be interested, such as *"When thou
drawest nigh unto a city to fight against it then proclaim peace
against it etc."* (Deut. 20:10 ff.) or *"When thou shalt besiege a
city a long time etc."*[14] (ibid. 19).

In the opinion of this Rabbi it is portions of international
law that were published by Joshua on the στῆλαι (blocks of
stone) which he set up.

---

[14] *Mekhilta* to Deut. published by Schechter in *Festschrift zu Israel Lewy's*
etc., Hebrew part, p. 189: לא כתבו עליהן אלא מה שאומות העולם רוצין כגון כי תקרב
אל עיר להלחם עליה וקראת עליה לשלום. אם שלום תענך וגו'. כי תצור על עיר ימים רבים וגו'
Comp. *Tosefta Sotah* VIII, 311 3 ff.

APPENDIX III (to p. 87, nn. 30, 31)

Jewish and Christian Codices

The Greek word פנקס, πίναξ, writing-tablet, is very common in rabbinic literature.[1] From the second century rabbinic sources it is obvious that the πίναξ often consisted of more than one tablet.[2] We are told in TP[3] that a Samaritan once dreamed[4] that he was dressed in a *pinax* of twelve tablets.[5] The dream may reflect the reality of the time.[6] The *pinaces* were made not only of tablets but also of some softer material. The *Mishnah*[7] explicitly mentions a *pinax* of papyrus. Another bit of relevant information dates from a somewhat later period. On Gen. 28:13 (*The land whereon thou liest to thee will I give it and to thy seed*) Bar Kappara[8] remarks: "[The Lord] folded the earth like a *pinax* and put it under his (i. e. Jacob's) head."[9] The com-

---

[1] See Krauss *LW*, p. 466, s. v. פנקס; L. Blau, *Studien zum althebräischen Buchwesen* (Budapest 1902), p. 17 ff.; S. Krauss, *Talmudische Archäologie* III, p. 306 ff.

[2] *Mishnah Shabbath* XII. 5; *Tosefta Sotah* XV. 1, 321₁₆ and parallel in *TP* ibid.

[3] *Ma'aser Sheni* IV. 9, 55b.

[4] It is an incident of the second half of the second century, as we learn from the report (ibid.) that the Samaritan turned to R. Ishmael b. R. Jose for the interpretation.

[5] *Midrash Ekha Rabba* I, ed. Buber 26b, reads: he was *carrying* a *pinax* of 24 tablets.

[6] A *pinax* of nine tablets is reproduced by W. Schubart, *Das Buch bei d. Griechen und Römern*[2], p. 24. This seems to be the largest number of tablets known to have been bound in one *pinax*.

[7] *Kelim* XXIV. 7. The passage is not later than the middle of the second century.

[8] Flourished at the end of the second and the beginning of the third century.

[9] *BR* LXIX. 4, 793₈. Comp. *TB Nidda* 30b.

parison apparently refers to the folding of papyrus (or parchment) so as to make a codex.[10]

Thus פנקס, πίναξ, in rabbinic literature is sometimes identical with codex.

In ancient Jewish sources, the פנקסים, πίνακες, codices are usually synonymous with records. To examine one's *pinax* merely signified to examine one's records.[11] The *pinax* also contained the record of a business man.[12] In the case of R. Ishmael[13] it served him as a record of his private memoranda; he noted there a mishap that occurred to him on the Sabbath.[14] It is evident that rabbinic literature mirrors the general practice of the time. The codex in antiquity was used for all the purposes cited above.[15]

We have pointed out above (p. 84 ff.) that an ancient injunction prohibited the publication in writing of the Oral Law. However, rabbinic sayings and decisions were written down in epistles,[16] in private rolls[17] and, above all, on πίνακες, codices (or single tablets which could subsequently be bound in a codex).[18] Most of the Rabbis who are reported to have put down the *Halakhoth* of their masters on codices flourished in the first half of the third century. But the practice itself is undoubtedly much older. The employment of the note-book

---

[10] See F. G. Kenyon, *Books and Readers in Ancient Greece and Rome*, Oxford 1932, p. 101; C. C. McCown, *Harvard Theological Review* XXXIV, 1941, p. 232.

[11] *BR* LXXXI. 1, 968 and parallels referred to in the notes a. l.; ibid. 972₄; 1015₂; *Esther Rabba* I. 6, ed. Romm 3c; *Tanhuma* משפטים 5, end; *Targum* ps.-Jonathan, Gen. 39:11. Comp. also *Mishnah Aboth* III. 16, and *TP Rosh Hashanah* I. 3, 57a.

[12] *Mishnah Shebu'oth* VII. 5 and parallels.

[13] Flourished in the second half of the first century.

[14] *Tosefta Shabbath* I. 13, 1102₇, and parallels in *TP* and *TB* ibid.

[15] See Schubart, *op. c.* (above n. 6), p. 175; McCown, *op. c.* (above n. 10), p. 249; H. A. Sanders, *Michigan Alumnus Quarterly Review* XLIV, 1938, pp. 101a, 102b and 109b.

[16] J. N. Epstein, מבוא לנוסח המשנה, p. 699 ff.

[17] See above, p. 87 n. 29.

[18] *TP Kil'aim* I. 1, 27a; *Ma'asroth* II. 4, 49d; *TB Shabbath* 156a (three times) and *Menahoth* 70a.

was the most suitable way of indicating that they were writing the Oral Law for private, or unofficial use, and not for publication.

Now the Jewish disciples of Jesus, in accordance with the general rabbinic practice, wrote the sayings which their master pronounced *not* in form of a book to be published, but as notes in their *pinaces*, codices, in their note-books (or in private small rolls). They did this because otherwise they would have transgressed the law. In line with the foregoing we would naturally expect the *logia* of Jesus to be originally copied in codices.

Archaeological evidence, as is well known, fully corroborates this assumption. Among the early Christians both the Gospels and the Septuagint prevailed in a codex form.[19] Prof. C. H. Robert,[20] with his usual sagacity, rightly questions the general theory that the Christian predilection for the codex was dictated by economic reasons. We have seen that the first Jewish Christians, such as Matthew and Mark,[21] would follow the accepted Jewish practice and put down their ὑπομνήματα in codices.[22]

According to Jewish law the Scroll of the Law was to be written only on a parchment[23] roll.[24] However, these and many other restrictions may have been imposed only on the roll which was to be publicly read in the places of worship. For private liturgical purposes, the Jews wrote certain portions of the Torah

[19] See Schubart, *op. c.*, p. 119 ff.; Kenyon, *op. c.* (above n. 10), p. 95 ff. H. A. Sanders, *op. c.*, p. 107b; McCown, *op. c.*, pp. 224 ff., 237 ff.

[20] *The Journal of Theological Studies* L, 1949, p. 162.

[21] See Eusebius, *hist. eccl.*, II. 15.

[22] See Robert ibid. 161 ff.; ibid. XL, 1939, p. 253. Luke, the Gentile, could naturally act differently. He probably wrote his account in book form, with the intention of publishing it.

The reasons for the codex form of the LXX will be given below.

[23] And not on paper or דיפתרא, διφθέρα, which *TB* (*Megillah* 19a top and parallel) defines as a skin prepared with salt and flour but without gall-nut. Comp. the following note and *Mishnah Megillah* II. 2.

[24] See the minor tract *Soferim* I. 1–6, ed. Higger, pp. 96–99 and the parallels referred to in the notes ibid.

on διφθέραι[25] or papyrus as well as on parchment, as is well
illustrated by the famous Nash papyrus.[26] The Jewish children
began their education with the study of written tablets, and
from them they went on to the roll.[27] We do not know the exact
contents of these tablets, but it is likely that they included not
only the letters of the alphabet, but also verses of the Bible.[28]
Books of *Aggada* were in existence among the Jews, notwithstanding the violent opposition of some Rabbis.[29] Unfortunately
the rabbinic sources mostly refer to them as ספר, book, which
can mean both roll[30] and codex.[31]

We conclude with an interesting *Midrash* bearing on our

[25] See *Soferim* III. 6, p. 125. According to Aristeas (*Epistle* 176, Appendix
to Swete's *Introduction to the O. T. in Greek*, 1902, p. 549) the scrolls sent from
Jerusalem to Alexandria were διφθέραι on which the Law was inscribed in
golden characters. See *Soferim* I. 8, pp. 105–106 and comp. Blau, *op. c.* (above
n. 1), pp. 157 ff., p. 162. Χρυσόγραφοι were also in vogue among the Persians;
see B. Geiger in Krauss' *Additamenta ad librum Aruch Completum*, p. 331b,
s. v. פסחא II.

[26] On its date see W. F. Albright, *JBL* LVI, 1937, p. 145 ff. Comp. also
Bulletin of the American Schools of Oriental Research CXV (October 1949),
pp. 20–22.

[27] *Tanḥuma* quoted in *Or Zaru'a* I, 4b, top.

[28] See *TB Gittin* 60a, and comp. M. Friedmann, *Mekhilta*, Introduction,
pp. XXXIV–XXXV.

[29] See Strack, *Introduction to the Talmud and Midrash*, Philadelphia 1931,
pp. 13 ff., 243 ff.

[30] Also called טומוס, τόμος, *tomus*. We are told that word came to R.
Ishmael (see above n. 13) that a man had written a טומוס, *tomus*, of prayers.
When he went to check the report the owner threw the *tomus* into a pail of
water (*Tosefta Shabbath* XIII (XIV). 4, 128₃₁ ff.). The form of that *tomus*
can be determined. Instead of *tomus* TP (ibid. XVI. 1, 15c) employs תכריך,
roll. Another case of the alternation of these two words occurs in the phrase
טומוס של שטרות (*Tosefta Baba Kamma* IX. 31, 366₈), a *tomus* of documents, and
תכריך של שטרות (*Mishnah Baba Mezi'a* I. 8), a roll of documents. This establishes the presumption that the two terms are synonymous. Now the form
of the תכריך is described in *TB Baba Mezi'a*, 20b, where we are told that it
was made of sheets placed end to end [and then rolled together]. We can
therefore conclude that the *tomus* consisted of sheets pasted end to end and
then rolled in the form of a scroll. This was the usual procedure in the Mediterranean countries; see Schubart *op. c.* (above n. 6), pp. 172 and 180.

[31] Comp. *Sifre* I, 103, ed. Horovitz, p. 102. See L. Blau, *op. c.* (above
n. 1), p. 167, and Krauss, *op. c.* (ibid.), p. 307, n. 89.

subject. We read in *Tanḥuma*:[32] אמר ר׳ יהודה בר שלום כשאמר הק׳
למשה כתב לך בקש משה שתהא המשנה בכתב, ולפי שצפה הב״ה שאומות העולם
עתידין לתרגם את התורה ולהיות קוראין בה יונית והם אומרים אנו ישראל,[33]
ועד עכשיו המאזנים מעויין. אמר להם הקב״ה לאומות אתם אומרים שאתם
בני, איני יודע, אלא מי שמסטירין שלי אצלו הם בני ואי זו זו המשנה שנתנה
על פה "R. Judah b. Shalom[34] said: When the Holy One told
Moses *'write down'* (Ex. 34:27), the latter wanted the *Mishnah*
also to be in writing. However, the Holy One blessed is He
foresaw that a time would come when the nations of the world
would translate the Torah and read it in Greek and then say:
'We are Israel',[35] and now the scales are balanced!'[36] The Holy
One blessed is He will then say to the nations: you contend that
you are my children. That may be, but only those who possess
my mysteries are my children, i. e. [those who have] the
Mishnah which is given orally."

TP[37] states to this effect: אילו כתבתי לך רובי תורתי לא כמו זר
נחשבו מה בינן לאומות, אילו מוציאין ספריהן ואלו מוציאין ספריהן. אילו
מוציאין דפתריהן ואלו מוציאין דפתריהן "If I wrote down *the greater
part of my Law* would they (i. e. the Jews) not *be accounted as
strangers?* (Hos. 8:12). What would then be the difference
between them and the nations? These produce their books and
their διφθέραι and the others produce their books and their
διφθέραι!"[38]

---

[32] כי תשא 34. Comp. ibid. וירא 5; ed. Buber 6, 44b; *Pesikta Rabbathi* V,
ed. Friedmann, 14b. I copy from *Tanḥuma* ed. prin.

[33] The modern editions of *Tanḥuma* וירא erroneously read: ש ל ישראל,
but in ed. prin. ibid. the word של is not extant.

[34] Flourished in the middle of the fourth century.

[35] Ed. Buber וירא, 44b, reads: א, ף אנו ישראל, we are *also* Israel. This is a
correction of a learned scribe. The Christians did not assert that they are *also*
Israel, but they maintained that they are the ἀληθινὸς Ἰσραήλ (*const. Apost.*
VII. 36. 2), the *true* Israel. The Jews were, of course, (as was our learned
scribe) surprised at that claim. Tryphon the Jew is portrayed (Just. Mart.
Dial. CXXIII. 7) to have reacted in the same way. Τί οὖν; φησὶν ὁ Τρύφων.
ὑμεῖς Ἰσραήλ ἐστε; " 'What then', says Trypho, 'are you Israel' "?

[36] I. e. the Jews and the Gentiles have seemingly come with equal claims.

[37] *Pe'ah* II. 6, 17a; *Hagigah* I. 8, 76d.

[38] For the rabbinic definition of διφθέρα see above, n. 23. Here the word
seems to be synonymous with book; see Herodot. V. 58. The *Aggada* is often

In this homily the Christians are portrayed as producing the Septuagint in the form of books and διφϑέραι (and not specifically in the form of *pinaces*, codices) because, according to the Rabbis, they wished to stress that in regard to the Torah they were on a par with the Jews. They have the same books in the same form[39] as the Jews have. In reply the Rabbis emphasized that the Christians have no oral law. By the fourth century the Christian Bible had already long since been published; it was accessible and open to anyone who could read. The Jewish oral law remained recorded in secret (private) rolls[40] and in private codices. It constituted the mysteries[41] of the Lord which were published *orally* only for Israel. Its circulation in the form of private codices made it something like the secret hermetic *logos* concerning the regeneration and the rule of silence,[42] which was not to be published.[43]

It is natural that the prestige of the Gospels among the Christians engendered the desire to have them and the Septuagint in the same form. Both were subsequently published in the form of codices.

not very particular about the exactness of its terminology. Comp., however, Blau, *op. c.* (above n. 1), p. 93, n. 0.

[39] Tischendorf stated that the vellum on which the Vatican and Sinaitic codd. (See Swete, *op. c.* [above n. 25], pp. 126 ff., 129 ff.) are written came from antelopes. F. G. Kenyon, *op. c.* (above, n. 10), p. 86, remarks that, to his knowledge, this statement has never been verified. The Jews preferred to have the Torah written on parchment prepared from the skins of deer. See my note in *Tosefeth Rishonim* II, p. 139.

[40] See above, p. 87, n. 29.

[41] See the passage from the *Tanḥuma* quoted above.

[42] *Corpus Hermeticum* XIII, ed. Nock-Festugière, p. 200; see n. 1 ibid.

[43] See A. J. Festugière, Le "logos" Hermétique d'enseignement, *Revue des études Grecques* LV, 1942, p. 90. See ibid. p. 93 ff.

ADDITIONS AND CORRECTIONS

P. 6, n. 13. It is more plausible to assume that the statement of R. Isaac is independent of the difficulty raised in the other *Midrashim*. The Rabbi simply made a remark about the interesting connection between the name Laban and its bearer. The later *Midrashim* utilized this comment for their own problems.

P. 50, n. 34. W. Riedel cited most of the pertinent material bearing on the word פסח. His article came to my attention when this book was already set in pages. The reference to Riedel would otherwise have been included in the text and not in a note.

P. 142. Prof. Elias Bickerman kindly informs me that *R. P.* Roland De Vaux explained the "Awakeners" in a similar way. His article was published in the *Bulletin du Musée de Beyrouth* which appeared, according to Dr. Bickerman, sometime after World War II. This Bulletin has been inaccessible to me.

P. 178. See also J. Brand in מנחה ליהודה (*Jubilee Volume in honor of Rabbi J. L. Slotnik*), p. 12 ff.

ADDITIONS AND CORRECTIONS TO
GREEK IN JEWISH PALESTINE

This volume was warmly received by the prominent specialists in the subject. The author took notice of the reviews by A. D. Nock,[1] Ralph Marcus,[2] G. Allon,[3] Johanan (Hans) Lewy[4] and Henri Grégoire.[5] He is very grateful to the eminent scholars who took the trouble to analyze the book and to present it to the general reader. Their useful suggestions were always accepted with thanks, and some of them will appear in the following corrections.[6]

A few words are in place about the review of my lamented friend Mr. G. Allon. H. Lewy[7] noted that Allon had attributed to Lieberman "a thesis" which he never proposed and that he had omitted Lieberman's many qualifying words, so that his "perhaps" was converted by Mr. Allon into a "certainty". We shall add here two more examples in support of H. Lewy's charge. Allon ascribes to me[8] the assertion that even in the midland centers of Palestine the prayers for rain were uttered in Greek only. This absurdity was correctly refuted. What happened was that one word was altered in the quotation from my book. Whereas I stated:[9] "The people *sometimes* said their special prayers in Greek," I was quoted as writing: "The people *always* said their prayers in Greek" (לא אמרו אלא יונית). Again, he reported in my name[10] that R. Eleazar took the sentence παρὰ βασιλέως ὁ νόμος ἄγραφος from a *juridic* source

---

[1] *Anglican Theological Review*, XXV, April 1943, p. 223 ff.

[2] *Historia Judaica* V, 1943, p. 73 ff.

[3] *Kirjath Sepher* XX, 1943, p. 76 ff.

[4] *Zion* X, 1945, p. 197 ff.: דרכים חדשות בחקר ההיליניזם היהודי.

[5] *Renaissance*, vol. II-III, New York 1945, p. 470 ff.; *Byzantion* XVII, 1944–1945, p. 384 ff.

[6] The figures mentioned below in connection with these scholars refer to the pages of their respective reviews.

[7] P. 198, n. 3.

[8] P. 76b.

[9] P. 30.   [10] P. 84b.

(מ.מקור משפטי").[11] Allon contended that the phrase was a current *proverb*. However, I stated clearly:[12] "R. Eleazar . . . began his explanation with a Greek *proverb*: παρὰ βασιλέως etc."[13]

In short, Allon would often be right in his arguments if his starting point were correct. Instead he combats a fiction, attributing to me statements which I never made, and sometimes even said just the opposite.[14] We fully subscribe to Prof. Lewy's request:[15] "I beg the reader to compare Lieberman's actual words with the 'thesis' that Mr. Allon has ascribed to him."

We cannot help adding the following observation. He who knows the conditions under which the late Mr. Allon labored will not be too harsh with him for his errors. Furthermore, he was not familiar with the English language, and, in some cases, he may have relied on a wrong translation. Indeed, his premature death is a great loss to Jewish scholarship. יהי זכרו ברוך.

We can now proceed.

P. 1 (and p. 20). There were a thousand young men in my father's house etc. See above p. 104 ff.

P. 9. On πρωτογάμια see now Lieberman, Rays from the East, *Mélanges Grégoire*,[16] p. 411.

P. 22 and n. 47. See above p. 76 n. 240.

P. 29. On the passage from Cleomedes, see now Johanan (Hans) Lewy in ספר דינבורג, p. 104 ff. Comp. p. 106, n. 3 ibid.

P. 40. Prof. R. Marcus observed:[17] "Lieberman *seems* to suggest that the nominative verb משכן is etymologically related to the root משך[18] etc." I never derived משכן from משך etymologically.[19] It was simply maintained that משך is identical with

---

[11] The quotation marks are Mr. Allon's.

[12] P. 37.

[13] The source of the *proverb* was recorded on p. 38, n. 51.

[14] He occasionally ventured an argument on *Halakhic* grounds. This was tacitly dismissed in *Tarbiz* XX, 1950, p. 109 and n. 28 ibid., p. 116 ff.

[15] P. 198, n. 3.

[16] *Annuaire de l'Instit. de Philol. et d'Hist. Orientales et Slaves* IX, 1949.

[17] P. 75.

[18] This is the opinion of S. D. Luzzatto in his *Epistles* VI, p. 997.

[19] A similar mistake was made by Allon, p. 85, who thought that I preferred the reading משכן to משך. Comp. also n. 26 ibid.

משכן signifying "to seize by order of the court." I was not aware that this meaning of משך is not listed in any dictionary.

However the point can be proved from many sources. משך is the literal equivalent of ἕλκειν and *trahere*. The latter was a technical term for coercive summons to court.[20] From the rabbinic sources it is obvious that this verb signified general seizure by order of the authorities. We read in *Midrash Mishle*:[21] לא נ מ ש כ ו עשרה הרוגי מלכות אלא בחטא מכירתו של יוסף "The Ten Martyrs were *seized* only for the sin of the sale of Joseph." Similarly, it is stated in the *Midrash*:[22] וכמה מ ש ו כ י ן עתיד למשוך מכם "How many *prisoners* will he (i. e. Edom, Rome) seize from among you!"[23] Again we read in *Sifra*:[24] יכול מ ו ש כ ו ויצא, and the parallel passage[25] formulates it: שלא י מ ש כ נ נ ו ויצא. Thus, משך can safely be identified with משכן, to seize,[26] to arrest, to imprison.[27]

P. 50. See Prof. Grégoire's elucidating comments in *Byzantion* XVII, p. 387.

P. 72. On מצוה, ἐντολή, and φιλέντολος, see now Lieberman, *JBL* LXV, 1946, p. 69 ff.

P. 102, n. 51. Mediaeval rabbinic authorities[28] assert that

---

[20] See Le Blant, *Les actes des martyrs*, p. 144. Comp. also James II.6, and Liddell and Scott s. v. ἕλκω II. 3.

[21] I, ed. Buber, 23a. This is also the reading of *Midrash Haggadol*, Gen., p. 565, ed. Margulies, p. 637, bot.

[22] *Debarim Rabba*, ed. Lieberman, p. 20.

[23] Comp. *Sifre* II, 24, ed. Finkelstein, p. 34, where שובין (capture, imprison) seems to be the equivalent of מושכין in our source. Similarly, *Midrash Tehilim* XXII, 16, ed. Buber, p. 188, reads: שנשבית אל פרעה לילה אחד instead of ש מ ש כ ה פרעה לילה אחד; see *GJP*, p. 40.

[24] בהר IX. 2, 110b.

[25] *TB Baba Kamma* 113b, top, according to two mss. See דקדוקי סופרים ibid., 139a, bot., n. 5.

[26] Comp. also קונטריסים ed. H. Yalon II, p. 80.

[27] This identification will perhaps illuminate an obscure expression in *Koheleth Rabba* IV.14, where בית הסורים is rendered בית נידרא. The latter is perhaps Aramaic for בית משיכה, prison.

[28] Naḥmanides in his commentary to Lev. 18:19; Rabbi Joshua Ibn Shu'ib in his *Derashoth* ibid., 50d; Rabbi Simeon Duran in his מגן אבות on *Aboth* II. 11; Rabbi Abraham Saba in his צרור המור to Deuteronomy, ed. Venice 1546, 130a, and others.

when a woman looks in the mirror at the beginning of her *menses* she sees *guttae sanguineae*. Naḥmanides[29] quotes it in the name of Aristotle. Rabbi Simeon Duran[30] is more specific; he cites it from the book שינה ויקיצה, i. e. *de somno et vigila*.[31] The passage can be found in Aristotle's *De somniis* II, 459b. The Rabbi probably had an Arabic translation which included both books together.

P. 121, n. 39. The reference to *Pesikta deR. Kahana*, 104a, n. 81, has nothing to do with the subject treated. I was misled by Jastrow, Dictionary s. v. אליקי. The correct interpretation was already given by de Lara, (see *LW* II, p. 50, s. v. אלאיקי). The word איקי is also extant in Palestinian Syriac,[32] and אליקי or אלאיקי is certainly על איקי, i. e. על מגן, in vain.

P. 123. The oath כך וכך occurs also in II Aboth deR. Nathan XIX, p. 40.[33]

P. 126, n. 91. On monuments to dogs in antiquity, see F. Cumont, *Recherches sur le Symbolisme Funéraire des Romains*, p. 509.[34]

P. 133. "For אימרא is the exact translation of κριός — ram". Prof. Marcus remarked (p. 75): "אימרא is rendered 'ram' and equated with κριός; but the latter regularly translates איל in the LXX, whereas אימרא usually means 'lamb'." On the whole the observation is correct. One may say with *TB*:[35] תורה תורה אימרא בדיכרא מיחלף לך "Torah, Torah! You have confused the lamb with the ram." However, there is no doubt that in Palestine אימרא signified both lamb and ram. In our case I followed the opinions of Resh Lakish, Bar Kappara and R. Ḥiyya,[36] all of whom explained אימרא in our *Mishnah* to

---

[29] תורת ה' תמימה, Vienna תרל"ז, p. 26.

[30] In his philosophic work מגן אבות, 41b. Comp. ibid. 65b.

[31] Steinschneider, *Die hebraeische Uebersetzungen*, p. 153, n. 338, remarked that it is not extant in Averroes.

[32] Col. II. 18, cod. Damascus, ed. F. Schulthess, Berlin 1905, p. 75.

[33] See n. 1 ibid. It is to be found in the שאילתות ed. Rabbi N. Z. Berlin, III, p. 212.

[34] Additions to pp. 405, n. 4 and 439, n. 6.

[35] *Zebaḥim* 77a.

[36] See *TP Nedarim* a. l. 37a; *Bereshith Rabba* LVI.9, 602 ff.

mean ram. אימרא is also translated ram (איל) in *TP 'Abodah Zarah*.[37] Comp. also *TP Berakhoth* IX.2, 13c, and *TB Rosh Hashana* 26a.

P. 137. The example of a Jew swearing by the sun is very striking etc. Prof. Nock remarked (p. 223): "The references to an oath 'by heaven and by earth' and the denial by Maimonides of the validity of swearing 'by heaven, by earth, *by the sun* and by similar objects' should now be brought into connection with the oath 'under Zeus, earth, the sun' in a society which must be deemed to be of Jewish origin in south Russia."[38] As to Prof. Goodenough's objection (*JQR* XLVII, 1957, p. 223, n. 9) comp. R. Taubenschlag, *The Law of Graeco-Roman Egypt* etc., New York 1944, p. 73, n. 150. Indeed among the documents recently discovered by Prof. Y. Yadin in the Judean desert (so far the most important discovery for Jewish history and literature of the tannaitic period) there is a Greek document which states that Babtha (a Jewess) swore by the τύχη of the emperor,[39] a forbidden oath, see *Scholia* III, Jerusalem 1959, p. 81, n. 42.

The words of Maimonides, who probably drew from a now lost rabbinic source, clearly indicate that the Jews swore by the *sun*. In his ספר המצות[39a] Maimonides rules that it is forbidden to swear by the *stars*, but that it is legitimate to do so if one has their Creator in mind; it is like *swearing by the sun* and thinking of the Lord of the sun etc. If we combine both statements of Maimonides[40] we derive the rule that the Jew was permitted to swear by the sun when he had its Creator in mind, but even then the oath was not legally binding. Some crooked Jews employed an oath which was considered binding by the Gentiles, but had no force in Jewish law.

---

[37] III. 2. 42d, top.

[38] J. B. Frey, *Corpus Inscr. Iudaic.* I, No. 690; Nock, *Conversion*, p. 63.

[39] Even in a Jewish center in Palestine, in Beth She'arim, a Greek epigram (probably of the third century) on a tombstone of a Jew reads: ἐπ<ε>ὶ ἤϑελε Μοῖρα κραταιή. "For such was the wish of the powerful Moira." The interesting epigram was published by Prof. M. Schwabe in the *Bulletin of the Jewish Palestine Exploration Society*, VI, 1939, p. 107.

[39a] Positive commandments 7, ed. Dr. Ch. Heller, 1946, 37a.

[40] I. e. of the יד החזקה and the ספר המצות.

This circumstance may shed light on an obscure passage hitherto totally misunderstood. A responsum by Rab Hai b. Nahshon *Gaon*[41] records:[42] חס וחלילה לעשות כן בנדר ובשבועה כי דבר גדול הוא. ובא אלינו איש חכם וחסיד זקן ודרש בישיבה ופן תשא עיניך השמימה וראית את השמש זה נדר. ואת הירח זו שבועה. ואם אתה עובר או מערים על שום אחד מהם, מיד ונדחת, וצריך תשובה גדולה שאין תשובה כמותה. מאי טעמא משום דהשם נוטל נקמה ממך ואתה משתחוה[43] בסבה זו לעובדי השמש והירח ועל כן כתיב בתריה העידותי בכם היום וגו' כי אבוד תאבדון "Heaven forbid that one should do so (i. e. to circumvent the law) in vows or oaths, for that is a serious matter. There came to us a pious, learned old man and taught in the School: It is written (Deut. 4:19), '*And lest thou lift up thine eyes unto heaven and behold the sun*' — that means to make a vow[44] by it[45] — '*and the moon*' — that means to swear by it.[46] If you transgress or circumvent either of them,[47] then, '*thou hast gone astray*' (ibid.) and are required to do the most severe penance. For the Lord will wreak vengeance upon you, and you will on this account be considered on a par with those who worship the sun and the moon. That is why it says further on (ibid. 26): '*I call heaven and earth to witness against you this day that ye shall utterly perish*'."

The thundering language of the old Rabbi indicates that some ignorant[48] and crooked Jews abused the oath by the luminaries. It was accepted by their neighbors as if it were legally binding. The same situation probably existed at all

[41] Flourished in the ninth century in Sura, Babylonia.

[42] *Geonic responsa* שערי תשובה No 143.

[43] Read משתווה.

[44] Comp. *Mishnah Sanhedrin* VII.6.

[45] *Const. Apost.* V.12, derives from the same verse the injunction against swearing by the luminaries.

[46] According to our explanation there is nothing mysterious in the teaching of the old man. See Hazan's note a. l., 54b, and Dr. B. M. Lewin, אוצר הגאונים *Nedarim*, p. 23, n. 12.

[47] I. e. either the vow or the oath.

[48] For such an oath is invalid only when it concerns the swearer himself, *e. g.* a self imposed oath not to eat or drink etc. The case is different in human relations when the intention of the adjurer must be taken into account. The great sin of חילול השם, profanation of His name, is involved here.

times and in all places. Some eight hundred years before the time of our old man, Martial declared.[49]

ecce negas iurasque mihi per templa Tonantis
non credo: iura, verpe, per *Anchialum.*

There! You deny it, and swear to me by the Thunderer's
    Temple
I don't believe you: swear circumcised one, by Anchialus.[50]

Martial requires that the Jew swear an oath *more iudaico.*

P. 140. ἀγ[άπ]ην θεῶν. This reading is correct. See C. H. Roberts, *Journ. of Egypt. Arch.* 39, 1953, p. 114 (Prof. Nock).[51]

P. 152. On the Oriental proverbs used by Petronius and their rabbinic parallels, see M. Hadas, *American Journal of Philology* L, 1929, p. 378 ff. (Nock, p. 224, n. 3).

P. 158. εἶδες τὸν φίλον σου, εἶδες τὸν θεόν σου. "When you have seen your friends, you have seen your Lord." The proverb is probably taken from Tertullian:[52] vidisti, inquit, fratrem, vidisti dominum tuum. "When you have seen a brother, says [Scripture], you have seen your Lord." This corroborates my conjecture (ibid., n. 95) that the reference is to Gen. 33:10.

P. 165. On the expression קפץ עליו הדבר "The *davar* jumped upon him" see now Lieberman *JBL* LXV, 1946, p. 67 ff.

Pp. 175–176. בן יום in the sense of "immediately," "instantly" occurs also in *Tosefta:*[53] נעשה תם בן יומו "He becomes a *Tam* (harmless) immediately." It is also extant many times in *Sifra,*[54] in *Bereshith Rabba*[55] and in *Midrash Yelamdenu.*[56]

Ibid. The phrase בר שעתיה in the sense of "instantly" is also

---

[49] *Epigr.* XI. 49.

[50] I. e. by היכלא, by the Temple of Jerusalem, as correctly explained by H. Seyrig, *Annuaire de l'Inst. de Philol. et d'Hist. Orientales et Slaves* VII (1939–1944), p. 283. See ibid., p. 287, n. 21 and my note ibid., p. 288.

[51] The correction in the first edition of this book is void.

[52] *De oratione* 26.

[53] *Baba Kamma* II.2, 347[31].

[54] בחוקותי I, 110d.

[55] X. 4, 77[2].

[56] See ליקוטים, Grünhut V, עקב, 126a.

found in *Midrash Job*:[57] עשת ... ש ע ת ה ב ת עושה שהיתה הארץ
ב ת ש ע ת ה... מיד. Hence it is clear that בת שעתה means מיד,
instantly.[58] The expression was still in vogue in Palestine during
the *Geonic* period:[59] אינו יכול לחזור בו אפילו ב ן ש ע ת ו "He cannot change his mind even immediately."[60]

Both terms have a very early origin. A Ugaritic tablet[61]
reads:[62] [64] כתר בנם עדתה. [63] אשתם כתרבן ים "I shall make [it], O Kothar,
immediately. O Kothar, instantly."

P. 188. See the excellent article of Prof. Henri Grégoire,
Revue de l'Université de Bruxelles XXXVI, 1931, p. 257 ff. and
n. 1, p. 258 ibid.

[57] As quoted in *Yalkut Hamakhiri* Is., p. 252.

[58] Comp. also *TP Pesaḥim* VIII.8, 36b top: ונקבר בשעתיה "And he was
buried immediately."

[59] *Responsa geonica* ed. S. Assaf, *Mekize Nirdamim*, Jerusalem, 1942,
p. 123.

[60] I. e., after the transaction took place.

[61] II AB, col. VII, l. 15 ff.

[62] According to the correct explanation of A. D. Singer, *Bulletin of the
Jewish Palestine Exploration Society* XI, May 1944, p. 22. Prof. H. L. Ginsberg has kindly drawn my attention to it.

[63] בן יום.

[64] בן עת.

KEY TO ABBREVIATIONS

Allen, T. W.	*Homer, the Origins and the Transmission*, Oxford, 1924.
b.	*ben* (the son).
BK	*Baba Kamma*.
BR	*Bereshith Rabba*, quoted by chapter and page, ed. Theodor and Albeck, Berlin 1903–1929.
CGL	Corpus Glossariorum Latinorum, ed. G. Loewe, G. Goetz et F. Schoell.
CII	Corpus Inscriptionum Iudaicarum, ed. P. J. B. Frey, 1936.
CIL	Corpus Inscriptionum Latinarum.
CMG	Corpus Medicorum Graecorum.
CSEL	Corpus Scriptorum Ecclesiasticorum Latinorum.
Daremberg et Saglio	Dictionnaire des antiquités grecques et romaines, Paris 1877–1919.
Dornseif, F.	Das Alphabet in Mystik und Magie, Berlin 1922.
FHRA	Fontes Historiae Religionis Aegyptiacae, by Th. Hopfner, Bonnae 1922–1925.
Ginsburg C. D.	Introduction to the Massoretico-Critical Edition of the Hebrew Bible, London 1897.
GJP	Greek in Jewish Palestine, New York 1942.
HUCA	Hebrew Union College Annual.
Jastrow, M.	A dictionary of the Targumim, the Talmud Babli and Yerushalmi, and the Midrashic Literature.
JBL	Journal of Biblical Literature.
JQR	Jewish Quarterly Review.
Liddell and Scott	A Greek-English Lexicon, 1937.

LW	Griechische und lateinische Lehnwörter im Talmud, Midrasch und Targum, von S. Krauss, Teil II, 1899.
LW I	Idem I, 1898.
MGWJ	Monatsschrift für Geschichte und Wissenschaft des Judentums.
OLZ	Orientalistische Litteratur-Zeitung.
PG	Patrologia Graeca.
PL	Patrologia Latina.
PW RE	Pauly-Wissowa Real-Encyclopädie der classischen Altertumswissenschaft.
R.	Rabbi
REJ	Revue des études juives.
Schubart W.	Das Buch bei den Griechen und Römern, Berlin-Leipzig, 1921.
Schürer E.	Geschichte des jüdischen Volkes im Zeitalter Jesu etc., Vierte Auflage, Leipzig 1901–1909.
Syl.[3]	Sylloge Inscriptionum Graecarum, ed. W. Dittenberger, Leipzig 1915–24.
TB	Talmud Babylonicum.
TP	Talmud Palaestinense.
Terminologie I	Die älteste Terminologie der jüdischen Schriftauslegung, ein Wörterbuch der bibelexegetischen Kunstsprache der Tannaiten, von W. Bacher, Leipzig 1899.
Terminologie II	Die exegetische Terminologie der jüdischen Traditionsliteratur, idem, Leipzig 1905.
ZAW	Zeitschrift für die alttestamentliche Wissenschaft.

INDEX I

Hebrew and Aramaic Words

INDEX II

Latin and Greek Words

[1] The words marked with an asterisk are omitted by Liddell and Scott (in the last edition) and Sophocles.

INDEX III[2]

Bible, Targum, LXX, Apocrypha and Rabbinics

[2] Only passages explained or paralleled are listed in this Index.

[3] Pages and line in ed. Zuckermandel.

[4] Chapters and pages in ed. Horovitz.
[5] Pages in ed. Hoffmann.
[6] Folios in ed. Weiss.
[7] Section and pages in ed. Horovitz.
[8] Section and pages in ed. Finkelstein.
[9] *Parasha* and pages in ed. Horovitz.

[10] Chapter and pages in ed. Schechter.
[11] Chapter and pages in ed. Theodor-Albeck

INDEX IV

Ancient and Mediaeval non-Rabbinic Sources

Porphyrius Tyrius 142, 145[10], 163
Protevangelium Iacobi 76[240], 167
Prudentius 145[9]

Quintilianus 87[35]

Rhacenditus Ioseph 56[76], 68[168]

Sardianus Ioannes 59, 59[92]
Sardianus Melito 137[87]
Scholia to Aristophanes 42[38], 117[13], 174[95]
Scholia to Hermogenes 56[73]
Scholia to Homer 36[53], 37[55], 57, 42, 44[52]
Scholia to Sophocles 132[44]
Seneca 27[52], 192
Servius (grammaticus) 152[39]
Silentiarius Paulus 190
Silius Italicus 151[38]
Simplicius (philosophus) 114[99]
Sosibius 65, 79
Strabo 136[77]
Suetonius 17, 63[132]
Suidas 137[87]
Synaxarium Constantino-politanum 10[36]

Tacitus 85[16]
Tertullianus 17, 111, 112, 137[87], 138[90], 149[20], 216

Thaumaturgus Gregorius 105[36]
Theodoretus 117[11]
Theon (rhetor) 67
Theophanes Nonnus 189[68], 190[80]
Theophrastes 145 ff., 181 ff.
Titus Livius 161[72], 165[12]

Varro 11
Virgilius 52[50], 114, 145[9], 151[38], 152[40], 157[36]

Xenophon Ephesius 196[24]

Zenodotus 36

INSCRIPTIONS AND PAPYRI

Acta fratrum Arvalium 179[5], 146[12]
Beth She'arim Inscriptions 113[89], 214[39]
The Black Stone of Esarhaddon 76
Dittenberger, Sylloge³ 136[77], 140[11], 164[4]
CII 214[39]
North-Semitic Inscriptions 168[7], 139[5]
Ramsay, Cities and Bishoprics etc. 164[2]
Ugaritic tablets 217
Pap. Louvre (Magic) 114[7]

INDEX V

General

Acclamations 16 ff.
acrostic 79 ff.
acrostic in Homer 79 ff.
acrostics in rabbinic literature 80[263]
adoratio of the edict, *not* introduced by Diocletian 9[34]
Ἀφροδίτη Οὐρανία 132
Aggada, thirty-six rules of 68[168]

Alcmeon, the anecdote about 171
Alexandrian grammarians 27
"Alexandromania" 7
ἀληθινὸς Ἰσραήλ 207[35]
Altar, built of victims' ashes 162
Altar, raven-scarer of 174
Altar, worshipped 163
anagram 74